Florida Indians and the Invasion from Europe

FLORIDA INDIANS

and the Invasion from Europe

Jerald T. Milanich

University Press of Florida

Gainesville   Tallahassee   Tampa   Boca Raton   Pensacola   Orlando   Miami   Jacksonville

Copyright © 1995 by the Board of Regents of the
State of Florida
Printed in the United States of America on acid-
free paper   ∞
All rights reserved

00 99 98 97 96 95   6 5 4 3 2 1

Library of Congress Cataloging-in-Publication Data

Milanich, Jerald T.
   Florida Indians and the invasion from
   Europe/Jerald T. Milanich
       p.   cm.
   Includes bibliographical references (p.) and
   index.
   ISBN 0-8130-1360-7 (acid-free paper)
   1. Indians of North America—Florida—
Antiquities.   2. Indians of North America—
Florida—History.   3. Florida—History—To 1565.
4. Florida—History—Spanish colony, 1565–1763.
I. Title.
E78.F6M554   1995
975.9′01—dc20   95-7951

The University Press of Florida is the scholarly
publishing agency for the State University System
of Florida, comprised of Florida A&M University,
Florida Atlantic University, Florida International
University, Florida State University, University of
Central Florida, University of Florida, University
of North Florida, University of South Florida, and
University of West Florida.

University Press of Florida
15 Northwest 15th Street
Gainesville, FL 32611

For M and N

CONTENTS

ILLUSTRATIONS

Modern Florida

 **PREFACE**

In the summer of 1992, almost five hundred years to the day after Christopher Columbus set sail on the voyage that opened the Western Hemisphere to European powers, my mail brought copies of several colonial-period documents recently discovered in Cuban archives by noted historian Eugene Lyon. Scanning the eighteenth-century texts piqued my curiosity. In the pages of the parish records of the church of Nuestra Señora de la Asunción in the town of Guanabacoa, the historians had located a death registry containing the names of thirty American Indians from Florida. Among them was Juan Alonzo Cabale, identified as an "Indian of the Timucuan nation." Timucua-speaking peoples had once occupied the northern half of peninsular Florida, but only a very few individuals were known to have survived past the 1730s.

Juan Alonzo's entry, dated November 14, 1767, noted he had been born at Nuestra Señora de la Leche, in St. Augustine, Florida. That Spanish Franciscan mission village was located on the northern edge of St. Augustine, capital of Spain's Florida colony. Today a Catholic shrine with the same name, Nuestra Señora de la Leche, still exists near the location of the colonial-period mission.

Other records examined by Lyon in the archives of the city council of Guanabacoa indicated that Juan Alonzo had been among the native peoples taken by Spaniards from St. Augustine to Cuba as a result of the international negotiations that ceded St. Augustine and all of

Florida to Great Britain in 1763. At the time he arrived in Cuba, Juan Alonzo was fifty-five years old.

The story of the Timucua, whose ancestors had lived for hundreds of generations in what is now northern Florida and southeast Georgia, is a bittersweet saga. They were among the first Native Americans living in what is now the mainland United States to come in contact with people from Europe following Columbus's 1492 voyage. But they also were among the first native groups that succumbed to the invasion from Europe; in that historical encounter were the seeds of a demographic catastrophe.

At the time of contact with members of the expedition of the Spaniard Juan Ponce de León, who landed on the Atlantic coast of Florida in 1513, Timucua speakers numbered as many as 150,000. For over twelve millennia their ancestors had resided here, making a living from the land by fishing, collecting shellfish, hunting, gathering wild plants, and sometimes cultivating crops. Thousands of archaeological sites—village middens and sand mounds—dot the landscape, offering testimony to their presence.

In the early sixteenth century many of those villages were inhabited. But 250 years later, the once populous Timucua apparently were reduced to a single individual, Juan Alonzo Cabale, who died in a land far from his birthplace and the home of his ancestors.

Who were the Timucua and the other native groups of Florida, people with names like Calusa, Jororo, and Saturiwa? Where did they come from? Where did they live? What happened to them? These are questions we can answer using information gathered from archaeological excavations and from the interpretation of documents left behind by the colonial powers who sought to settle La Florida and place the native groups under their sway. Indeed, the history of native peoples is so entwined with the histories of the French and Spaniards in Florida that the story of the native peoples after 1513 cannot be told without also telling the story of the people who invaded their land. To understand the history of the native people of this period is to understand the nature and tempo of French and Spanish colonization and its impact on those same native people.

In the end, the Spanish conquest of Florida proved catastrophic for the native groups. Although they successfully adjusted to many aspects of their new world, the Timucua, the Calusa, the Jororo, and their neighbors could not maintain their numbers in the face of diseases carried to North America from Europe and, perhaps, Africa. Epidemics and ill health resulting from the stresses of colonization and the servitude it brought eventually overcame them. Slave raiding into Florida in the late seventeenth and early eighteenth centuries by English colonists from the Carolinas and by their Indian allies also took a heavy toll. No descendants of the original Florida Indians have survived. One small group of Apalachee Indians who had fled west from Florida are known to have been living in Louisiana between 1763 and 1834, but they, too, vanished.

This book relates the story of those American Indians, the ancestors of Juan Cabale and neighboring groups in Florida, and their interactions with, first, Spain, then France, and then Spain once again, as those monarchies sought to control Florida and its people during the 250 years following Juan Ponce de León's landing in Florida. Using archaeological data and information gleaned from Spanish, French, and English documents, we will trace the histories of the indigenous groups from their precolumbian roots into the seventeenth and eighteenth centuries while providing insights into the impact of colonialism.

That Florida has a history pre-dating the 1820s is not fully realized by many residents and visitors, much less other Americans living elsewhere in the United States. People are not aware of the native groups who once lived here. That French colonists, American Indian villagers, and Spanish soldiers and priests of the sixteenth and seventeenth centuries walked trails that have become twentieth-century highways is not a part of the knowledge learned by every schoolchild. Consequently, another aim in writing this book is to bring to my readers a sense of history and place, to correlate modern towns and places with past events and people. Florida's colonial history is all around us. We have only to look for it.

I have tried to write a book that is both factually correct and accessible to students and other people, who, while not historians or archaeologists, are interested in the history of Florida and the people who once lived there. Although it is impossible to cite all of the scholarly studies that past and present colleagues have written about the early colonial period, I have provided a number of references and footnotes (collected in the back of the book) intended to guide readers, especially students who wish to pursue their own research, to additional information.

The first of two introductory chapters examines the nature of the documentary record and the archaeological evidence that are used in subsequent chapters to tell the story of the native people and those who invaded their land, conquering them. The second summarizes the history of the native people who lived in Florida prior to 1492. A companion volume to this one, *Archaeology of Precolumbian Florida,* published in 1994 by the University Press of Florida, recounts that 12,000-year history in more detail.

The remainder of the book is organized into three parts, each with a brief introduction. Part I, comprising chapters 3, 4, and 5, focuses on the various native Florida Indian groups at the time they were first encountered by the French and Spaniards. In many instances, we can correlate those groups with precolumbian cultures known from archaeological inquiry. I was especially interested in locating the native groups on Florida's landscape, tying the past to modern places.

The three chapters in Part I are not mini-ethnographies, however. For most native groups we simply do not have sufficient archaeological and historical information to describe their cultures fully. It is only where the more intense interactions between native groups and Europeans occurred that there were descriptions of what those groups were like. As you will see, in many instances we still have much to learn.

Part II, which includes chapters 6, 7, and 8, provides an introduction to European attempts to explore, conquer, and settle La Florida. Beginning with the expedition of Juan Ponce de León, Spain and then France made efforts to establish a colony in La Florida. The expeditions of Pánfilo de Narváez, Hernando de Soto, Tristán de Luna, Juan Ribault, René de Laudonnière, and others were attempts to place a permanent colonial presence in La Florida. None was successful.

The goal of colonization was finally realized in 1565 with the founding of San Agustín, Spanish St. Augustine. Once the colony was established, its founder and governor, Pedro Menéndez de Avilés, turned toward pacification of the people who lived there and to exploitation of their lands.

One way to accomplish both aims was to bring the native people to Christianity. Chapters 9 and 10 in part III focus on the Spaniards' efforts to win the hearts of the Florida Indians and control their bodies. Particular emphasis is given to the impact of the mission system on native groups, especially the Timucua-speaking peoples of northern Florida and the Apalachee Indians of the eastern panhandle.

The final chapter in part III, chapter 11, relates the demise of the indigenous native groups. Epidemics, which probably began as soon as the first contact with Spaniards took place, were a major reason why native societies could not maintain a level of population that allowed them to continue to exist as ethnic groups. Another blow was the destruction of the Spanish missions in the first decade of the eighteenth century. Carolina militia, aided by Native American allies, caused the abandonment of the missions, scattering and enslaving the native population and leaving Florida open to raids by Indian warriors and slavers from the north. Native people taken as slaves in Florida could be sold in Charleston to provide labor for local plantations or be exported to plantations in the West Indies. These raids were the final assault.

Some of the raiders remained to take advantage of the recently abandoned fields and settlements. Other groups, mainly Creek Indians, also entered the state, leaving their home territories in Alabama and Georgia to repopulate locales in northern Florida and, later, central Florida. These people were called *cimarrones,* a Spanish word meaning "wild, untamed." Today we call them Seminoles. A concluding Epilogue provides a brief introduction to the history of the Seminole peoples in Florida.

Although those of us living in Florida tend to think of our fast-growing state (soon to become the third most populous of the fifty United States) as central to many events in the modern world, this was not its position in the Spanish empire. The colony of La Florida was at the northernmost edge of an empire that encompassed much of the Caribbean, Mexico, and Central and South America. Historians often refer to Florida and the other Sun Belt states as the Spanish borderlands, which indeed they were. La Florida's location on the periphery of the Spanish empire and the lack of mineral wealth that could be wrested from its ground or from the native people who lived there conspired to assure that St. Augustine would be a backwater compared to the populous Spanish, Indian, and mestizo towns in Mexico and points south.

But even so, La Florida was a part, albeit a small one, of the Spanish empire in the Americas. The diplomatic and military maneuverings of the colonial powers often were felt in La Florida just as they were in other colonies in the Western Hemisphere. Spanish St. Augustine and the native people of Florida felt the impact of wars taking place in distant lands and of treaties negotiated an ocean away.

The indigenous Florida Indians did not survive the conquest of North and South America that followed in Columbus's wake. The Timucua speakers, as well as the Calusa, Jororo, Mocoso, Apalachee, Mayaca, Hobe, and other Florida Indians, bore the brunt of colonial expansion and ultimately were engulfed by it. Many other groups north and west of Florida did survive the colonial era, and their descendants today continue to live in the United States. Those descendants include the Seminole Indians who live in modern Florida and Oklahoma.

By learning about the Florida Indians of the colonial period, we can better appreciate the histories of the Seminole and other present-day American Indian societies and understand their contributions to our world. It is important to remember that all our histories have been shaped by the tumultuous events set in motion five centuries ago.

In writing this book I have drawn heavily on the work of past and present archaeologists, ethnohistorians, and historians. Some of those individuals graciously read and critiqued specific chapters. Robert Austin, Paul Hoffman, George Luer, Eugene Lyon, William Marquardt, Rochelle Marrinan, Bonnie McEwan, Rebecca Saunders, John Worth, and Brent Weisman all gave me the benefit of their respective knowledge. John Hann read the entire manuscript and made a considerable effort to correct facts and interpretations, as did David Hurst Thomas and Nancy Marie White. I am very grateful to all of these colleagues.

My thanks are extended to Jan Coyne, my cartographer, and to Donine Marlow, Robin Shulman, and Ann Cordell, who helped me find information and references. Many individuals and institutions were gracious in providing photographs or other illustrative materials; their contributions are noted in the illustration legends. The Carnegie Endowment of Washington granted permission to quote from Robert

Chamberlain's translation of a Spanish document, the *requerimiento,* published by that organization in 1948.

I am also indebted to the staff of the University Press of Florida, and to Jonathan Lawrence, my copyeditor, for their encouragement and assistance.

Searching for the Past

1 The past is everywhere, if one only knows where and how to look. Nowhere in the United States is this more true than in Florida, where twelve thousand years of human history lie beneath our feet in archaeological sites. During a small portion of those twelve millennia, the period after 1513, there also are written accounts of events that occurred and the people who lived there. Archaeologists and historians study these records of the past, whether artifacts from an archaeological site in downtown Tallahassee or letters written by a sixteenth-century St. Augustine official.

The first step in our journey to early colonial Florida will be to examine the nature of these records. We will see that artifacts and documents are voices from Florida's past.

The Native Presence

Calusa, Ocale, Apalachee—these are the names of a few of the many Florida Indian groups encountered by Spaniards in the sixteenth century. As the Spanish and the French sought to colonize the state, they would come in contact with many more native groups, adding their names to the written record. In total, the names of nearly one hundred individual groups are known. At the time of Juan Ponce de León's first voyage to Florida, in 1513, the sum of their respective populations was about 350,000: 50,000 Apalachee in the eastern panhandle, 150,000

Timucua speakers in northern peninsular Florida (with more in southern Georgia), and another 150,000 people in central and southern Florida and the western panhandle.[1]

Evidence for the precolumbian existence of Florida's people is found everywhere in the state, although the archaeological sites that comprise that evidence continue to be destroyed by looters and by oftentimes uninformed agricultural and commercial developers. Beginning in the late nineteenth century, commercial mining destroyed many of the large precolumbian shell heaps—archaeological sites—found around Tampa Bay and in the central portion of the St. Johns River drainage. The shell dug from sites was used to pave the roads in a host of Florida towns. Other sites, such as those on Biscayne Bay, fell in the twentieth century to the construction of hotels, homes, and businesses. As incredible as it may seem, this destruction of our past continues even today. Mounds are bulldozed for fill dirt, and backhoes dig peat from ponds in which people buried their dead thousands of years ago. In Florida, as elsewhere in the United States, there is little protection for the past. This is in marked contrast to many other countries, where the past is considered part of a national heritage that belongs to all and must be carefully managed for future generations.

The archaeological record of the early colonial period—two and a half centuries of interaction between native peoples and colonial powers—is even more endangered because it is so ephemeral and fragile. Outside of colonial St. Augustine and south and west of the seventeenth-century missions and ranches of northern Florida, the archaeological evidence for native cultures in this period—a small portion of the twelve thousand years of American Indian history—is only a thin veneer across the state. A handful of Venetian glass beads found in one archaeological site, broken Spanish crockery in a second, a Portuguese copper coin in still another—these are the clues that help archaeologists to identify American Indian sites of the early colonial period.[2]

Such artifacts, originating in Europe or in European colonies in the Americas, reached native hands as gifts, through trade or purchase, as items salvaged from ships wrecked along Florida's coasts, and as items recycled from Spanish camps, garrisons, ranches, and missions. Ultimately they made their way into archaeological sites, having been deposited as trash, lost, or deliberately placed there. To people who had never seen an iron hatchet or a multicolored glass bead before, these European-derived artifacts were as exotic as moon rocks were to a subsequent generation of Americans. European tools and trinkets were sought after and highly valued.

The desire of native people to obtain these exotic items was intense. One documented example comes from the 1930s, when three Australians led an expedition into highland New Guinea. Metal tools and other goods brought by the Australians were as valued and sought after by the villagers as thousand-dollar bills falling from the sky would be to us today. Villagers, who at first thought the white Australians were spirits, were anxious to trade food and even relatives to obtain iron tools.[3]

In Florida archaeologists can date many European-derived artifacts to a particular period, providing at least some indication that a specific native Florida Indian site was occupied, for example, in the early sixteenth century as opposed to the early seventeenth century. The archaeological study of colonial-period artifacts manufactured in Europe, the Far East, and the Spanish colonies of the Americas is an important focus of historical archaeology. Many such studies have focused on items from Spanish Florida.[4] Historians also have provided important perspectives on the material culture of colonial Florida, including objects likely to be found in archaeological sites.[5]

Although the quantity of European artifacts found at any one colonial-period American Indian site is small (at least in sites away from St. Augustine and the mission provinces in the northern third of the state), the number of individual sites with such artifacts is amazingly large. In the western panhandle and the coastal and interior regions of the central and southern peninsula, for example, Florida archaeologists have found small quantities of European artifacts in a host of aboriginal sites. That these artifacts are widespread indicates that native groups lived throughout Florida in the early colonial period and that they were in contact, either direct or indirect, with Europeans. The impact of the European presence must have been similarly widespread.

Although this information on the distribution of sites is important, it is in some instances all that is known about some regions of the state. We know little about the people who lived in areas of Florida outside the mission provinces. There have been few in-depth archaeological studies of colonial-period native cultures in the western panhandle or central Florida, for example. Often the archaeological record is fragmentary, undiscovered, or unstudied.

One obvious solution to this problem is to consult historical documents. But the archival record can be just as biased and, at times, as incomplete as the archaeological one. For example, there are tantalizing Spanish documents from the late seventeenth and early eighteenth centuries that mention the Jororo Indians in central Florida. Those documents tell us that the Jororo existed and provide small amounts of other information, but we cannot as yet confidently tie the Jororo to specific sites or to an archaeological culture (see chapter 4). For most Florida groups we do not have the more or less continuous paper trail that we have for the Apalachee Indians and for some of the Timucuan groups. Unfortunately, for many native groups we know little except their name and where they probably lived.

Even when we do have documents about a specific group, we must be cautious in determining who the group actually was. When asked by a Spaniard or Frenchman who they were, sixteenth-century Timucua speakers at a village near modern Jacksonville probably answered, "We're us." And who are the people living in that other village? "They're the others." What is this place called? "Our land." Given the problems of communication between French or Spanish speakers and speakers of a Timucuan dialect or the language of the Calusa, it is no wonder that some of the names for specific groups listed in European sources translate from native languages into English as "our land" or "that town."

The situation is further confused by the European practice of using a native place-name to refer to the native group residing at that place, or using the same name to refer to a chief, or using a chiefly title as a place-name or as the name of a group. And when people living at a specific location moved away and a new group moved in, Europeans might refer to the second group by the same name as the first. In still other instances, the Spaniards used a Spanish place-name to refer to a native group. The result is that the names used to refer to specific groups often probably are not the names those groups used to refer to themselves.

Given all of these caveats, one might well wonder: How can we know anything about these people if we are not even certain who they were? The answer is that, despite the shortcomings of the archaeological and historical records, there is information on many of the Florida native groups, albeit it at times very limited. The groups did exist. In many cases the same names, whether correctly applied by the Spaniards or not, appear repeatedly in historical accounts spanning generations. Each of a number of groups can be correlated with specific artifacts, archaeological sites, and a geographical area.

Were there major native groups in Florida that did not interact with Europeans and which, consequently, remain largely unknown? Probably not as many as we might think. The Europeans, and especially the Spaniards, made an effort to explore and learn about Florida and the native people who lived there. It was to the benefit of the colonists to learn about the land so they could avail themselves of its resources. When the entire gamut of archival sources from the sixteenth, seventeenth, and eighteenth centuries are considered, we can be confident that nearly all of the major native groups are mentioned.

Even so, there are a few places with archaeological remains indicating the presence of colonial-period populations for which there are few or no historical accounts, such as in the lower Kissimmee River Basin, just north of Lake Okeechobee. Who were the native groups responsible for the many earthwork and midden sites found along and near the river? Archaeology and historical research still have much to tell us about the Florida Indians.

The European Presence

Every year, like swallows returning to the Spanish mission of San Juan de Capistrano in California, tourists come to the former Spanish town of St. Augustine in northeast Florida. After considerable hassle finding a place to park their automobiles, they walk down St. George Street through the heart of the historic district, searching for some bona fide sign of our Hispanic heritage. Founded in 1565, this mecca for tourism rightfully has been crowned the oldest continuously occupied European-founded town in the United States (with an asterisk noting that what is meant is the U.S. mainland, as towns in Puerto Rico are certainly older).

After passing through the gauntlet of T-shirt, sunglasses, and postcard purveyors, the Castillo de San Marcos, a national monument administered by the National Park Service, looms across the greensward at the end of St. George Street like an oasis of authenticity. Here at last, in the thick coquina walls of this imposing fortress, tourists can find the *real thing,* a relic of Spanish Florida (throughout this book, *Florida* refers to the modern state, *La Florida* to the Spanish colony).

La Florida was a Spanish colony for 236 years—from 1565 to 1821, except for a twenty-year period (1763–83) when it was an outpost of the British Crown. Purists might argue that La Florida first became a part of Spain in 1513, when Juan Ponce de León so claimed it for his sovereign. Spain, however, was unable to establish a permanent settlement during the half century following Juan Ponce's voyage, a time when Florida continued to be home to hundreds of thousands of people who did not know who the King of Spain was, and a time when the French Crown sent its own expeditions to Florida to plant a colony.

Today, outside of the walls of St. Augustine, little tangible, aboveground evidence remains of Florida's heritage as a Spanish colony. Outside of St. Augustine and nearby Fort Matanzas National Monument, a visitor cannot find buildings or even ruins from the sixteenth and seventeenth centuries. We have no restored missions like those at Capistrano for people to visit. And, except for Fort Matanzas, which was originally built in 1742, none of the Spanish garrison buildings and forts established in several places along the Florida coasts, including Pensacola, are still visible. Nor can any of the Spanish ranches or coastal fisheries be seen. This is one reason the public knows so little about the early Spanish colonial period and its relevance to our history.

But ample evidence of Spanish activities in Florida does exist, albeit underground, where the trowels and shovels of archaeologists are needed to expose it, or in archives, where the skills of historians must be employed to uncover dusty data. Excavations and document searches do provide a picture of the early-colonial-period Spanish activities in Florida. And, thanks to a number of state agencies and educators, modern residents and visitors can not only learn about Spaniards and their interactions with American Indians in textbooks and museum exhibitions, but they can visit actual locations where the events of the colonial period were played out across the Florida landscape.

For instance, beginning at the Hernando de Soto National Monument west of Bradenton, one can drive the De Soto Trail to Tallahassee

The Castillo de San Marcos in St. Augustine.

and on to the Georgia border. The route is marked with signs, and the story of the early-sixteenth-century de Soto expedition is told in roadside exhibits. In Tallahassee one can visit the site of the late-seventeenth-century Apalachee Indian–Franciscan mission of San Luís, where archaeologists Gary Shapiro and Bonnie McEwan have uncovered homes and the council house of the native villagers, as well as the church and other buildings of the mission and the adjacent small Spanish settlement and fort.[6] Project historian John Hann has uncovered documentary information about not only San Luís and the Apalachee, but about other Florida missions and people as well.[7] Few modern Floridians are aware that as many as 140 mission churches were established in La Florida in the seventeenth and early eighteenth centuries, a number that dwarfs the double handful of California

Archaeologists Bonnie McEwan and Charles Poe of the Florida Bureau of Archaeological Research examining a bottle fragment in the wall of an excavation unit at the mission of San Luís in Tallahassee (courtesy of the Florida Bureau of Archaeological Resources).

missions that followed in the next century and which are so well known today.

In St. Augustine the story of Spanish Florida is also being told, even while archaeologists continue to uncover the remains of the pre-1763 town. Excavations beneath parking lots and in the backyards of modern St. Augustinians have yielded millions of artifacts and resulted in many hundreds of pages of information about the town and its people.[8] St. Augustine may be the most archaeologically studied Spanish colonial town in the Americas, and once visitors make their way past the tourist-oriented hoopla they can learn a great deal in exhibits, museums, and military reenactments.

So there is evidence of the early colonial period in Florida. The early Spanish presence did leave marks all across Florida. Some marks, like those left by Juan Ponce, are so faint we can trace them only in documents. Others, like those of de Soto, are heavier on the land, and we can find and interpret them at places along the route he and his army followed from Tampa Bay to Tallahassee. Heaviest are the marks left by

John Hann, historian for the
Florida Bureau of Archaeological Research's San Luís project.
Hann, the most widely
published historian on Florida's
Spanish missions, carries out
much of his research at the site
of that late-seventeenth-century
mission.

the seventeenth-century Spanish missions and haciendas and by the
colonists who lived in St. Augustine, the capital of Spanish Florida.

In chapters 3 through 11 we will look at these marks, evidence left in
the earth and written on paper. They will bring us the story of the
events and people that were responsible for helping to shape a new
world.

Interpreting the Past

In this book the emphasis is on the native Florida Indians who lived
here at the dawn of the European invasion, a time that began shortly
after the initial voyage of Christopher Columbus. These native groups
were the descendants of people who had been in Florida for thousands
of years before the first Spaniards landed.

Archaeologists have given the precolumbian cultures of Florida
names taken from nearby modern places like Belle Glade or St. Johns
or Fort Walton, because we do not know what names the precolumbian people used to refer to themselves. And although we can

delineate the geographical regions of specific archaeological assemblages (for example, the region of the Alachua culture), in most cases we simply do not know how many different ethnic groups might have been associated with that assemblage. Social terms, symbols, and the like must have been present and used by the people to differentiate their own group from others, but in many cases we have not as yet learned to recognize such evidence. To delineate ethnic differences we must also have the help of documentary descriptions. Archaeology does provide methods and theories for understanding the past, but it is limited in the types of human behavior it can recover. In other words, there are many things archaeology cannot tell us about the native peoples of Florida.

Written documents provide information not recoverable from archaeological excavations. Archival materials provide firsthand observations that allow us to place sixteenth-century names on places, archaeological sites, and the groups represented by archaeological assemblages. Documents also allow us to read about actual individuals and events and, occasionally, to tie them to archaeological evidence. The quality of information and, thus, the level of detail regarding some colonial-period American Indians in Florida is much greater than the data we can glean from archaeology alone. Not surprisingly, our knowledge of colonial-period native peoples generally is more detailed than it is for precolumbian cultures.

But documents, like archaeological data, do not provide all the answers. The priests, soldiers, and functionaries responsible for the archival records we have today were simply doing their jobs, recording information on supplies needed or used, salaries paid, disputes settled, converts made, and so forth. They were not trained anthropologists or historians. With one or two wonderful exceptions, they were not seeking to provide descriptions of the native peoples and their interactions with Spanish and French colonists.

In addition, documents are often generated as a result of specific incidents. One example is from the late 1690s, when Franciscan priests attempting to found a new mission were unceremoniously kicked out of a native town near Fort Myers by its Calusa Indian villagers and forced to make their way southward along the coast to the Keys. Governmental investigations regarding the incident and the reasons for the failure of the mission effort resulted in a large collection of remarkable

Hale Smith (right) and a crew member at the 1947 Florida Park Service excavation of the Scott-Miller site, an Apalachee Indian-Spanish mission in Jefferson County. The archaeological investigations were the first to be carried out at a Florida mission (courtesy of the Florida Museum of Natural History).

Spanish documents describing the lower southwest Florida coast and its native people at that date.

In a sense, documentary coverage of colonial Florida is happenstance. Documents provide only part of the total picture, often only at a single point in time and focusing on a single event or a series of related events. Documents also can seek to convince the reader of the writer's point of view. Consequently, documents, like artifacts, have to be studied and interpreted. We must understand the context of a document and the intent of its author. Is the author a soldier stationed at a mission garrison who is seeking to cast the missionary priests in a bad light by overstating the disruptive behavior of the Franciscans toward the mission villagers? Or is the document a letter to the king from a disgruntled priest seeking more supplies for his mission by stretching the truth about the lack of food and the hardships he faces? Documents have to be weighed and used with care, and often we must read between the lines. And we must take into consideration that what is

Archaeologist Rochelle Marrinan (back right) and members of the 1994 Florida State University archaeological field school at the site of mission San Pedro y San Pablo de Patale, east of Tallahassee. The landowners of the site, Frank Bilek and his wife, the late Eveline Bilek, have been strong supporters of research at the site since 1984 (courtesy of Rochelle Marrinan).

being described is for a specific time and place and may not be applicable to earlier or later periods.

But even so, in combination with one another, archaeology and archival records are powerful tools for understanding the past. And when the methods and approaches of other disciplines also are focused on early colonial Florida, even greater understanding emerges. In Florida such interdisciplinary research dates from 1946 with the excavations and historical investigations of John Griffin, Hale Smith, and Mark Boyd, all working under the auspices of the Florida Park Service.[9]

Another notable early scholar was Charles Fairbanks, who, beginning in the early 1950s, while a professor at Florida State University, and later at the University of Florida, managed to replicate himself numerous times, producing many generations of graduate students who expanded his interests and accomplishments in historical archaeology. Historical archaeology also was advanced by John Goggin, who preceded Fairbanks at the University of Florida, and by Hale Smith, who joined the faculty of Florida State University after leaving the Florida Park Service in the late 1940s.

Archaeologist and historian John Worth of the Fernbank Museum of Natural History, transcribing and translating a microfilmed copy of a Spanish document into his computer (courtesy of John Worth).

Today new generations of historical archaeologists, many of them Fairbanks's students or students trained by his students, are continuing the work begun by Boyd, Fairbanks, Goggin, Griffin, and Smith. In their pursuits, these recent scholars—people like Kathleen Deagan, Rochelle Marrinan, Bonnie McEwan, and Brent Weisman—have collaborated with a cadre of historians—notably Amy Bushnell, John Hann, Paul Hoffman, Eugene Lyon, Albert Manucy, and John Worth, the latter trained as both an archaeologist and a historian.[10] Together these archaeologists and historians, whose publications are often cited in this book, are providing new vistas on the events and people of the colonial period.

We are hearing new voices from the land—voices from a time when a new world was taking root. Today we live in that new world, a world encompassing East and West that traces its origin to 1492 and the initial voyage of Christopher Columbus, a Genoese dreamer sailing under the flag of Spain. As we shall see, however, the onset of that new world was the beginning of the end for the Indians of Florida. Two and a half centuries after the voyage of Juan Ponce de León to the Florida peninsula, the descendants of the precolumbian Indians were no more.

Before turning to those 250 years, we will first gain some understanding of the precolumbian history of Florida's native peoples and of their locations at the dawn of the invasion from Europe. We begin with an overview of the nearly twelve thousand years during which people lived in Florida prior to Columbus's fateful voyage.

An Old World and Its People

| | To stand on top of a midden where native American In-
| 2 | dian houses stood hundreds of years ago and look out
| | across the wet savanna surrounding Lake Okeechobee
| | is a heady experience. To walk beside an earthwork
| | built by human hands more than two thousand years
| | ago can actually raise goose bumps.

To stand on top of a midden where native American Indian houses stood hundreds of years ago and look out
across the wet savanna surrounding Lake Okeechobee
is a heady experience. To walk beside an earthwork
built by human hands more than two thousand years
ago can actually raise goose bumps.

I was able to do both in the summer of 1966 when I was an undergraduate student in a University of Florida archaeological field school
held at the Fort Center site. It was an experience that many people
should be able to enjoy. Indeed, history and archaeology, both disciplines that study the past, are of great interest to many people. Every
year tourists travel to archaeological sites to learn about people who
lived long ago and, perhaps, to seek some of that same feeling of awe
that I enjoyed.

Fort Center was the first archaeological site I had ever knowingly
been on. I say knowingly because it turns out that during the late 1950s
I had spent many youthful hours walking around on top of an archaeological site that extended along the shore of a shallow lake I fished
near the small town of Lockhart in Orange County, Florida. It was
more than twenty years later that I learned there had been a site on
that lake. My enlightenment came when archaeologists were called to
the lake to examine a portion of a precolumbian dugout canoe that had
been found preserved in the lake bottom. Not only had my uneducated
teenage eyes completely missed the presence of an archaeological site,

the waterlogged wooden canoe might well have been one of those underwater snags I tripped over when I waded the lake, casting for bass.

Unfortunately, this anecdote does not have a happy ending. When archaeologists visited the lake in the 1970s it was little more than a mudhole. Commercial interests had used up the water for irrigation, and local residents found the canoe while exploring the dried, cracked mud that was exposed when the water disappeared. Worse, the landscaping of lots and the construction of homes had pretty much destroyed the site, leaving only some artifacts—such as pottery and sun-cracked bones of animals eaten for food—on the badly eroded ground surface. The canoe itself, exposed for some months, was badly rotted and cracked.

The lessons of this anecdote are straightforward. The first is that archaeology, history, and the past are people pleasers. Visitors who might not come to Florida to catch the sun will come to walk through the castillo at St. Augustine or visit archaeological sites in state and national parks. The second lesson, already mentioned in chapter 1, is that archaeological sites are a fragile resource and must be carefully managed. Fortunately, archaeologists are getting better at managing that resource and are educating officials from state and federal agencies. Even better, the public is learning that environmental conservation and archaeological site preservation can go hand in hand.

The same commercial interests that cause water to disappear from lakes are often the forces that destroy archaeological sites. Purchasing a tract of coastal wetlands so it can be put in public ownership and kept for all to admire and experience is a positive process that can preserve archaeological sites located in those wetlands. In Florida, land-purchase initiatives such as the Conservation and Recreation Lands program have assured that archaeological sites and the information they contain are being preserved. State and national parks and other agencies, such as the U.S. Forest Service and local preservation boards administered under the Florida Division of Historical Resources, also are doing their part. As a consequence, residents and tourists in Florida can learn about the precolumbian past by going to museums and by visiting parks and preservation areas where they can see exhibits and experience archaeological sites in their natural settings.

In the remainder of this chapter we will see that the precolumbian Florida Indians were closely linked to their environments. The very saltwater and freshwater marshes and wetlands that we value today provided a large portion of their livelihood. To learn about the past is to learn about past environments, to learn about the land. Let us begin our journey into the past by taking a giant step back, a step of twelve millennia.

Paleoindians—The First Floridians

Twelve thousand years ago, what is now the state of Florida was first settled by American Indians whose ancestors had entered North America from eastern Asia during the Pleistocene epoch, the Great Ice Age. Because so much water was tied up in glaciers, sea levels were as many as 350 feet lower than present, exposing a huge land bridge between present-day Siberia and Alaska. Hunter-gatherers in search of game and other foods easily traveled across this land bridge, which was at least as wide as the distance from Orlando to New York City.

These early hunter-gatherers, now called Paleoindians, entered Florida at about the same time they moved into other parts of what is now the United States. Evidently their nonsedentary lifestyle and a new world filled with plant and animal foods never encountered previously by humans enabled—perhaps stimulated—them to quickly colonize the Americas. Their campsites are found across North America, from Alaska to south Florida.

At the time of the Paleoindians, the same lowered seas that created a transcontinental bridge between northeastern Asia and northwestern North America gave Florida a total landmass about twice what it is today. The Gulf of Mexico shoreline was more than one hundred miles west of its present location. During this period Florida was also much drier than today; many present-day rivers, springs, and lakes did not exist, and even groundwater levels were significantly lower. Viable plants needed to be able to grow in these dry, cool conditions, so scrub vegetation, open, grassy prairies, and savannas were common.

Sources of surface water, so important to Paleoindians and to the animals they hunted for food, were limited. The Paleoindians sought water in deep springs, like Little Salt Spring in Sarasota County, or at watering holes or shallow lakes or prairies where limestone strata near the ground surface provided catchment basins. Such limestone deposits are most prevalent from the Hillsborough River drainage north

Approximate extent of Florida's shoreline during the Paleoindian period, with sea levels 130 to 165 feet below those of today.

through peninsular Florida into the panhandle. Paleoindians hunted, butchered, and consumed animals at these watering holes, leaving behind their refuse, artifacts that can be studied and interpreted by modern archaeologists.

Today, with higher water levels, many of these catchment basins are flowing rivers, such as the Ichetucknee, Wacissa, Santa Fe, Aucilla, and Chipola. Paleoindian camps with bone and stone weapons and tools, including distinctive lanceolate stone spear points, are found underwater in deposits at the bottoms of these rivers, as well as at land sites

Paleoindian and Archaic site locations.

nearby. Found with the tools are bones of animals the Paleoindians hunted, some exhibiting butchering marks. A number of the animal species hunted by Paleoindians became extinct shortly after the end of the Pleistocene epoch, perhaps in part because of human predation. They include mastodon, mammoth, horse, camel, bison, and giant land tortoise. Other animals that provided meat for the Paleoindian diet, such as deer, rabbits, and raccoons, continue to inhabit Florida today.

After about 9000 B.C., as glaciers melted and sea levels rose, Florida's climate generally became wetter, providing more water sources around which the Paleoindians could camp. These late Paleoindians moved between water sources less frequently and established and occupied camps for longer periods of time. Archaeological sites corresponding to these larger, late Paleoindian camps have been found in the Hillsborough River drainage near Tampa, around Paynes Prairie south of Gainesville, near Silver Springs, and at other locations in northern Florida.

Archaic-Period Cultures

Over time the tool kits of the Paleoindians changed as people altered their lifeways to adjust to the new environmental conditions that confronted them. A wider variety of stone tools began to be used, and many of the stone points originally used to hunt the large Pleistocene animals were no longer made. These changes were sufficient by 7500 B.C. for archaeologists to delineate a new culture, the Early Archaic.

The environment of the Early Archaic peoples was still drier than our modern climate, but it was wetter than it had been in earlier times. Early Archaic peoples continued to live next to wetlands and water sources and to hunt and gather wild foods.

One remarkable site of this period is Windover Pond in Brevard County. Excavations by Glen Doran and David Dickel of Florida State University revealed that between 6000 and 5000 B.C. human burials were placed in the peat in the bottom of the shallow pond. The peat helped to preserve an array of normally perishable artifacts and human tissues, including brains from which scientists have recovered and studied genetic material.

Artifacts from the pond include shark teeth and dog or wolf teeth, which had been attached with pitch to wooden handles for use as tools. Other tools were made from deer bone and antler, as well as from manatee and either panther or bobcat bone and from bird bone. Bone pins, barbed points, and awls were found preserved in the peat, along with throwing stick weights made from deer antler. The latter were used with a handheld shaft to help launch spears; throwing sticks probably also were used by Paleoindians. Remains of plants, including prickly pear and a wild gourd fashioned into a dipper, were also preserved, as was a well-developed and sophisticated array of cordage and fiber fabrics and matting. Fibers taken from Sable palms and saw palmettos and other plants were used in the twining and weaving.

After 5000 B.C. the climate of Florida began to ameliorate, becoming more like modern conditions, which were reached by about 3000 B.C. The period from 5000 to 3000 B.C. is known as the Middle Archaic. Sites from this period are found in a variety of settings, some very different from those of Paleoindians and Early Archaic times, including for the first time along the St. Johns River and the Atlantic coastal strand. Middle Archaic peoples also were living in the Hillsborough River drainage northeast of Tampa Bay, along the southwest Florida coast, and in a few south Florida locales. Sites are also found in large numbers in interior northern Florida. The presence of a larger number of surface water sources than had been available in earlier times provided many more suitable places for people to live.

By 3000 B.C., the onset of the Late Archaic period, essentially modern environmental conditions were reached, and expanding populations occupied almost every part of the state. Wetland areas were heavily settled. Numerous Late Archaic sites are known to be present in coastal regions in northwest, southwest, and northeast Florida and in the St. Johns River drainage. Such sites are characterized by extensive deposits of mollusk shells, the remains of thousands of precolumbian meals. At both marine and freshwater wetland settlements, fish and shellfish were dietary staples, as they were for generations of later native Floridians as well.

Late Archaic groups probably lived along most if not all of Florida's coasts, but many sites have been inundated by the sea-rise that continued throughout the Archaic period. This is certainly true around Tampa Bay, where dredging has revealed extensive shell middens that today are underwater.

Slightly before 2000 B.C. the Late Archaic villagers learned to make fired-clay pottery, tempering it with Spanish moss or palmetto fibers. Sites with fiber-tempered pottery, some associated with massive shell middens, are distributed throughout the entire state, down to the Florida Keys. By the end of the Late Archaic period, at 500 B.C., regional groups were making many new types of fired-clay pottery. Because different groups made their ceramic vessels in specific shapes and decorated them with distinctive designs, archaeologists can use pottery as a tool to define and study specific cultures. In a few instances we can trace, albeit incompletely, the evolution of these regional cultures from 500 B.C. into the colonial period.

1 northwest
2 north
3 north-central
4 east and central
5 north peninsular Gulf coast
6 central peninsular Gulf coast
7 Caloosahatchee
8 Okeechobee Basin
9 Glades

Post–500 B.C. regions of precolumbian Florida.

Post–500 B.C. Regional Cultures

Regional cultures, each with a distinctive style of pottery, tended to live within one major environmental or physiographic zone where they developed an economic base and other cultural practices well suited to that particular region and its various habitats and resources. East Florida, including the St. Johns River drainage from Brevard County north to Jacksonville, the adjacent Atlantic coastal region, and the many lakes of central Florida, was the region of the St. Johns culture. Like the Late Archaic groups that preceded them, the St. Johns people made extensive use of fish and shellfish and other wild foods. By about 100 B.C., the St. Johns people were constructing sand burial mounds in which they interred their dead. Each village had a leader or leaders who helped coordinate activities, such as communal ceremonies. Vil-

St. Johns culture sites.

lagers most likely were organized into a number of lineages or other kin-based groups, each of which probably had a name and distinctive paraphernalia or other symbols of membership.

When a village grew too large for its residents to be supported easily by local resources, one or more lineages broke away and established a new village nearby. Traditions and shared kinship and origins served to tie old and new villages together. Such a social system probably was present in nearly all of Florida at this time.

Although squashes and gourds may have been grown in gardens even in the Archaic period, it was probably not until after A.D. 750—several hundred years later—that some of the northerly St. Johns peoples began to cultivate corn. Food production, in conjunction with hunting, collecting, and fishing, could support larger human populations. Many more post–A.D. 750 St. Johns villages are known than earlier sites, reflecting this population increase.

Agriculture, important to native groups in the central portion of peninsular Florida and the eastern panhandle, led to changes in lifeways. After about A.D. 1000, some of the groups living along the northern St. Johns River constructed large mounds to serve as bases for temples or as residences for chiefs. Larger populations, a desire to understand and control such things as agricultural fertility and rainfall, and the need for more social cooperation in order to maintain fields and protect territory led to more complex political organization and new beliefs and ceremonial practices.

With agriculture, the roles of village leaders were replaced by those of chiefs and religious figures, who exercised control over people and sought to bridge the gap between the villagers and the supernatural. Often these chiefly and religious officials were associated with special objects and symbols, visible reminders of their power. Through alliances or the threat of military force, some chiefs sought to extend their hegemony and increase their control of territory. At times they controlled outlying villages and village chiefs.

Many of these St. Johns–region villages were inhabited in the sixteenth century when Europeans first came to east Florida. Beginning at this time, we have written records left by the French and the Spaniards offering firsthand descriptions of the early-colonial-period descendants of the St. Johns people. Those descendants include many eastern Timucuan groups who lived along and near the St. Johns River and its tributaries, groups with names like Saturiwa and Utina (see chapter 5). As we shall see in chapter 7, the French and the Spanish visited these groups in the 1560s and came face-to-face with native chiefs who ruled portions of the St. Johns River drainage north of Lake George.

In north and northwest Florida and on the Gulf coast from Cedar Key north, the earliest post–500 B.C. regional culture was the Deptford culture. Village sites characterized by the distinctive Deptford pottery (decorated with check-stamped and grooved-surface designs applied by malleating the surface of the ceramic vessels with carved wooden or clay paddles before they were fired) are especially numerous adjacent to the salt marshes and tidal streams of the Gulf coast. Smaller camps are found inland.

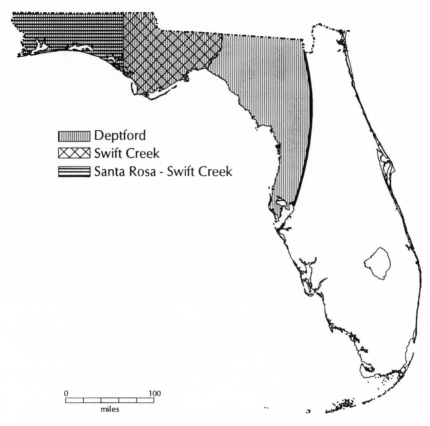

Deptford, Swift Creek, and Santa Rosa–Swift Creek regions in northwest and peninsular Florida. Deptford sites are earlier than Swift Creek and Santa Rosa–Swift Creek sites in the panhandle.

In the panhandle, increased use of interior wetland and forest resources, especially the rivers and lakes in Gadsden, Leon, and Jefferson counties, led to the replacement of the Deptford culture by the Swift Creek culture. Swift Creek, with its distinctive pottery stamped with geometric designs, was related to the Santa Rosa–Swift Creek culture that followed Deptford in the westernmost panhandle. Influenced by cultures to the north of Florida, the late Deptford and Swift Creek societies were associated with a rich variety of ceramic, shell, stone, and even copper items, some traded into the state from the north. Many of these objects display stylized animal motifs representing the same species important to later native Floridians.

The Weeden Island culture and its coastal and inland regional vari-
ants appeared after about A.D. 250 from Sarasota County north along
the Gulf coast to Alabama, as well as in the interior of north and northwest Florida. Weeden Island, named for a site in Old Tampa Bay in
Pinellas County excavated in the early 1920s, emerged out of the Deptford, Swift Creek, Santa Rosa–Swift Creek, and related cultures present
in that large area. Weeden Island–period villages, often with burial
mounds and other mounds in association, are found in a variety of inland and coastal settings. In each area villagers practiced distinctive lifeways while sharing many aspects of Weeden Island ideology and social
and political organization.

One Weeden Island variant culture was the Cades Pond culture of
Alachua County and the western portion of Putnam County. Cades
Pond peoples lived in villages adjacent to extensive wetlands, lakes,
wet prairies, and marshes, where they could fish and gather waterbirds
and a wide variety of other wetland-dwelling animals. They also
hunted in the adjacent forests and collected acorns, hickory nuts, and
persimmons. Numerous Cades Pond mounds are known.

Weeden Island variant cultures also are found around Tampa Bay
(the Manasota culture) and along the north peninsular Gulf coast, the
latter the location of another important site, Crystal River in Citrus
County. In those coastal regions people continued to practice many of
the same patterns of subsistence as did their Late Archaic ancestors.
But, like other Weeden Island villagers, they built mounds and manufactured and traded for ornate ceramic vessels and other objects dis-
playing a rich array of symbols important to their beliefs. The ceramic
complex associated with mounds is the defining characteristic of the
Weeden Island cultures.

Cultivation of corn appeared among the northern Weeden Island
cultures sometime after A.D. 750, about the same time as in the St.
Johns region. In the eastern portion of northwest Florida, maize agriculture became particularly important to aboriginal subsistence, providing, after A.D. 1000, the economic base for the development and
elaboration of the Fort Walton culture, which eventually stretched
from the Aucilla River west through the panhandle. Fertile inland
areas, especially the Tallahassee Hills zone of Leon and Jefferson counties and the upper Apalachicola River Valley, supported a number of
Fort Walton villages, some with large mounds built as platforms on

Weeden Island cultures.

which to erect the temples and residences of chiefs and religious leaders. The Lake Jackson Mounds is one such site.

Fort Walton was the most politically complex precolumbian culture in Florida. Separate political units, each consisting of a number of villages, village chiefs and other officials, and outlying agricultural homesteads, all united under a paramount chief, vied with one another for power and territory. The Apalachee Indians (see chapter 5) encountered by Spanish expeditions in the early colonial period were the descendants of precolumbian Fort Walton populations.

Agriculture also was added to the economic system of the late–Weeden Island–period culture of north peninsular Florida, which was east of the Aucilla River, north of the Santa Fe River, and west of the St. Johns River drainage. Named the Suwannee Valley culture, the people of this post–A.D. 750 culture never practiced agriculture as extensively as did their Fort Walton neighbors. The descendants of Suwannee Valley populations were the Timucua-speaking groups of Madison, Suwannee, Hamilton, and Columbia counties who witnessed the passage of the Hernando de Soto expedition in 1539 (see chapters 5 and 7).

Further south in north-central Florida, from the Santa Fe River to Belleview in Marion County, another culture replaced the Weeden Island–period Cades Pond culture by about A.D. 600. The Alachua culture represents the migration of a new population into Alachua and western Marion counties from the river valleys of southern Georgia. It is uncertain if this intrusive culture was associated with farming when it first appeared in north-central Florida, but by about A.D. 1250, if not before, it is certain that maize was being cultivated. Early in their history in Florida, Alachua settlements expanded westward into eastern Levy and Dixie counties to locales such as Manatee Springs State Park and around Chiefland. The Potano Indians were descendants of the Alachua population.

Around Tampa Bay, a huge estuary capable of supporting large human populations, the Weeden Island–period culture developed into the Safety Harbor culture after about A.D. 900. Safety Harbor sites are found along the Gulf coast from Charlotte Harbor north to the Withlacoochee River in Citrus County. The Safety Harbor people on Tampa Bay probably were not farmers, though villagers just north of Tampa Bay did grow corn. However, corn was not as important to their diet as it was in northwest Florida.

Safety Harbor sites, some containing huge heaps of oyster and other mollusk shells as well as sand mounds and village areas, once dotted the shoreline of Tampa Bay. Today only a few of these large sites exist, such as the Madira Bickel Mound State Archaeological Site. The colonial-period Uzita, Mocoso, Pohoy, Tocobaga, and possibly the Ocale Indians were all Safety Harbor groups. Like other north Florida native societies, all of these Tampa Bay–region peoples were in contact with Spanish expeditions in the sixteenth century (see chapter 4).

Lifeways of the various regional cultures of southern Florida were also well established by 500 B.C. The vast savanna around Lake Okeechobee, called Lake Mayaimi by Florida natives, was the home of the Belle Glade culture. Archaeological evidence from one site suggests

Late precolumbian cultures of northern and west-central Florida.

that by as early as 400 B.C.—shortly after the end of the Late Archaic period—the Belle Glade peoples grew small amounts of maize. But the practice seems to have been abandoned by A.D. 500 or so, possibly because of increasingly wet conditions.

The Belle Glade peoples built a remarkable series of villages, each containing mounds and earthen embankments and other earthworks, some in geometric shapes. They also dug ditches and canals. One such complex site is Fort Center in Glades County, where numerous wooden carvings of animals were found preserved in a pond. Belle Glade villagers continued to live around the lake and in the Kissimmee River drainage into the colonial period. Wetlands and savannas provided them with a rich assortment of fish, birds, turtles, alligator, and other animals, as well as plants.

Late precolumbian cultures of southern Florida.

Along the mangrove coasts and estuaries of southeast Florida, the coasts of the Ten Thousand Island region, and the coast of Monroe County north of the Florida Keys, a distinctive regional culture developed. These Glades-culture people lived by fishing, gathering shellfish, and collecting plants and other animals. Numerous Glades sites also are found in the Everglades and other areas of interior Florida south of the Okeechobee Basin.

Glades archaeological sites once covered the shores of the Florida Gold Coast and the counties north to Indian River County. Where huge precolumbian shell heaps once were on Biscayne Bay, today there are high-rise buildings. Scattered sites, however, are still visible in a few places, such as in Jonathan Dickinson State Park and the Fort Pierce Inlet State Recreation Area. In Dade County the colonial-period descendants of the Glades populations were the Tequesta Indians. To the north were groups such as the Boca Ratones and the Santaluces, names given to the natives by the Spaniards (see chapter 3).

Another coastal-oriented culture, the Caloosahatchee, occupied the southwest coast from Charlotte Harbor south into Collier County. The largest shell mounds in Florida today are found there, such as at Cayo Costa State Park and in the J. N. "Ding" Darling National Wildlife Refuge. Large and small shell heaps are found on nearly every coastal island and the adjacent mainland, especially in Charlotte Harbor, Pine Island Sound, and San Carlos Bay.

The Caloosahatchee peoples, ancestors of the Calusa Indians (see chapter 3), also built mounds of shell and earth to serve as the bases for temples. And they dug ditches and canals similar to those of the Lake Okeechobee Basin, a region to which they were connected by the Caloosahatchee River, to create a canoe highway.

These were the major native cultures of precolumbian Florida. In the next three chapters we will look in more detail at their early-colonial-period manifestations, the various native groups who lived in Florida when Juan Ponce de León first sailed the coastline of Florida. In these and subsequent chapters we shall see how historical documentation, in combination with information gleaned from the archaeological record, can reveal the story of the Indians of Florida and their interactions with explorers and colonists from Spain and France.

Indigenous People

 **PART I**

The past, when viewed from the present, is often romanticized. Perhaps that is one of the reasons people enjoy thinking about precolumbian and early-colonial-period Florida. But was the past truly idyllic? Did the precolumbian native inhabitants of Florida enjoy a carefree life, living in harmony with one another, free from disease and warfare, as some modern faux Indians have claimed? Of course not. The precolumbian groups of Florida at times struggled to survive; they did attack one another, and some groups and individuals were successful in spreading political domination over others.

Over the long term, the archaeological record indicates that the precolumbian groups in Florida did make successful adjustments to the land and to one another. But there were good times as well as bad, times of famine and times of relative plenty. And bioarchaeologists who have studied the bony tissues of precolumbian Florida people tell us they suffered from endemic diseases, such things as treponematosis (a form of nonvenereal syphilis), spina bifida, osteomyelitis, and arthritis.

In the early colonial period, as more and more people from Europe arrived on the scene, life for the native Florida Indians only became more difficult. Introduced diseases and the colonial system reduced populations, caused alterations of traditional political systems, and disrupted what had previously been adequate subsistence systems.

Bioarchaeological analysis of a sixteenth-century native population from west-central Florida and two seventeenth-century mission-related native populations, one from northeast and one from north peninsular Florida, have documented the changes in diet and health that occurred during the colonial period. Lisa Hoshower's (1992) bioanthropological study of Timucua speakers indicates that, in general, mission villagers suffered a lifetime of dietary and disease-related stress. We will return to this topic in part III.

It is certain that the presence of the Spaniards had a profound impact on Florida's native people. To understand that impact we must be cognizant of both the nature of precolumbian societies and the nature of Spanish colonization. It is also true that to understand the Spanish colonization of Florida, especially the activities of the Spaniards, we must understand the nature of the native American societies. In his book *The Spanish Frontier in North America,* David Weber (1992) has shown this to be true of Spanish colonial activities all across the southern United States, the Spanish borderlands.

In Florida, Spanish settlements were restricted to the northern third of the state. It is no coincidence that this region was the home of the Apalachee Indians and the Timucua speakers, both of whom cultivated maize and other crops, food needed to support the Spanish colonists. Because of the nature of their economies, these same native groups tended to be sedentary, maintaining villages with larger populations than nonagriculturists. Larger, sedentary populations provided more opportunities for Spanish missionaries to make converts and more labor for colonial endeavors. Also, the Apalachee and some of the Timucua-speaking groups maintained more centralized political systems, making it easier for the Spaniards to co-opt the upper echelons of native polities and control relatively large populations.

The native groups of central and southern Florida were not maize farmers and most probably did not cultivate any crops. Villages and populations were probably smaller and less densely distributed than in northern Florida. Consequently, the establishment of missions and the control of native populations were much more difficult in the southern two-thirds of the state than in the northern third.

The Spaniards never were successful in their attempts to maintain garrisons and missions in central and southern Florida. In the late seventeenth century, as the native population of Timucua disappeared

Geographical division of Florida into southern, central, and northern regions.

under the onslaught of disease and the rigors of colonization, threatening the labor force needed to sustain the La Florida colony, the Spaniards refocused mission efforts on southwest and central Florida, but these attempts also failed. By that time the English colonial presence in the Carolinas precluded any redirection of Spanish initiatives northward into the native farming populations of interior Georgia and South Carolina. Spain's La Florida colony was destined to fail.

In the three chapters of part 1 that follow, the state of Florida is divided into three geographical sections and the native groups in each are delineated. It might have been more historically and ethnographically precise to divide the groups into two chapters, the northern Apalachee and Timucua-speaking agriculturists in one and all the other groups in the second, but doing so would have resulted in a very long chapter. Instead I have opted to separate the southern two-thirds of peninsular Florida from the northern third along a line drawn from Cape Canaveral northwest to Lake George on the St. Johns River and then southwesterly to the coast at the mouth of the Withlacoochee River. The resulting southern portion of peninsular Florida is further divided by a line drawn from Fort Pierce across the northern end of the Lake Okeechobee Basin to Charlotte Harbor. The outcome nicely divides Florida into three almost equal geographical portions.

We first will look at the native groups in the southernmost third of the state and then consider groups in central and northern Florida. My goal is not to provide ethnographies for these groups but to locate them on the landscape and provide information that can be useful in understanding the impact of the European invasion.

One caveat merits repeating. In delineating these groups it is necessary to rely on many of the same colonial documents that were generated by the colonial process itself. For instance, to know the Jororo existed is to know that the Spaniards tried to missionize them. I cannot describe the Jororo apart from their colonial context; I cannot write about them as if they existed apart from the European presence. To understand early colonial Florida is to understand the interactions between native people and the people from France and Spain who came to La Florida.

Native People in Southern Florida

3 The first time I visited state-owned La Costa Island on the southwest Florida coast, I was awestruck by the extensive shell mounds and middens on this seven-mile-long island. The immense piles of food refuse, some deliberately deposited to form mounds and other shellworks, are extraordinary archaeological sites. But impressive as they are, the La Costa Island sites are only a few of many archaeological sites that still exist along Florida's southwestern Gulf coast. Huge middens and mounds composed of hundreds of thousands of oyster and *Busycon* shells and other debris dot many of the islands in coastal Charlotte and Lee counties.

The size and number of archaeological sites in southwest Florida did not escape the Spaniards who visited the region in the sixteenth century and who also must have marveled at the huge heaps of oysters and *Busycons*. As early as the 1530s, a Spanish navigation rutter called the region "La Costa de Caracoles," literally "the coast of shells."[1] La Costa de Caracoles might well have provided the name for modern La Costa Island.

This world of immense island archaeological sites and shallow, grassy-bottomed waters was the realm of the Calusa Indians, one of the first mainland native groups in the United States to come in contact with Spaniards after Columbus's initial voyage. In this chapter we will learn who these native people were, a people whose archaeological remains were so extensive that they still today bear witness to their world.

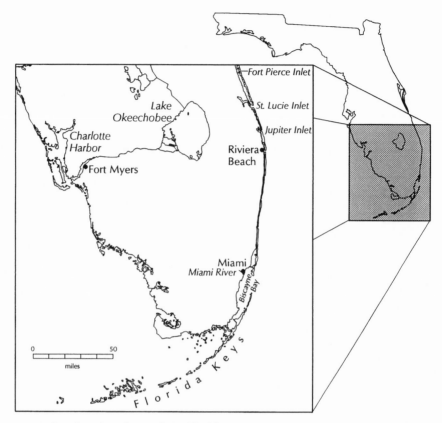

Modern locations in southern Florida.

Calusa of the Southwest Coast

The Calusa Indians were the most important aboriginal group in southern Florida in terms of population size and density, political and military power, and influence. In the early sixteenth century they inhabited the coastal region of southwestern Florida including Charlotte Harbor, Pine Island Sound, San Carlos Bay, and Estero Bay. Sites once associated with the Calusa also were found on the mainland, especially along the Caloosahatchee River.

Archaeologists have named the precolumbian archaeological culture in this region the Caloosahatchee culture and traced its unbroken history back to 500 B.C.[2] Even after they were gone from Florida, the Calusa's renown was apparent to the Seminole Indians, who gave the Caloosahatchee River its name, "River of the Calusa."

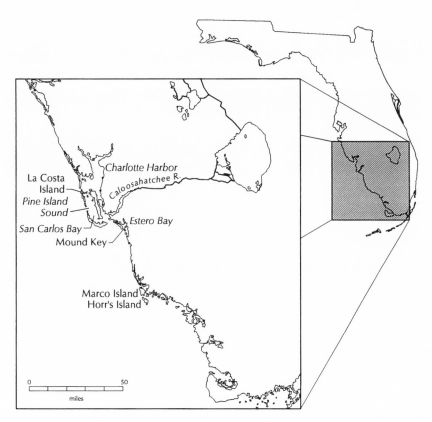

Archaeological site locations in southwest Florida.

Pottery made by the late-precolumbian ancestors of the Calusa is very similar to that found at contemporaneous sites in the Lake Okeechobee Basin, suggesting close ties between the coast and the interior Belle Glade culture. A mid-sixteenth-century account written by a Spaniard named d'Escalante Fontaneda, who had been shipwrecked in south Florida in about 1545 when he was ten years old, suggests that at that time the Calusa chief, called Carlos in Spanish accounts, controlled at least a portion, if not all, of the villages in the Okeechobee Basin. Fontaneda, freed by the Calusa as a sign of goodwill when Pedro Menéndez de Avilés visited the Calusa in 1566, wrote:

Running from south to north between Habana [Havana, Cuba] and Florida, the distance to the Tortugas [Dry Tortugas west of Key West] and the Martires [the Florida Keys] is forty leagues; twenty leagues to the

Martires, and thence [an]other twenty to Florida—to the territory of Carlos, a province of Indians, which in their language signifies a fierce people, they are so-called for being brave and skillful, as in truth they are. They are masters of a large district of country, as far as a town they call Guacata, on the Lake of Mayaimi, which is called Mayaimi because it is very large. Around it are many little villages.[3]

Lake Mayaimi is, of course, the native name for Lake Okeechobee and the source of modern Miami's name.

Fontaneda also names a number of villages subject to the Calusa chief, both coastal towns and those around Lake Okeechobee. The list suggests that the Calusa maintained alliances reaching all across southern Florida to the Atlantic coast:

I will [list] the villages and towns of the . . . [chief] Carlos. . . . First, a place called Tanpa, a large town, and another town which is called Tomo; and another Juchi; and another Soco; another by the name of Ño, which signifies town beloved; another Sinapa; and another Sinaesta; and another, Metampo; and another Sacalo pada; and another Calaobe; another Estame; another Yagua; another Guaya; another Yguebu; another Muspa; another Casitoa; another Tatesta; another Coyobea; another Juton; another Tequemapo; and another with the name Comachica quise; also Yobe and two other towns in that territory, the names of which I do not recollect. Besides there are others inland; on the Lake of Mayaimi; and it, Mayaimi, is the first; and another is Cutespa; another Tavagemve; another Tomsobe; another Enenpa, and there are twenty towns more whose names I do not remember.[4]

Tanpa, the basis for the name of the modern city of Tampa, was a village at the mouth of Charlotte Harbor where the Calusa maintained a large mullet fishery; the Bay of Tanpa was Charlotte Harbor.[5] Later Spaniards mislocated the harbor, assigning the name to Tampa Bay. Tatesta is certainly the Tequesta Indians, a native group whose settlement was at the mouth of the Miami River in modern Miami. Yobe (oftentimes spelled Hobe) is the name of another group that was located on the southeast Florida coast and which is the source of the name of modern Hobe Sound, near where they lived.

Muspa, also mentioned by Fontaneda, was probably on Marco Island, or possibly on Horr's Island immediately to the south. A seem-

ingly accurate sixteenth-century account locates Muspa at 25°45' latitude, near Marco Island. It says that the point of Muspa is distinguished
by "three little groves on top of it that are about half a league distant
from one another."[6] The groves were probably clumps of trees growing
on the top of the high, parabolic sand dune system found on Horr's Island and the southern end of Marco Island and encompassing modern
Caxambas Bay. European-derived, mostly Spanish artifacts have come
from sites on both islands, including the Key Marco site.[7] If Muspa
were a Calusa town, and if it were located on Marco Island, it is evidence that the territory of the Calusa Indians extended down the coast
to the Ten Thousand Islands.

Remarkably, Muspa and Casitoa are names of places appearing in
documents as late as 1698, a century and a half after Fontaneda first
mentioned them.[8] Even later, in 1710, the chief of Muspa, along with
Calusa chiefs and other chiefs of south Florida villages, went to Cuba as
part of a group of 280 Florida Indians. Many died, and the others returned to the Florida Keys in 1716 or 1718.[9] These people may have
been pushed south out of their traditional territories when Creek and
other native groups from the north raided the length of the Florida
peninsula in the early eighteenth century (see chapter 11).

Artifacts derived from the Spaniards, including silver and gold items,
glass and metal beads, ceramics, and iron objects, have been recovered
at a host of sites along the coast and in the Okeechobee Basin, including
the lower Kissimmee River drainage just to the north.[10] Archaeologists
agree that many of these artifacts came from wrecked Spanish ships
that were salvaged by native people. In the sixteenth and seventeenth
centuries, Spanish fleets sailing from Veracruz carrying wealth from
the Americas back to Spain were lost along the Florida coasts, victims
of hurricanes and storms. When salvaged, objects from Mexico and
Central and South America, as well as Spain, found their way to the
Florida Indians. With the cargoes came the ships' crews and passengers
and, at times, native people from elsewhere in the Americas who were
on the ships when they wrecked.

The salvaging of Spanish ships and the division of spoils among
chiefs was described by Fontaneda and by two shipwrecked Spaniards
who were ransomed by the French about 1564 from a native chief
living on the Atlantic coast south of Cape Canaveral. First, Fontaneda's
account:

A silver disc incised with an eye-in-hand motif from the Lake Okeechobee Basin; the disc, which has a central hole, is 3.5 inches in diameter (see Sears 1982:59–67; courtesy of the Florida Museum of Natural History).

I desire to speak of the riches found by the Indians of Ais, which perhaps were as much as a million . . . or over, in bars of silver, in gold, and in articles of jewelry made by the hands of Mexican Indians, which the [ship] passengers were bringing with them. These things Carlos divided with the caciques [chiefs] of Ais, Jeaga, Guacata, Mayajuaco, and Mayaca, and he took what pleased him, or the best part.[11]

The French officer who had the Spaniards ransomed recorded what he learned:

I questioned them about the places they had been. . . . They answered that fifteen years ago [about 1550] three ships, including one they had been on, were wrecked across from a place named Calos, in the shallows called The Martyrs [the Florida Keys] and the King of Calos had recovered most of the treasure in the ships and saved most of the people, including several women. Among them were three or four young married gentlewomen who with their children were still staying with this King of Calos. . . . [The

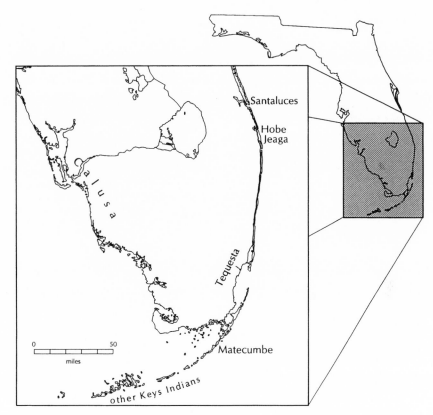

Native groups in southern Florida.

King] was the most handsome and the tallest Indian of the region, a great warrior and one who had many subjects under his authority. They told me furthermore that he had a great deal of gold and silver.[12]

When Spanish soldiers led by Pedro Menéndez visited Calos in the 1560s, they quickly bartered with the Calusa for the gold and silver, taking the wealth that the native peoples had salvaged.

The Ais Indians mentioned in Fontaneda's account lived from Cape Canaveral southward into St. Lucie County, while the Mayaca lived to the northwest in the St. Johns River drainage below Lake George (see chapter 4). The Jeaga Indians, described below, lived along the southeast Florida coast and, as we have seen, the Guacata were in the Okeechobee Basin. Just who the Mayajuaco were is uncertain. Possibly they also were an inland group living in the St. Johns drainage and/or the lakes of Seminole County if they were not the same group known as the Mayaca (see chapter 4).[13]

Other than shipwrecks, another source of the European-derived items found in Calusa sites was a Spanish garrison and Jesuit mission established in the 1560s in the Calusa capitol town of Calos, believed to have been on Mound Key in Estero Bay, south of Fort Myers (see chapter 8).[14] At that time, and apparently throughout the seventeenth century, the chief of the Calusa and his family lived at Calos. But earlier in precolumbian times, the Calusa's main town may have been elsewhere along the coast, such as at the Pineland site on Pine Island in coastal Lee County. Pineland, like Mound Key, features canals, large mounds, and middens.[15]

In the 1960s, Father Clifford Lewis, a Jesuit historian, made several archaeological reconnaissances of Mound Key. He found Spanish pottery, including fragments of sixteenth-century olive jars. Some of those ceramics may have served as containers for oil, wine, and other supplies brought to Calos by the Spanish in the 1560s. Lists of such provisions from 1566–67 include 1,360 fanegas of maize, 91 barrels of flour, 5 barrels of vinegar, 57 barrels of wine, 150 arrobas of oil, 1,500 arrobas of meat, 250 boxes of manioc cakes, 630 quintales of biscuits, 300

One of the large mounds at Mound Key. A person standing on top of the mound provides an idea of the scale. This photograph was taken by Father Clifford Lewis in 1967 (courtesy of the Florida Museum of Natural History).

earthenware jugs of wine, 300 ropes of garlic or onions, 100 hens, 30 goats, 2 arrobas of wax, and 6 bottles of honey.[16]

When Pedro Menéndez first visited the Calusa chief, he presented the chief and his family with food, clothing, beads, scissors, knives, bells, mirrors, hatchets, and machetes. Later, a Jesuit priest returning from Havana brought fishhooks, knives, sickles, adzes, nails, and iron to give to the Calusa.[17] No wonder many Spanish artifacts have been found in southwest Florida.

The Mound Key site, location of Calos, is a roughly circular island crosscut by a Calusa-built canal. However, a large, deep canal cut into the island is a modern artifact, the result of a barge being used to mine shell from the archaeological site for commercial purposes. Today most of Mound Key is owned by the state of Florida and is protected against further disturbances.

Several large, artificial mounds built of earth and shell served as platforms for temples and other important buildings. One is more than thirty feet high. Middens, some several yards thick, cover portions of the island. The Calusa and their precolumbian ancestors must have lived at Mound Key for many generations.

Modern Mound Key and its setting in Estero Bay, once called the Bay of Carlos, still resemble a description written by a Spanish geographer in the 1570s:

> The Bay of Carlos, which is called Escampaba in the language of the Indians . . . is at 26½ plus degrees [latitude; it actually is at 26°24' north latitude]. Its entrance [Big Carlos Pass] is very narrow and full of shallows, as a consequence of which only [small] boats are able to enter. Within it is spacious, about four or five leagues in circumference, although all subject to flooding. There is a little island [Mound Key] in the middle that has a circumference of about a half league, with other islets around it. On this [island] Cacique Carlos had his headquarters and presently his successors have it there [as well].[18]

Father Lewis was not the only person to recover Spanish and other artifacts from Mound Key. In the nineteenth century a large array of sixteenth- and early-seventeenth-century European-derived artifacts were recovered from that small island, some of which subsequently were exhibited in 1895 in Madrid at the Columbian Historical Exposition. Today the objects are in the collections of the University Museum

Metal ornaments and crosses from the Mound Key site. All are made of silver, except for the small cross. The woodpecker ornament is 9.75 inches long (courtesy of the Florida Museum of Natural History).

at the University of Pennsylvania and the National Museum of the American Indian.[19] Most of the artifacts were dug out of the top of a large mound at Mound Key. Some are objects salvaged from wrecked ships.

The collection contains a variety of gold, silver, and copper ornaments, including embossed disks; scraps of copper; amber, silver, gold, and glass beads; a small piece of sheet gold; lead ornaments and musket balls; an iron key; and an assortment of Spanish and Mexican pottery. Several of the gold beads are thought to be from Ecuador.[20] Among the ornaments are a silver, crested bird very similar to several others found at sites west of Lake Okeechobee, and three small, incised silver tablets, one of which was found in 1937. Overall, many of the objects are like those from other south Florida sites.

The tablets are particularly interesting. At least fifty similarly decorated tablets have been found in southern Florida, south of a line from the northern side of Tampa Bay to Cape Canaveral, although most are from the southwest coast, the Kissimmee River drainage, and the

Silver woodpecker ornament (8.75 inches long) from the Lake Okeechobee Basin (courtesy of the South Florida Museum, Bradenton; photograph by David Dye).

western portion of the Lake Okeechobee Basin. Most are made of silver, at least one was crafted from a hammered Spanish coin, and a few were fashioned out of gold or copper.[21]

The design on one side of most of the tablets includes what archaeologist John Griffin suggested may be a sun/fire motif on the back of a stylized spider.[22] Other scholars see other animals depicted. If a spider is represented, the tablets may symbolize a fire-origin myth similar to that recorded from the Cherokee Indians in the late nineteenth century by anthropologist James Mooney:

> In the beginning there was no fire, and the world was cold, until the Thunders . . . who lived up in the Upper World, sent their lightning and put fire into the bottom of a hollow sycamore tree which grew on an island. The animals knew it was there, because they could see the smoke coming out at the top, but they could not get to it on account of the water, so they held a council to decide what to do. . . . [In succession, Raven, Screech Owl, Hooting Owl, Horned Owl, a blackracer snake, and a blacksnake all failed in attempts to bring the fire back.] [A]t last the [Water Spider] said she would go. . . . How could she bring back the fire? "I'll manage that," said the Water Spider; so she spun a thread from her body and wove it into a *tusti* bowl, which she fastened on her back. Then she crossed over to the island and through the grass to where the fire was burning. She put one little coal of fire into her bowl, and came back with it, and ever since we have had fire.[23]

Wooden tablet with what appears to be a spider motif, excavated by Frank Hamilton Cushing at the Key Marco site in the late nineteenth century. The painting was done by Wells Sawyer, who accompanied Cushing. The size of the tablet is uncertain; probably it was 5 to 6 inches long (see Gilliland 1989; courtesy of the Smithsonian Institution).

Some of the tablets are incised on the reverse side with quarter moons or other motifs. Similar sun/fire and spider motifs have been found on a number of stone and wooden tablets in southwest Florida. In a few cases, other motifs appear on tablets of the same shape.

Just what these tablets were used for is uncertain. The iconography, the shape of the tablets, and the motifs on the two sides were probably complex, and the symbolism inherent in the objects may have had multiple meanings. The distribution of the tablets appears to correlate with the geographical distribution of Calusa activities. At least one author has suggested the distribution reflects the extent of Calusa political influence.[24]

As noted above, the sixteenth- and early-seventeenth-century European-derived objects from Mound Key, including the small metal tablets and the stylized bird ornament, are very similar to items from several sites on the west side of Lake Okeechobee.[25] This similarity certainly supports Fontaneda's observation that the Calusa and the people living in the Lake Okeechobee Basin were linked politically. Distribution of these artifacts, including the tablets, also seems to correlate with the distribution of salvaged goods described by Fontaneda in the mid-sixteenth century. Perhaps the distribution of these tablets in some fashion correlates with the geographical alliances governing the division of shipwreck booty made between the Calusa chief and the other south Florida chiefs.

In the sixteenth century the Spaniards saw in the chief of the Calusa a leader whose powers over his people resembled the power of the Spanish monarchs. Indeed, some of the Spaniards called Chief Carlos *el Rey* ("the king"). Carlos and the Calusa chiefs who followed him were imposing individuals who enjoyed political power that reached throughout southern Florida. Vassal chiefs paid them respect and tribute, including feathers, hides, and mats, as well as food items and captives.[26] Whether or not the precolumbian chief of the Calusa was as powerful as Carlos is a topic of discussion among scholars. Some maintain that at least some of Carlos's importance was tied to the distribution of wealth salvaged from Spanish ships.

To support their society, the Calusa depended heavily on fish and shellfish taken from the shallow-bottomed inshore waters of the Gulf of Mexico and the many adjacent estuaries. When Pedro Menéndez was feasted by the Calusa chief he was served boiled and roasted fish and raw, boiled, and roasted oysters, "without anything else."[27] This bounty from the grassy-bottomed tropical waters of southwest Florida was literally a harvest from the sea. Every indication is that the precolumbian ancestors of the Calusa similarly depended on marine waters.

But the lifeways of the precolumbian Calusa would not endure. When the Spanish entered the lives of the Calusa Indians they introduced the native people to another world. Goods salvaged from shipwrecks and items brought to the Calusa by Spanish priests and the military could only have whetted the collective desire of the native peoples to obtain more such items, which had been unknown before the coming of the Europeans. New foods also were introduced, including corn, which the Spanish priests brought to bribe the Calusa to attend classes to learn the catechism.[28] The Calusa, like the other south

Metal disc with embossed dots around the periphery, from the Lake Okeechobee Basin (4.75 inches long). The central "button" once covered a perforated wooden toggle which was placed through a hole in the center of the disk in order to attach it (courtesy of the South Florida Museum, Bradenton; photograph by David Dye).

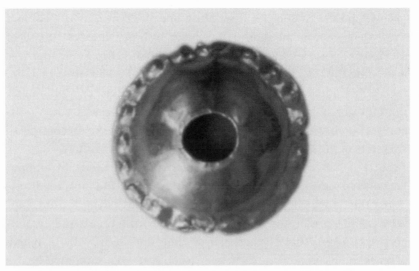

Gold, conical-shaped concha with embossed dots around the edge (2 inches in diameter), Lake Okeechobee Basin (courtesy of the South Florida Museum, Bradenton; photograph by David Dye).

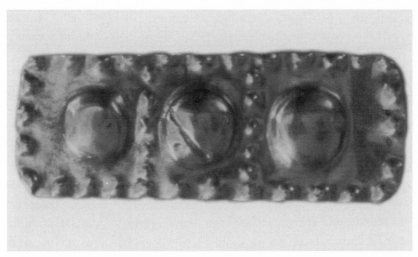

Embossed gold ornament (3.4 inches long), Lake Okeechobee Basin (courtesy of the South Florida Museum, Bradenton; photograph by David Dye).

Florida native peoples, did not grow corn, and they may have viewed it as an exotic delicacy.

But despite Spanish intervention into their lives, the Calusa Indians of the sixteenth and seventeenth centuries, like other Florida Indians, were not mere dupes caught up in the events of the colonial period. As much as they could, they maintained their way of life and took an active role in trying not only to influence their place in the new world unfolding around them but also to turn that world to their advantage. As we shall see in chapter 8, the Calusa chief sought to co-opt Pedro Menéndez and his military might to punish enemies of the Calusa. And the Calusa, both in the period of Jesuit missions in the 1560s and that of the Franciscan missions in the 1690s, were not averse to using diplomacy as well as guile to obtain the material items offered by the Spanish.

The Calusa did not always welcome Spanish priests and soldiers with open arms. Although they did interact with the Spaniards and sometimes accede to Spanish wishes, they did so only when it was in their own best interest. Perhaps the most graphic example of the feelings the Calusa harbored toward Spaniards dates to 1697, when Franciscans came to Calos to establish a mission. The Calusa ridiculed the priests, laughing at them and throwing mud and soot on them when they tried to preach. Some of the hecklers "turned around and showed them [the priests] their buttocks."[29] The priests were expelled, forced to canoe down the coast to seek safety in Cuba. Along their arduous journey they were harassed, thrown into the Gulf, relieved of their supplies, and, ultimately, left naked. When found by a Spanish ship at Matecumbe Key, they were nearly dead from hunger.

The Calusa could reject the priests and the religion they represented and gain some measure of pride by ridiculing them, but they dared not kill them. The Calusa knew the might of the Spanish. In the encounter between the Calusa and the Spaniards, the native people were not on equal footing, at least in terms of military might. Ultimately, as we shall see in chapter 11, this disadvantage, as well as the diseases brought to Florida by Spaniards and other Europeans, led to the total destruction of the Calusa. Today we have only artifacts, archaeological sites, and the information found in archives to help us understand the Calusa Indians, one of the first native societies in the mainland United States to encounter the European invasion.

Tequesta of the Miami Area

Despite modern housing and commercial development in southern Florida, we can still envision some part of the natural world of the Calusa. Canoeing the inshore waters south of Fort Myers Beach offers at least a bit of the ambience of the region when they canoed the same coastline hundreds of years ago. Unfortunately, the same is not true of the coast of southeast Florida, especially Dade County, home of the Tequesta Indians, which once also featured numerous shell middens, though smaller ones than those in southwest Florida. Middens once were especially prevalent around Biscayne Bay, including near the mouth of the Miami River. Similar sites were found north along the Gold Coast and beyond in Broward, Palm Beach, St. Lucie, and Martin counties. Other, much smaller, sites were inland on the small tree "islands" along the eastern edge of the Everglades.

In the first decade of the twentieth century, visitors to the Miami Beach–Biscayne Bay locale saw these sites, some of which had been occupied by the precolumbian ancestors of the Tequesta Indians. But almost none of the large sites survived the onslaught of the real estate boom that began in Florida in the 1920s. The same combination of sea and sand that made the region hospitable to American Indians and drew real estate entrepreneurs in the early part of this century continues to draw people to the region. As modern resident and tourist populations increase, archaeological sites are leveled to make room for the buildings and other amenities that modern Floridians and tourists require. The material heritage of the Tequesta and other native people of southeast Florida has been almost totally erased from the landscape.

Fortunately, archaeologists have been able to study some of the sites in southeast Florida. Scientists from Florida Atlantic University have an ongoing project investigating extant sites in the Palm Beach County area. In addition, avocational archaeologists affiliated with chapters of the Florida Anthropological Society and archaeologists of the Florida Archaeological and Historical Conservancy and the National Park Service continue to study sites in southern Florida, including along the Gold Coast and in nearby inland areas.

The archaeological culture associated with these sites and the material culture of the Tequesta Indians have been named the Glades culture, which can be traced back in time at least to 500 B.C.[30] Glades sites are found throughout most of south Florida, excepting the region of the Calusa Indians on the southwest coast and the Lake Okeechobee Basin region. The Tequesta, however, seem to have been restricted to the general Dade County area.

Their main village was on the Miami River near the coast. López de Velasco describes the location:

> At the very point [of land] of Tequesta there enters into the sea a freshwater river, which comes from the interior, and to all appearances runs from west to east. There are many fish and eels in it. Alongside it on the north side is the Indian settlement that is called Tequesta, from which the point takes its name.[31]

Archaeological excavations have been carried out at the Granada site, an extensive shell midden on the north side of the Miami River at or near the location of the Tequesta village.[32] The site contained colonial-period glass beads and metal objects, as well as precolumbian artifacts.

What were the Tequesta like?[33] Unfortunately, our first documentary descriptions of the Tequesta are relatively sparse and come from the 1560s, two generations or more after initial Spanish contact and several decades after the salvage of Spanish shipwrecks and the redistribution of their contacts had been ongoing in southern Florida.

The archaeological information from the precolumbian period provides no evidence that the Tequesta were organized in as complex a fashion as the Calusa. There are no village sites with large mounds thought to have been associated with a paramount chief like the Calusa's. Yet documents from the 1560s and later periods do indicate there was a head chief of the Tequesta, who resided in their main village and controlled several other villages and their leaders. The chief's brother had high social status and could represent the chief. So at least in the colonial period there were some similarities to the Calusa political system.

But Tequesta political organization was only a dim reflection of that of the Calusa. The Tequesta chief ruled over a much smaller population and did not control outlying, non-Tequesta villages or chiefs. The Tequesta chief was forced to show allegiance to the Calusa chief, maintaining that alliance through exchange marriages of chiefly relatives. Even so, on at least one occasion the chief of the Tequesta was not above trying to instigate his own initiatives and challenge Calusa authority. When he failed, he had to face the wrath of the Calusa chief.[34]

Spanish documents provide additional descriptions of the Tequesta. They tell us there were "leading men," perhaps respected elders or warriors or relatives of the chief. Both these individuals and the chief had high status. Writing in the last quarter of the sixteenth century, López de Velasco described the special treatment awarded each of these high-status individuals upon his death:

> When a cacique or leading man dies, they take him apart and remove the larger bones from the body and they bury the little bones with the body. And in the cacique's house they place a large box and they enclose the large bones in this box and the whole village comes there to adore and they hold these bones as their gods.[35]

This describes very accurately the treatment of human bodies as reconstructed from archaeological evidence from large portions of Florida during the precolumbian period.[36] Burials resulting from this process—interment of the large bones—have been found just south of

Calusa territory on Horr's Island in Collier County and in Broward County.[37] One of the mounds in the Boynton Mound complex in Palm Beach County may also have contained similar burials.[38] European-derived beads were found in both the Collier County and Palm Beach County sites.

One reason the Tequesta did not develop larger populations may have been that their subsistence base did not allow it. Although they made their livelihood by fishing, collecting plants and animals (including shellfish), and hunting, the waters of Biscayne Bay and the surrounding estuaries and adjacent islands and mainland could not produce the large amounts of food that the Calusa could harvest from their environment.

The languages spoken by the Tequesta and other native groups in south Florida remain unknown. Other than place-names and proper names, only a handful of native words were recorded in Spanish documents. That small amount of linguistic data suggests that the languages were different from the Timucua language and the Apalachee language spoken in northern Florida. One documentary account says the language of the Tequesta was "similar to or the same as Calusan." In 1570 a priest observed that "in Carlos [the region controlled by the Calusa] there were twenty-four languages in the thirty chieftainships." That same account notes the people speaking these languages "did not understand one another," suggesting these were separate languages, not dialects.[39]

In the eighteenth century, at the time Florida native groups were being raided and, in some instances, displaced, by marauding native groups from more northerly states, Spanish priests returned to south Florida. In 1743 a Jesuit mission was established for a brief time at the mouth of the Miami River where the Tequesta's main village had once been. Documents relevant to that mission no longer refer to the Tequesta, but they do mention two other groups, the Santaluces and Boca Ratones (see below).[40] The former lived two days' travel north, and the latter, greatly reduced in number, were living with other refugee groups at the mission. Both groups provided place-names still apparent today: St. Lucie County and the town of Boca Raton. Boca Raton (which translates into English as "Rat Mouth") probably derived its name from a small coastal inlet, perhaps the one still called Boca

Raton Inlet today. Both names are examples of the use of Spanish names to refer to native groups.

Jeaga, Hobe, and Santaluces of the Southeast Coast

As one moves northward along the Atlantic coast from Dade County toward Cape Canaveral, there are variations in the Glades archaeological culture. One variation is in the East Okeechobee subregion, largely Palm Beach County, where archaeologists have recently described an archaeological assemblage called the Riviera Complex. That complex is thought to be associated with the Jeaga Indians, one of the groups mentioned by Fontaneda.[41] Large numbers of what are described as sixteenth-century glass beads, as well as a few gold and silver beads and two cut crystal beads, were excavated from a Palm Beach County site.[42] The mound may have been associated with the Jeaga.

Farther inland, in the Lake Okeechobee Basin, sites are associated with the Belle Glade complex, a different archaeological culture, one associated with the Guacata and other native groups said by Fontaneda to live around the lake.[43] Many of those sites also contain European-derived artifacts.

North of the Jeaga, in coastal Martin County, were the Hobe Indians. During the early colonial period, native groups must have lived in coastal Broward County, because Spanish artifacts have been found there as well.[44] Both the Jeaga and the Hobe, as well as other groups, are named in a 1675 Spanish document that lists the groups on that Atlantic coast south of Cape Canaveral as the Ais, Santaluces, Jeagas, Jobeses (Hobe), Viscaynos, and Matecumbes.[45] The Viscaynos, from whom modern Biscayne Bay derives its name, may be the Tequesta, while the Santaluces, mentioned above, probably lived near a sixteenth-century Spanish garrison called Santa Lucía, thought to be located near modern Port St. Lucie. The Matecumbe were in the Florida Keys.

Of these groups, the best known is the Hobe, who rescued a group of American English colonists whose ship was wrecked in 1696 during a storm on the coast about five miles north of Jupiter Inlet. This location is well documented by one of the shipwrecked men, who used a quadrant salvaged from the wreck to shoot the sun and determine that their location was 27°8' north latitude, just north of Jupiter Inlet. One of those shipwrecked, Jonathan Dickinson, wrote a remarkable account of the wreck and of the native people they encountered as the survivors made their way northward along the coast to Spanish St. Augustine. Without his account we would know little about the Hobe or the Ais, to the north.[46]

Dickinson and his fellow passengers viewed the Hobe and the other native people as bloodthirsty, pagan cannibals and were constantly in fear of their lives. The native peoples, who consistently sought to intimidate the colonists and, thus, to control them, seem mainly to have been interested in salvaging what they could from the shipwreck and then sending the passengers away.

In order to protect Spaniards who were wrecked on that shore, the military government in St. Augustine had made it clear to the native groups that the survivors of wrecks were to be protected and turned over to Spanish authorities. They also required the native people to report the presence of non-Spaniards. The native people received payment from the military government for rendering these services. These interactions with Spaniards provided an opportunity for the native people to trade ambergris. Highly valued in Europe as an ingredient in perfumes, ambergris was collected by Florida Indians from the beaches, where it washed ashore after being deposited in the Atlantic by whales. On his trek northward, Dickinson observed such a trade: five pounds of ambergris for a mirror, ax, a knife or two, and tobacco.

When their ship—already partly broken up from when it ran aground in the storm—washed up on the beach, Dickinson and the other survivors salvaged their luggage, trunks, and chests and set up a camp. The hogs and sheep on board had been washed away and had swum to shore, where they were wandering about. In no time at all, several Hobe appeared, whom Dickinson described as frothing at the mouth. They soon were followed by a larger contingent, including the leader of the Hobe, also frothing at the mouth. Perhaps they were chewing tobacco or another substance.

Word of a wrecked ship and the promise of booty spread quickly, and the chief and other Hobe soon came to oversee the salvage operation. Dickinson distributed tobacco and pipes, hoping to ensure good intentions on the part of the Hobe. After threatening the shipwreck victims to gain their cooperation, the Hobe proceeded to take the chests and trunks and most of the survivors' clothes, as well as corn and other goods. They left behind the rum, sugar, and molasses, which were taken later when the Hobe returned to strip the site. Perhaps the rum, sugar, and molasses were valued commodities to which another chief whose military might the Hobe feared had a standing claim. That person may have been the chief of the Ais, who lived north of St. Lucie Inlet in Indian River and Brevard counties (see chapter 4). When Dickinson and the other colonists reached the Ais and their chief learned of the shipwreck, he immediately went to claim his share of the booty, which included Spanish coins.

After the Hobe completed their initial salvage of the ship, the natives took Dickinson's contingent about five miles south to their main village on Jupiter Inlet. (A large shell midden that marked the spot in the early twentieth century has been destroyed.) Dickinson describes the Hobe men as wearing a loincloth made of woven vegetable fibers, with their long hair worn in a bun "tied in a roll behind [their heads] in which stuck two bones shaped one like a broad arrow, and the other a spearpoint."[47] Hobe men and women later donned clothing taken from the colonists.

Some of the Hobe houses—small wigwams made by sticking poles into the ground, bending them over and tying them to make a dome-shaped framework that was thatched with palmetto fronds—were built on the shell middens. Later, in their journey northward, Dickinson and the other colonists saw the benefits of such a location when a storm-driven high tide flooded another native village in which they were staying; only the houses on the highest parts of the shell heaps were spared.

The diet of the Hobe was like that of other coastal groups. They speared fish, some of which were drumfish, and gathered oysters and clams, coco plums, sea grapes, and palm berries. Night fishing was done from a canoe using a torch. Two canoes could be made into a catamaran by tying poles between them and placing mats on the pole frame for passengers. Although the Hobe depended largely on marine foods and plants collected near the shore, they also hunted deer and used the hides as blankets. Gourds were used as rattles and dippers. These probably were made from small, hard gourds that grew semiwild around villages. Dickinson noted the Hobe and their neighbors "neither sow nor plant."[48]

While at the Hobe village, Dickinson witnessed a native ceremony that, from the viewpoint of a cold, hungry shipwreck survivor who thought he might be killed and eaten by his hosts at any minute, must have been an extraordinarily blood-curdling event:

> Night came on; the moon being up, an Indian, who performeth their ceremonies stood out, looking full at the moon making a hideous noise, and crying out acting like a mad man for the space of half an hour; all the Indians being silent till he had done: after which they all made fearful noise some like the barking of a dog, wolf, and other strange sounds. After this, one gets a log and sets himself down, holding the stick or log upright on the ground, and several others getting about him, made a hideous noise, singing to our amazement; at length their women joined consort making the noise more terrible. This they continued till midnight.[49]

This Hobe ceremony, led by a native priest and involving chanting, must have been as foreign to Jonathan Dickinson as Dickinson's own wedding ceremony would have seemed to the Hobe.

At a native village just to the north, probably at St. Lucie Inlet and perhaps occupied by the Santaluces, Dickinson saw the people brew and drink a special tea called black drink. The drink is made from the parched leaves of the yaupon holly plant (*Ilex vomitoria*), which grows wild along the Florida coasts north of the more tropical regions. It was used as a ceremonial tea by a very large number of southeastern American Indians, including nearly all of the groups in northern Florida. Archaeological evidence suggests it has a long history in Florida.[50] Dickinson described the ceremony in detail:

> In one part of this house where the fire was kept, was an Indian man, having a pot on the fire wherein he was making a drink of the leaves of a shrub (which we understood afterwards . . . is called caseena), boiling the said leaves, after they had parched them in a pot; then with a gourd having a long neck and at the top of it a small hole which the top of one's finger could cover, and at the side of it a round hole of two inches diameter, they take the liquor out of the pot and put it into a deep round bowl, which being almost filled containeth nigh three gallons. With this gourd they brew the liquor and make it froth very much. It looketh of a deep

brown color. In the brewing of this liquor was this noise made which we thought strange; for the pressing of this gourd gently down into the liquor, and the air which it contained being forced out of the little hole at top occasioned a sound; and according to the time and motion given would be various. This drink when made, and cooled to sup, was in a conch-shell first carried to the Casseekey, who threw part of it on the ground, and the rest he drank up, and then would make a loud He-m; and afterwards the cup passed to the rest of the Casseekey's associates, as aforesaid, but no other man, woman nor child must touch or taste of this sort of drink; of which they sat sipping, chatting and smoking tobacco, or some other herb instead thereof, for the most part of the day.[51]

Dickinson and the other shipwreck survivors, guided by natives, made their way north past Cape Canaveral, traveling up what is today the Intracoastal Waterway, the Indian River and Mosquito Lagoon. North of the cape they met a party of Spaniards, who helped guide them to a Spanish outpost at Matanzas Inlet and then to St. Augustine. Eventually they traveled northward to Charleston, then an English colonial town. Were it not for the unfortunate shipwreck, we would know almost nothing about the native people of Martin County.

Matecumbe and Native Groups of the Florida Keys

American Indians also inhabited the Florida Keys, which the Spaniards called the Martyrs. Archaeologists have located a number of pre-columbian sites—typically shell middens—within the Keys, and human occupation of the region stretches back at least to A.D. 800. The archaeological assemblage found at the precolumbian Keys sites is a variant of the Glades assemblage.[52]

By the time of extensive Spanish contact in the region, forty years or so after the onset of shipwreck salvaging by the native peoples, the chiefs of groups living in the Keys were subject to the Calusa chief. Because of their geographical position, the Keys were well known to the sixteenth-century Spaniards whose ships plied the coasts of southern Florida and the Straits of Florida:

From the farthest point of the mainland, which [southernmost Monroe and Dade counties] is at 25 degrees, it [the upper Florida Keys] runs toward the sea [the eastern Gulf of Mexico] on a northeast-southwest orientation until at 24^1/$_2$ degrees it becomes a chain of shoals, full of little islands that they call the Martyrs [the lower Florida Keys]. And they are countless, with the greater part of them inhabited by Indians subject to the cacique [chief], Carlos, great archers and spear throwers. One may sail among them [the islands] with light-draft vessels and canoes. . . . The long and big island, which is at the end of the Martyrs, is also inhabited by Indians, like the others, whose cacique is called Matecumbe.[53]

Modern-day Upper and Lower Matecumbe keys derive their names from Chief Matecumbe.

Fontaneda's sixteenth-century account mentions two other villages or locations in the Keys, Cuchiaga and Guarugunbe, and both also are mentioned by López de Velasco (who may have gotten his information from Fontaneda). Cuchiaga also is named in two late-seventeenth-century documents. Still another village, Tancha, is noted as being in the Keys.[54]

By the late seventeenth century, the Spaniards had assigned names to a number of islands and locations in the Keys and generally referred to the native peoples of those locations by those names. Many of those designations are still in use: Key of Huesos (Key of Bones, today Key West), Key of Vacas (Key of Cows, today Vaca Key), Key Largo, Bahia Honda (Deep Bay), and the Key of Matecumbe.[55]

The native people living in the Keys were organized into groups, each occupying a different locale or island. There is no archaeological or documentary evidence suggesting they were anything other than small groups that were forced to pay tribute—perhaps shipwreck booty—to the Calusa chief. Like their Glades culture neighbors to the north, they lived by fishing, hunting, and collecting wild plants and animals, including sea turtles that came ashore to lay eggs.

During the later colonial period, native people moved back and forth between the Keys and Cuba, both of their own volition and by Spanish intervention. William Sturtevant has reviewed documents indicating that remnants of the Calusa, Mayaimis, and other southern Florida natives were resettled in the Keys by the Spanish in 1716 or 1718. These people had been taken to Cuba in 1711, where most had died of sickness.[56] They were needed to provide labor for Spanish fishing efforts, some of which were centered in the Florida Keys in the early eighteenth century. Descendants of these native laborers, perhaps joined by other south Florida Indians, continued to live in the Keys until as late as 1763.[57]

In the next chapter we will delineate some of the native groups who lived in central Florida, including those on the Atlantic and Gulf coasts north of the Jeaga and the Calusa. Again, archaeological and documentary evidence combine to allow us to associate groups with archaeological cultures and locations within colonial and modern Florida.

Native People in Central Florida

4
In 1696, when Jonathan Dickinson and his fellow shipwreck survivors traveled the Atlantic coast north of the Jeaga, they entered the territory of the Ais Indians. That region stretched from Fort Pierce to Cape Canaveral and encompassed the adjacent mainland, probably including a section of the St. Johns River in Brevard County. West of the Ais, in the south-central area of the state, from Orange County south into Osceola County and parts of Polk and Highland counties, lived another native group, the Jororo. To the north of the Jororo within the St. Johns River drainage, from Seminole County north to Lake George, were the Mayaca Indians.

Two of these three groups, the Jororo and the Mayaca, are often mentioned together in Spanish documents. The basis for this linkage is the fact that both groups spoke a language the Spaniards called Mayaca.[1] Both also were the focus of missionary efforts in the 1690s. Some Spanish documents also suggest a linkage between the Jororo and Mayaca Indians and the Ais Indians to the east, but the reasons for that are unknown.

The Jororo and the Mayaca were relatively far away from the major Spanish mission provinces and settlements in north Florida. To reach the Jororo villages, the Spaniards first traveled to Mayaca, probably via the St. Johns River, and then went overland to the Jororo. Spaniards sometimes referred to the peninsular region in which the two groups lived as *la rinconada,* a Spanish word meaning a corner or nook, a place

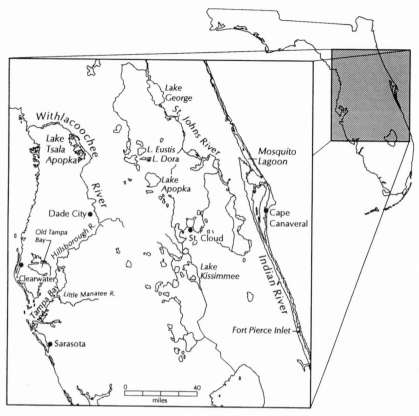

Modern locations in central Florida.

away from major activities. In 1702 the Spanish governor of La Florida described la rinconada as "a stretch of land in the shape of a horseshoe, which in the two extremities [has], in the one, the Presidio [St. Augustine], and in the other, the port of San Luís de Apalachee, which are seventy or eighty leagues distant from one another."[2] To the Spaniards this was the hinterlands, a region where people lived, but one well apart from the areas where there was a strong Spanish presence. To reach either the Jororo or the Mayaca was difficult because they did not live on the coast, nor were they easily accessible by river transportation, at least by Spanish watercraft.

As a consequence of their location, the Jororo and the Mayaca remained relatively isolated from Spanish initiatives. It was only after the native populations at the northern missions were severely decimated that the Spaniards began to make a major effort to place missions in la rinconada (see chapters 9 and 11). Thanks to John Hann's

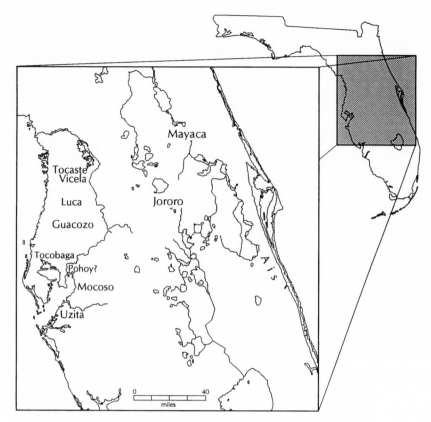

Native groups and towns in central Florida.

discovery of documents regarding an attempt to missionize the
Mayaca and Jororo in the late seventeenth century that we know
much about either group at all.

Other native groups also lived in central Florida. West and southwest of the Jororo and the Mayaca, in the region immediately around
and near Tampa Bay, were the Uzita, Mocoso, Pohoy, Tocobaga, and
others, most of which had interactions with Spanish explorers and
sailors in the sixteenth century. In this chapter all of these native
groups are further delineated and, as much as possible, tied to archaeological assemblages and locations in modern Florida.

Ais of the Central East Coast

Like the Jororo and the Mayaca, the Ais were geographically outside
the main thrust of Spanish colonial initiatives. But because they

controlled a coastal region where Spanish ships wrecked, their presence generated a documentary record, albeit a small one relative to the Calusa.

The large bay at the north end of the Indian River was known to the Spanish, and perhaps the native people, as the Bay of Ais. Its northern end was across the Bar of Ais just west of the southern end of the Mosquito Lagoon (and modern Kennedy Space Center). Modern Indian River, a saltwater lagoon that stretches southward past the Fort Pierce Inlet to the St. Lucie Inlet, was called the River of Ais; its southern mouth was said to be at 27 degrees north latitude.[3]

The Ais included a number of towns, each with its own leader, who were subject to a single chief, the chief of Ais. At about the same time that Dickinson was among the Ais, a Spanish bishop noted that the Ais chief had many fewer people and vassals than did the Calusa chief.[4]

One of the Ais towns in which Dickinson stayed was Jece, perhaps an Anglicized form of Ais. The town was four to five miles north of the Fort Pierce Inlet on the Indian River. Within the town was the chief's house, twenty-four by forty feet in size, with walls and roof thatched with palmetto fronds. Low benches formed seating platforms in the interior, which was partitioned.[5] This house contrasted with the smaller, simpler, wigwamlike houses occupied by the villagers.

The Ais alliance may have been at least in part the result of the presence of the Spanish (and possibly the French) and the wealth wrecked ships brought. But like the Tequesta, the Ais were subject to Calusa domination and were forced to maintain an alliance with the Calusa chief. Even so, the Ais were more powerful than the less numerous Jeaga; the Ais chief could claim a share of the booty from Dickinson's ship wrecked in Jeaga territory.

The archaeological assemblage that correlates with the Ais is the Indian River culture, a variant of the St. Johns culture.[6] Pottery found at precolumbian archaeological sites in Ais territory is a mixture of St. Johns wares and sand-tempered wares. The Indian River ceramic assemblage is distinct from those of the Mayaca and Timucuan regions and those of south Florida.

Indian River sites are found along the coast and in the adjacent marshy headwaters of the St. Johns River in Brevard, Indian River, and northern St. Lucie counties. In that region the freshwater St. Johns River and its marshy headwaters are only ten to fifteen miles from the coast. The people probably gained their livelihood by utilizing both the

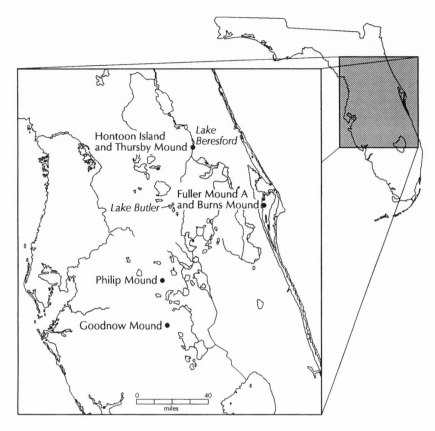

Archaeological site locations in central Florida.

coastal lagoons and other marine habitats and the freshwater inland marshes and other wetlands. Shell middens and other sites, including mounds containing human burials, are found in both locales. Like the Jeaga and Hobe to the south, the Ais lived by fishing, hunting, and collecting wild foods. They did not cultivate crops.

The Cape Canaveral area contains a large number of archaeological sites, including two mounds—the Fuller Mound A and the Burns Mound—in which European-derived glass beads have been found.[7] Just to the west of the cape, in easternmost Orange County, Spanish artifacts have been found in sites on the St. Johns River, probably in Ais territory.[8] Extensive salt marshes once were found in the vicinity of the cape, whose Spanish name, Cape Cañaveral, means cape of cane or reed fields, referring to those salt marshes, once the most extensive along the Atlantic coast south of St. Augustine. These salt marshes could have supported larger populations than those to the south.

In 1692 Spanish authorities were asked by a Mayaca or Jororo chief to provide missions so the people could become Christians.[9] The Spaniards took this request to include the Ais Indians. However, it is not certain that any missions were ever established in their territory.

Jororo of South-Central Florida

Prior to the research of historian John Hann, the name of the Jororo was practically unknown to scholars of the native Florida Indians. His research utilized documents reporting the establishment of Spanish missions among the Jororo in the late seventeenth century, a subsequent rebellion (which also involved the Mayaca), and the Spaniards' retaliation. Those archival records indicate the Jororo lived in south-central Florida, south of the Mayaca and west of the Ais, most likely from Orange County southward into Polk and Highland counties, west of the St. Johns River, which is very near the coast in that part of Florida. A large number of lakes are found in the Jororo region, a fact observed by a Spaniard in the late seventeenth century who noted the Jororo "lived on islands and very large lakes."[10]

The main village, called Jororo, was sixteen leagues from a Mayaca mission, which in turn was thirty-six leagues (about 120 miles) from St. Augustine. That was likely the distance overland from St. Augustine to the St. Johns River and downriver. In Jororo in the late seventeenth century, three missions were built nine leagues (about thirty miles) apart.[11]

Documentation regarding the Jororo missions mention several towns: Jororo itself, Atissimi, Atoyquime, and Piaja, the first three having missions. In the rebellion in 1696 the priest at Atoyquime, Father Luís Sánchez, was killed along with two native boys who assisted him in rites and a native chief who was becoming a Christian. Later, a Spanish soldier, part of a contingent sent to punish the natives responsible for the murders, was killed, as were two Guale Indians who had accompanied him.[12] Hann suggests that the name Atissimi, sometimes given as Jizime and Tisime, may be the source of the modern place-name Kissimmee.[13]

Initially the Spaniards were unable to find and punish the guilty parties because the soldiers were led astray by their native guides, who took them through "swamp areas and ponds,"[14] but later three of the natives involved in the murders were captured.[15] After that rebellion, some of the Jororo fled the area, one group to a town called Afafa on the St. Johns River, twenty leagues from St. Augustine, location in 1706 of a Spanish hacienda.[16]

Seventeenth-century Spanish artifacts, evidence for Spanish interaction with the native people of south-central Florida, have been found in Philip Mound, west of St. Cloud near Lake Marian in eastern Polk County, and in Goodnow Mound, near Sebring in Highlands County.[17] European artifacts also have come from sites on the east side of Lake

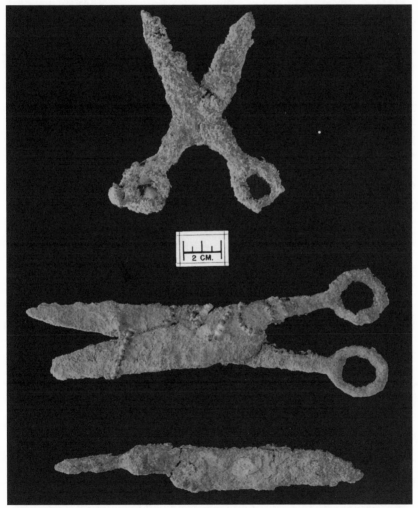

Two pairs of iron scissors and an iron knife blade excavated by John Griffin and Hale Smith (1948) from the Goodnow Mound in Highlands County. Strings of glass beads can be seen adhering to the middle scissors, which are 8 inches long. The photograph was taken by Griffin (courtesy of the Florida Museum of Natural History).

Apopka and from sites around the lakes immediately to the south in western Orange County. However, these latter sites may be too far north to have been in Jororo territory.

In 1693 a priest writing about the Jororo and Mayaca people noted, "on the whole [they] do not work at plantings. They are able to sustain themselves solely with the abundance of fish they catch and some wild fruits."[18] Like the south Florida Indians, they were hunter-gatherers.

It is not known what language the Jororo spoke other than that it was the same as the Mayaca, a language distinct from Timucua.[19] A Spanish document from the late-seventeenth-century period of the Jororo missions states that the people of Jororo and Mayaca "border on diverse nations with different languages,"[20] suggesting their language also was distinct from those of the south Florida Indians.

Mayaca of the Central St. Johns River

The first encounter between the Mayaca and Spaniards took place when an expedition led by Pedro Menéndez de Avilés sailed up (south-ward) the St. Johns River in the late 1560s. After crossing Lake George, the expedition came to a village of the Macoya Indians (another name for the Mayaca), which had been abandoned, presumably a strategic withdrawal by the native inhabitants.

After entering the village, Menéndez learned that the chief of the Mayaca did not wish the Spaniards to proceed any farther up the river. But Menéndez refused to honor this request and, manning oars, the Spaniards attempted to continue their journey. Several miles farther upstream, where the river narrowed, the Spaniards found the Mayaca had blocked their passage with "a row of stakes" across the river.[21] After breaking through the barrier, Menéndez managed to row farther, only to find that the river narrowed again, making it dangerous to continue, especially because Mayaca Indians, armed with bows and arrows, were observing the Spaniards' efforts. After more negotiations failed to gain him passage, Menéndez opted to retreat.

A Spaniard named Perucho, a former captive of the Ais who served Menéndez as an interpreter and guide, helped to convince the Spanish governor this was the proper decision, telling him the Mayaca were "many and very warlike."[22] The Mayaca were said to control the river from the point where the confrontation with Menéndez took place up the river (south) for an unspecified distance.

These descriptions place the Mayaca in the St. Johns River drainage south of Lake George in eastern Lake and western Volusia counties down to Seminole County. That portion of the river is characterized by large lakes and extensive marshes and contains numerous freshwater shell middens. Some of the latter, such as at Tick Island and Hontoon Island, are extensive. Burial mounds containing human burials, such as the Thursby Mound, also are present.

These archaeological sites all are associated with the St. Johns culture, as are the sites of the Timucua-speaking people to the north on the lower St. Johns River.[23] Investigations in the Lake Beresford area near Hontoon Island and Thursby Mound have established that Spanish olive jar potsherds and other European artifacts are common in sites there.[24] It may be that one of the Mayaca missions was in that general vicinity.

Little is known about Mayaca villages. At least one village may have been abandoned by the late mission period, when Spanish soldiers traveled to "ancient Mayaca" on their way to pacify the native people following the 1696 rebellion, which had taken place there and in Jororo. Hann suggests ancient Mayaca may be the site of the first Mayaca mission, San Salvador, in the early seventeenth century.[25]

Next we will turn to the Tampa Bay region, home of the Tocobaga and other native groups. The Calusa chief was apparently unable to hold sway over these groups until after the appearance of the Spaniards in the sixteenth century. Disease-caused population reductions and diplomatic and military maneuvering by the Spaniards in the 1560s may have altered the military and political balance of power that had existed previously among the Gulf coast native groups.

Tocobaga and the Central Gulf Coast Groups

Tampa Bay, a huge bight on the Gulf coast of Florida, is an estuary whose shoreline once featured both mangrove forests and saltwater marshes. The Hillsborough, Alafia, Little Manatee, and Manatee rivers flow into the bay, draining freshwater wetlands in Pasco, Hillsborough, Polk, and Manatee counties. This combination of salt and freshwater habitats presented the native peoples with a veritable larder of fish, shellfish, other wild animals, and plants.

It is not surprising that the indented shoreline of Tampa Bay and the adjacent islands and mainland bordering the Gulf of Mexico from

Sarasota to Clearwater—roughly one hundred miles of shore and coast—once was home to a number of native groups. Archaeological sites, especially shell middens and mounds, associated with those colonial-period groups and their precolumbian ancestors once blanketed those coasts and shores. Sites also were found along the freshwater rivers that flowed into the bay, especially around the river mouths, and at other mainland locations. The late-precolumbian archaeological culture associated with these sites is the Safety Harbor culture.[26]

Accounts from the 1539 Hernando de Soto expedition that landed on Tampa Bay, and documents from Pedro Menéndez de Avilés's voyage to Tampa Bay twenty-seven years later, provide information on a number of native groups: Uzita, Mocoso, Pohoy, and Tocobaga (around the bay proper), and Guacozo, Luca, Vicela, and Tocaste (north of the bay). In the seventeenth century the name Alafaias appears as another of the Tampa Bay groups. None of these groups appears to have been large; each consisted only of a single village or a group of villages with outlying homesteads. At times some groups formed alliances, and at the time of de Soto's expedition several groups were under the domination of an inland chief named Urriparacoxi, possibly a Timucuan, who lived well inland in a northeasterly direction.

The Uzita occupied the area from the mouth of the Little Manatee River southward to Sarasota Bay. This locality contains a number of Safety Harbor–period mound and village sites, including Harbor Key, the Bickel Mound, Snead Island, Pillsbury Temple Mound, Whitaker Mound, and the Thomas Mound and its adjacent village areas. Uzita territory may also have included inland sites, such as the Parrish mounds.

The Mocoso lived on the east side of Hillsborough Bay and on the Alafia and Hillsborough rivers. That area included the Mill Point site, the Fort Brooke Mound, and possibly the Bull Frog Creek and Picnic Mound sites. Although geographically close, the Uzita and Mocoso apparently spoke different languages.

After de Soto's army left Tampa Bay, the names of the Uzita and Mocoso do not appear again in Spanish documents.[27] No other expeditions were sent to either group, and no missions were ever established among them. We might guess that these two groups, who were among the first native Florida Indians to undergo sustained contact with

Spaniards, suffered greatly from disease epidemics and from having a significant number of individuals forcibly enslaved as bearers for de Soto's army. Remnants of both groups may have gone to live with other Tampa Bay groups, or they may have been known later by other names.

A third Tampa Bay group, the Pohoy, probably are the same people called the Capaloey in the de Soto narratives. In 1612 a detachment of Spanish soldiers traveling in small boats from the mouth of the Suwannee River to Tampa Bay, called the Bay of Pohoy, were sent to punish the Pohoy and their neighbors, the Tocobaga.[28] The two groups had been raiding missions to the north, and the Spaniards planned to retaliate.

It is probable that the people of Pohoy inhabited some part of upper Tampa Bay. In 1675 they were said to be living on a river six leagues from the Tocobaga, possibly on the Hillsborough River or the Alafia. In 1679 the Pohoy were subject to the Calusa Indians, who had extended their hegemony north to Tampa Bay.[29]

Documents from the first several decades of the eighteenth century, a time when remnants of the Tocobaga and the Pohoy were living in villages adjacent to St. Augustine, equate the Pohoy with the Alafaias, although other documents separate the two.[30]

Although the Tocobaga and the Pohoy were allied in 1612 when Spanish soldiers were sent against them, they were not always so friendly. In 1718 a village of Tocobaga, which had moved north to the mouth of the Wacissa River, was attacked by Pohoy Indians. Eight To-cobaga were killed and several more were taken captive.[31] Perhaps the Pohoy were settling old scores.

The de Soto expedition, which camped on the southeast side of Tampa Bay and seems not to have done any reconnaissance of the opposite side of the bay (near Old Tampa Bay), failed to encounter the Tocobaga Indians, whose name is so prominent in documents of the 1560s and later times.[32] A number of archaeological sites near the town of Safety Harbor on Old Tampa Bay contain Spanish artifacts, some of which probably came from the Menéndez excursion into the area in 1567 and may be from the town of Tocobaga.[33]

That Tocobaga was located on Old Tampa Bay in the vicinity of the modern town of Safety Harbor is certain. Juan López de Velasco de-scribes the location precisely:

The Bay of Tocobaga, [known] by the other names of [Bay] of the Holy Spirit or of Miruelo, is at 29¹/₂ degrees of latitude. The entrance has its passage to the west. . . . It would have three leagues at the mouth and three little islets in it on which there is nothing at all except sand and birds. On the northern side, within it the coast runs about two leagues from west to east and then an arm of the sea three leagues wide turns directly to the north, [penetrating] into the land for eighteen leagues up to the village of Tocobaga itself, a settlement of Indians where it terminates.[34]

The Bay of the Holy Spirit, Bahía de Espirito Santo, was the name de Soto gave Tampa Bay. The latitude given by López de Velasco is in error, about two degrees too far north. This is the same error that would so confuse Pánfilo de Narváez in 1528 when he searched for Tampa Bay and that appears in an early Spanish navigation rutter from that time (see chapter 6).

On his voyage to the Tocobaga, a two-day sail from Calos, Menéndez was accompanied by the Calusa chief and twenty of the latter's principal men. The chief tried to convince the Spaniards to raid the Tocobaga, or at least to allow his men to go ashore and burn the village. The Tocobaga and the Calusa had been warring for some time, perhaps since the balance of power in the Tampa Bay region had been altered by the impact of the de Soto expedition.[35]

To demonstrate both his power and his willingness to cooperate with the Spaniards, Chief Tocobaga summoned twenty-nine vassal chiefs, some of whom lived up to two days' travel away. The chiefs, along with one hundred principal men, assembled at Tocobaga's town, where fifteen hundred warriors armed with bows and arrows paraded before the Spaniards in a show of strength. Menéndez wisely persuaded Chief Tocobaga to send the Indian army away.

It seems clear that the Tocobaga Indians had considerable power in the region, perhaps controlling a number of other villages in the same fashion that the Jororo, Ais, and Mayaca maintained political control in their respective territories. Again, at least part of this power, and the reason for maintaining alliances over other villages, was tied to shipwreck salvage. Even as early as the time of the Narváez expedition in 1528, the native people around Tampa Bay were salvaging goods from wrecked ships. When Menéndez was at Tocobaga he found a Portuguese man who had been aboard a Spanish ship wrecked on the coast six years earlier. All of the other passengers had been killed by the Tocobaga; the man had survived by hiding in the woods for a month before being discovered and made a slave.

The Tocobaga were well aware of the native groups that lived to their east. One reason Menéndez wanted an alliance with the Tocobaga and to make them Christians (see chapter 7) was he thought there was a river passage from Tampa Bay to the St. Johns River to Mayaca territory, an idea the native people, with their tradition of canoe travel, assured him was true. But the Tocobaga advised Menéndez not to attempt such a passage with the few men he had brought to their village. They said that to go to Mayaca from Tampa Bay would not be wise because "the Indians on the way were numerous and warlike" and were enemies of the Tocobaga.[36]

All of the Tampa Bay groups were fishers who also hunted wild animals and gathered wild plants. But of the people living on the bay proper, only the Tocobaga had corn, and they may have gotten it from groups to the north. Members of the 1528 Pánfilo de Narváez expedition saw corn at Tocobaga, but the fields apparently were ten or twelve leagues away.[37] That would put them at about modern Dade City, where the de Soto expedition first observed cornfields.

As much as any other region of Florida, the documentary descriptions of the native people living on Tampa Bay, specifically the Uzita, correlate with archaeological evidence. A member of the de Soto expedition described the town of Uzita, believed to have been at the Thomas Mound archaeological site, on the Little Manatee River just upriver from Tampa Bay:

> The town was of seven or eight houses, built of timber, and covered with palm-leaves. The Chief's house stood near the beach, upon a very high mount made by hand for defence; at the other end of the town was a temple, on the top of which perched a wooden fowl with gilded eyes.[38]

The Tocobaga also maintained a temple in their main village, as probably did each of the towns of the native groups around Tampa Bay.

Another structure described in Spanish accounts is a charnel house. When soldiers from the de Soto expedition scouted the area around Uzita they found a Spaniard, Juan Ortiz, who had been held captive since 1528 (see chapter 6). Ortiz related how he first was held captive by Chief Uzita, who had ordered the Spaniard burned to death. But the chief's daughter pleaded for his life and Ortiz was spared. Instead of being put to death, Ortiz was made to guard a charnel house where bodies and bones of the dead were stored. The incident was related by one of de Soto's men:

> When Ortiz got well, he was put to watching a temple, that the wolves, in the night-time, might not carry off the dead there. . . . One night they snatched away from him the body of a little child, son of a principal man; and, going after them, he threw a dart at the wolf that was escaping, which, feeling itself wounded, let go its hold, and went off to die.[39]

Another version of the same incident is contained in a secondhand account of the de Soto expedition that utilized information provided years later by survivors. Although that account often embellishes and confuses events, the description of Ortiz and the charnel house rings true:

> The Cacique [chief] ordered to be inflicted upon the youth [Ortiz] another torment. . . . This was that day and night he should guard the remains of dead citizens placed in a designated section of a forest that lay at a distance from the town. These bodies had been put above ground in some wooden chests which served as sepulchres. The chests had not hinges and could be closed only by covering them with boards and then placing rocks or beams of wood on top of the board.[40]

After Narváez and his soldiers landed near the north end of Tampa Bay and marched inland to Tocobaga, they were shown wooden boxes in which corpses (perhaps bones) were stored, carefully wrapped in painted deer hides. Apparently, the boxes had originally been filled with goods being transported to or from New Spain (Mexico) and were salvaged from wrecked Spanish ships. Other items, including linen, cloth, feather headdresses, and gold, also had been salvaged from ships. The boxes were put to use holding bodies or bones, most likely in a charnel house.

Still another account, written in the 1560s, describes the process by which bodies were cleaned of flesh and the bones stored in a charnel house or temple:

> When a cacique [chief] from the leading ones dies, they break him into pieces and [macerate them] in some large jars and they [macerate them]

two days until the flesh separates from the bones and they take the bones
and they join one bone with another until they mount the man as he was
and they place him in a house that they have as a temple while they fast
four days. At the end of the four days they assemble all the people of the
village and go out with him to the procession and they [inter the bones],
making many reverences to him, and then they say that all those who go
to the procession gain indulgences.[41]

The layout of the village of Uzita, as described by the Spaniards, is
similar to the plan of Safety Harbor culture archaeological sites around
Tampa Bay. Such village sites typically have a platform mound, probably the base for the chief's house or temple, next to a plaza surrounded by village middens, marking where houses had been. One or
more burial mounds are present at each site, often located away from
the central village. Archaeological evidence of charnel houses also has
been found at Safety Harbor sites.

North of Tampa Bay, the de Soto expedition marched though several
other villages. The first was at the Plain of Guacozo, thought to be on a
north-south trail near Dade City in Pasco County. It was at this location, about fifty miles from their campsite on the Little Manatee River
and forty miles from Tocobaga, that the Spaniards saw the first native
cornfields in Florida. Farther north, near modern Lacoochee, they
came to another village, called Luca.

A third village, Vicela, is thought to have been near modern Is-
tachatta in northeast Hernando County. North of it on a large lake was
Tocaste, a village thought to be the Duval Island archaeological site at
the southern end of Lake Tsala Apopka in Citrus County.

European artifacts have been found at sites all around Tampa Bay
and at sites to the north in Pasco, Hernando, and Citrus counties. They
provide good evidence for the presence of native groups in the sixteenth and seventeenth centuries.[42]

The impact of these early Spanish entradas on the people around
and north of Tampa Bay may have been devastating. The relatively
small native population was hard hit by disease and warfare, a double
blow. Following de Soto's army's excursion through the region, the
Spaniards never again mounted an overland expedition to Tampa Bay
or the area immediately to the north. Perhaps they knew what those
sixteenth-century armies had done to the native populations.

The next chapter examines the native groups of northern Florida. It was there, the home of agricultural groups, that the Spanish would focus their colonial activities. It is no coincidence this was home to the largest Florida Indian populations.

Native People in Northern Florida

5 A large portion of northern Florida, that region north of a line across Florida from Cape Canaveral to Lake George and then west to the Withlacoochee River, was the focus of extensive Spanish missionary efforts in the seventeenth century. In the sixteenth century both Spanish and French explorations had penetrated portions of the region and encountered the Timucua and Apalachee Indians. In the seventeenth century this was the region of the Spanish mission provinces in Florida. These colonial efforts produced a voluminous documentary record about the native groups of the area. Equally large is the information gleaned from decades of archaeological investigations.

Less well known are the groups on the fringes of this region, those of the western panhandle and Marion and Sumter counties. Almost totally unknown is the northern peninsular Gulf coast, modern Levy, Dixie, and Taylor counties. With the exception of the Suwannee River, that region saw few Spaniards in the centuries following the de Soto entrada. Perhaps the area was too far from Spanish initiatives to warrant attention. Or, perhaps the impact of the Narváez and de Soto expeditions had been so severe it was known there was little left to colonize. Whether or not Timucua speakers lived in that coastal area is unknown.

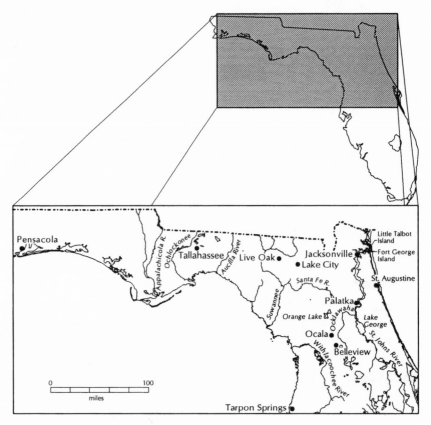

Modern locations in northern Florida.

Timucua Speakers

In the early sixteenth century, native groups who spoke dialects of the Timucua language occupied most of the northern third of peninsular Florida, from the Aucilla River east to the Atlantic Ocean and south at least through Marion County—perhaps into central Florida. Timucua speakers also lived in a significant portion of south-central and south-eastern Georgia. Their exact distribution in Georgia is uncertain, but documents from the mission period indicate they were living at least as far north and inland as a line drawn from Valdosta northeast through Waycross to the Altamaha River. This area includes Cumberland, Jekyll, and St. Simons islands along the coast.

Knowledge of the Timucuan language and its dialects comes almost entirely from the writings of a single Franciscan priest, Father Francisco

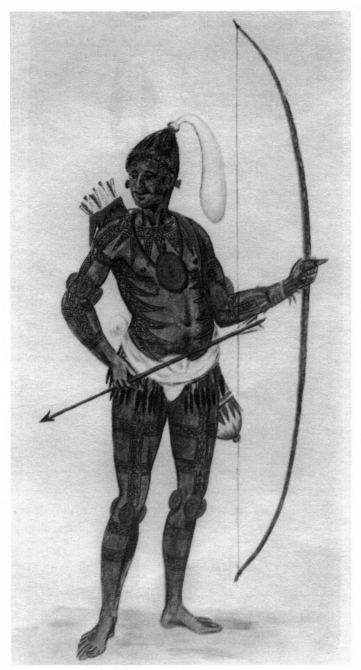

A Native American man from Florida, probably a Timucua-speaking person, painted by John White in the late sixteenth century (courtesy of the Trustees of the British Museum).

Pareja, who served the mission of San Juan del Puerto on Fort George Island north of Jacksonville in the late sixteenth and early seventeenth centuries.[1] Were it not for Pareja's interest in studying Timucua so it could be used by other Franciscans in Florida in ministering to native people, we would know almost nothing about the language.

In his writings Pareja mentions nine Timucuan dialects: Agua Dulce (fresh water), Icafui, Mocama (salt water), Oconi, Potano, Santa Lucia de Acuera, Timucua, Tucururu, and Yufera. The Agua Dulce dialect most likely was spoken by the groups living along the lower St. Johns River north of Lake George. Both the Icafui and Yufera dialects were spoken by Timucuan groups living in southeast Georgia, while Mocama was the dialect found along the coast from St. Augustine northward through southeast Georgia to the Altamaha River.

Less certain is the location of the Oconi dialect, said by Father Pareja in 1602 to have been spoken by a group three days' travel from Cumberland Island, Georgia. Recently discovered documents suggest Oconi was located in southern Georgia on the fringes of the Okeefenokee Swamp.[2] The location of another Timucua dialect, Tucururu, is similarly uncertain. A village called Tucuro was forty leagues from St. Augustine, probably in south-central Florida.[3]

The other Timucuan dialects can be better correlated with specific Timucuan groups or regions of groups. Potano was spoken by the Potano Indians, who lived in what is now Alachua County and northern Marion County. Santa Lucia de Acuera was associated with the Acuera Indians, thought to have been living on the upper reaches of the Oklawaha River in the vicinity of Lake Weir in southern Marion County. Timucua was the dialect spoken by the native groups north of the Santa Fe River in modern Columbia, Suwannee, and Madison counties.

It is their shared language that allows us to refer to these groups as Timucuan Indians. But in doing so, we should remember that in reality there was never a single group called the Timucua. Instead, there were a number of different, independent groups who spoke dialects of the same language. The many Timucua-speaking groups in northern Florida and southern Georgia were never united politically or ethnically. Indeed, some were at war with one another.

Generally the Timucua speakers are divided into two divisions, eastern and western.[4] The eastern groups lived from the St. Johns River drainage east to the Atlantic coast, including southeast Georgia.

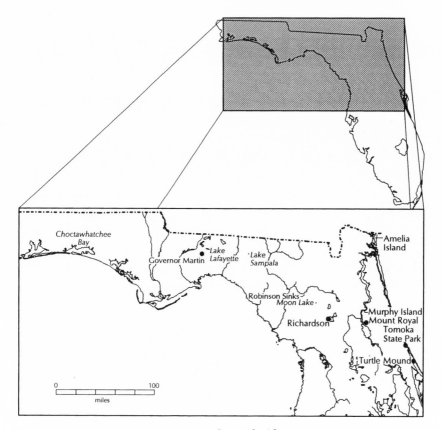

Archaeological site locations in northern Florida.

To the west, across northern Florida and south-central Georgia, were the western Timucua speakers. This division, a modern construct, is followed in this chapter.

Although the various Timucua speakers lived in different environmental zones, all of the groups derived at least a portion of their diets from the cultivation of plants. The precise importance of agricultural products—plants such as corn, beans, and squashes—to any specific groups is still being debated. To some of the eastern Timucuan groups, farming—especially growing maize—may have been less important than it was among western Timucua groups. All of the Timucuan groups also relied on hunting, fishing, and gathering wild foods, whether those foods were marine fish, acorns, or shellfish. And because contact between the groups had been ongoing for hundreds of years, many aspects of social, political, and religious life were shared.

One last bit of information that should be related before we look at the various Timucuan groups is the source of the name Timucua. When the French were among the Saturiwa and other groups living near the mouth of the St. Johns River, they were told that the enemies of these native allies were called Thimogona or Tymangoua. The territory of these Thimogona began two or three days' canoe travel upriver. It is clear that these enemies were other Timucua speakers and that the French also began to use the term Thimogona to refer to them.[5] Later, the Spanish and modern scholars would apply the name much more widely. It is probable that none of the Timucua speakers ever called themselves Timucua.

Eastern Timucuan Groups

The archaeological record for the colonial-period eastern Timucuan groups indicates that at one time native groups lived throughout the region. Sites containing sixteenth- and seventeenth-century European-derived artifacts have been found in numerous places along the St. Johns River. Colonial-period sites also have been recognized along the coast, including on Amelia Island, in St. Augustine, and farther south in Tomoka State Park, where one excavated site is thought to correlate with the early-seventeenth-century native village of Nocoroco. Still farther south, in Volusia County, on a narrow strip of land just north of Canaveral National Seashore and east of Mosquito Lagoon, is the huge shell mound that today is called Turtle Mound. This state historical site was the location of the village of Surruque noted in early-seventeenth-century documents.[6]

One of the first eastern Timucuan groups encountered by the French in 1562 was the Saturiwa, whose main village was located on the southern bank of the St. Johns River just inland from the river's mouth:

> One enters the harbor [the river mouth] . . . and on the left hand there is a pueblo of 25 large houses, where in each one live eight or nine Indians with their wives and children, because (those of) one lineage live together. The pueblo is called Saturiba.[7]

The French were told that Chief Saturiwa "had under his authority" thirty other chiefs, ten of whom were his brothers, and that the chief

Turtle Mound in Volusia County. The photograph was provided to the Florida Museum of Natural History in 1950 by Waldo H. Jones of Myrtle Beach, South Carolina, who had explored the site. In a letter, Jones described the sites at that time as "four hundred feet long, fifty feet high and one hundred fifty thick at the base" (courtesy of the Florida Museum of Natural History).

was "greatly feared in these regions."[8] Rather than referring to actual siblings, "brothers" probably meant the chiefs had formed alliances with Saturiwa. The territory of this Saturiwa-dominated alliance extended down the Atlantic coast perhaps as far as the later site of St. Augustine, location of the village of Chief Seloy.[9] Other allied chiefs lived on or near the St. Johns River. One chief was Emoloa, also called Emola, another was Casti, and another Malica, all three of whom lived westward from Saturiwa's village on the St. Johns River. In that direction that chief's territory extended upriver, perhaps as far as the south side of modern Jacksonville. Another of Saturiwa's vassals was Chief Alicamany on Fort George Island.[10]

The late-precolumbian–early-colonial-period archaeological ceramic assemblage present in the region controlled by Saturiwa is related to the Savannah series found along the Georgia and South Carolina coasts, rather than the St. Johns culture assemblage prevalent to the south.[11] It is possible that this difference in archaeological assemblages reflects ethnic differences that date back to the late precolumbian period.

North of Saturiwa's territory on Cumberland Island, Georgia, was another eastern Timucuan group, the Tacatacuru. They also are associated with an archaeological assemblage that is not the St. Johns culture.[12] Chief Tacatacuru seems to have controlled the groups along the northeastern Florida coast into southeastern Georgia. In that area, per-

"Rituals Observed by Saturiwa before Setting out on a Campaign Against His Enemies." De Bry's 1591 engraving depicts the chief and his vassal chiefs about 1564 (see Hulton 1977:I:146).

haps on Little Talbot Island, was the village of Caravay, sometimes called Calabay, Sarabay, Saravay, or Serranay. There were two other Timucuan groups with the same name, one near the mouth of the St. Johns River and one much farther upstream.

On the mainland in southeast Georgia were the Cascangue, Icafui, Yufera, and Ibi, also called Yui, all associated with a Savannah-related archaeological assemblage. The Yui may have lived the farthest inland, perhaps bordering on the Okeefenokee Swamp. Other Timucua speakers were living still further north, up to the Altamaha River.

There is no archeological evidence that Chief Saturiwa was a paramount chief like the Calusa chief. Instead, he seems to have had political power similar to that of the chiefs of the Mayaca, Tequesta, and Ais. Some of his vassal villages were located close to his village, so the populations of these villages could have been historically linked, starting as a single village that grew over time into numerous villages.

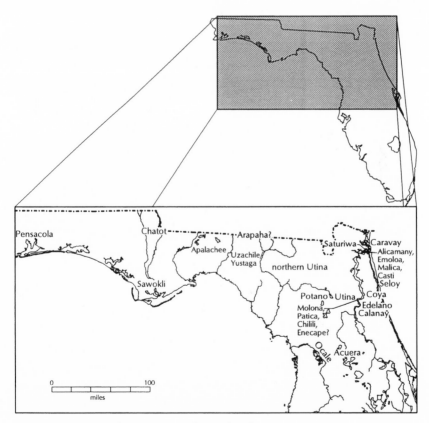

Native groups and towns in northern Florida.

Using information collected before many of the St. Johns River sites were destroyed, archaeologist John Goggin plotted site distributions on a modern map of the river.[13] The results show two dense regions of sites north of Lake George. One is from Jacksonville east to the mouth of the St. Johns River, a region that correlates the distribution of the late-precolumbian Savannah-related archaeological assemblage and the territory controlled by Saturiwa. South along the river is another dense distribution of sites, extending from about Palatka south to Lake George. This is probably a part of the territory controlled by another of the powerful eastern Timucuan chiefs, Chief Utina, an enemy of Saturiwa. From Palatka to Jacksonville there are relatively fewer sites, suggesting that area may have been a buffer zone between the Saturiwa-affiliated villages and those allied with Utina.

Chief Utina's main village, visited by both the French and the Spanish in the 1560s, was near Lake Grandin in northwestern Putnam County, near its boundary with Clay County.[14] It was on the east-west path that would become the major Spanish trail into northern Florida. Modern Clarkes Creek drains into the St. Johns River at about the point where the trail intersects the west side of the river, about seventeen miles from Utina's village. The same trail, often referred to by modern scholars as the mission road, runs from Picolata on the east side of the river to St. Augustine.

Utina's name is still found on the landscape in the word Etoniah. Etoniah Creek, now channelized, flows from the location of Utina's village southeast to the St. Johns River. Various forms of Utina/Etoniah appear on nineteenth-century maps, including It-tun-wah, It-tun-ah, Etinni, Itini, and Itina.

Utina's power and importance equaled or exceeded that of Saturiwa. One of Utina's vassal chiefs told the French that Utina controlled more than forty village chiefs, though that same chief could name only nine. Other documents give the names of others, although it is often difficult to locate a specific village on the modern landscape.

One of the villages was Coya, perhaps located near the mouth of Etoniah Creek north of Palatka. Coya was near the northernmost end of Utina's territory. A second village, Molona, was nearby. Just south of Coya, also on the river, was Patica; further south was Chilili, and then Enecape (also called Anacape), which was the location of the seventeenth-century Spanish mission of San Antonio de Enecape. San Antonio could be the mission found at the Mount Royal archaeological site by B. Calvin Jones of Florida's Bureau of Archaeological Research.[15] Mount Royal is just north of Lake George, on the east side of the St. Johns River. If it is true that Enecape was at Mount Royal, then the location shown for Enecape on the map on page 87 is too far north.

Enecape appears to have been near the village of Edelano, located on an island in the St. Johns River and said by colonial-period French visitors to have had an avenue three hundred paces long leading from the village to the river.[16] Most likely this was an earthwork like the long "roadway" or cleared earthwork that is still visible at the Mount Royal archaeological site. The island on which Edelano was located could have been Murphy Island, just south of Palatka. Earthworks were apparent on the island in the early twentieth century, and European-derived artifacts have been found in a mound on the island.[17]

On the other hand, if Edelano was another name for Enecape, then the "avenue" described by the French as being at Edelano could actually be describing the earthwork at Mount Royal. This would cause one to question all of the relative geographical placements provided by the French for villages along the St. Johns River.

Probably south of Edelano, according to the French, was the village of Calanay (also Zaravay or Saravai). It was said that if one traveled west from Calanay, from village to village, one would reach Tocobaga on Tampa Bay.[18] If Calanay were north of Lake George and a traveler took a southwesterly heading, this would indeed be possible.

Another group said to be affiliated with Chief Utina was the Acuera, who, as pointed out earlier in this chapter, most likely lived on the Oklawaha River, a region sometimes called Ibiniyuti. Acuera territory could well have extended southward from the Oklawaha River into Lake County, an area of numerous lakes. Spanish artifacts have come from a site on Lake Dora, perhaps the location of one of the Acuera missions.[19]

Several other Eastern Timucuan groups are also mentioned in sixteenth-century accounts, but they were not on the St. Johns River and their locations are very uncertain. They include the Eclavou, Onachaquara, and Omittagua, possibly all of whom lived east of the river, and the Astina, who were to the west.[20]

Western Timucuan Groups

A third powerful Timucuan chief, one also said to be an enemy of both Chief Saturiwa and Chief Utina, was Potano. The Potano Indians were one of the western Timucuan groups encountered by the de Soto expedition in 1539 and by subsequent Spaniards and Frenchmen prior to the arrival of Franciscan missionaries in the 1580s. The Alachua archaeological culture with which the Potano are correlated can be traced back hundreds of years.[21]

When the de Soto expedition entered the territory of the Potano, the region from about Belleview north to the Santa Fe River, the Spaniards noted they had entered a region of greater agricultural bounty than anything they had seen since leaving Tampa Bay. This is not surprising, since the loamy soils of the highland region that extend through this part of Florida are better suited for the type of agriculture carried on by the native people than are the soils of central, southern, and northeastern Florida.

An advance party from the de Soto expedition stayed at several Potano villages, recording their names. Today we can approximately locate nearly all of these towns, which are arranged in a roughly north-south line following the line of march along native trails. Each can be correlated with an individual archaeological site or a group of sites.[22]

The southernmost village, Itaraholata, has not been located. Most likely it was in western Marion County, west or west-southwest of present Morriston and Lake Stafford, near the border of Marion and Sumter counties (in a southerly direction from Williston). Potano, the next town, was on the western shore of Orange Lake, perhaps at the Richardson archaeological site north of Evinston. Less likely locations are on the western side of Levy Lake and on the southwestern end of Paynes Prairie in Alachua County. The village of Potano later would be moved to the vicinity of the Devil's Millhopper, just north of Utinamocharra.

Utinamocharra, the third village, was in the cluster of archaeological sites immediately east of Moon Lake, on the west side of Gainesville. Those sites, located in the late 1940s, have been destroyed by modern development.

To the north was a town the Spanish called Malapaz, probably the large Alachua-culture archaeological site near the town of Alachua. The fifth village, Cholupaha, which may have been just outside Potano territory, was within the very dense cluster of archaeological sites near the Robinson Sinks in northwest Alachua County, just south of the Santa Fe River. Spanish artifacts, mainly seventeenth-century items, have been recovered at or very near the presumed location of all four of these latter towns. Other site clusters are known for the Alachua County area, and many contain evidence of having been occupied during the late precolumbian period.

Immediately north and northwest of the Potano, the de Soto expedition encountered a large native population, the people often referred to by modern scholars as the northern Utina, another western Timucuan group.[23] The northern Utina were composed of a number of separate villages, at least some of which had powerful chiefs who maintained alliances with one another.

The expedition marched through the northern Utina region in the summer of 1539, stopping at the towns of Aguacaleyquen, Uriutina, Napituca, and two others, all located along a network of trails that led from the Santa Fe River (and Cholupaha), past the Ichetucknee River, and north to the vicinity of Lake City. There another trail (or trails) led west to the Suwannee River across modern Columbia and Suwannee counties. Like the Potano region to the south, this also was a good agricultural region, and the native people cultivated corn and other plants. The northern Utina can be correlated with the Suwannee Valley archaeological culture, many sites of which are present in Columbia, Hamilton, and Suwannee counties.[24]

The first northern Utina village where de Soto's army camped was Aguacaleyquen, thought to be located just east of the Ichetucknee River. Further north, near Lake City, perhaps by Alligator Lake, was an unnamed small village. Next, west of Lake City, perhaps in the cluster of sites near the Indian Pond site in western Columbian County, was the village of Uriutina. Farther west was a village called Many Waters, probably east of Live Oak and near lakes Peacock and White, where more sites are clustered. Still another village, Napituca, was farther west, perhaps near modern Live Oak or to the south of that town. As was true of the Potano region, the archaeological sites of the Suwannee Valley culture occur in clusters in the zone of the best agricultural soils.

The towns of Aguacaleyquen, Uriutina, and Napituca all had village chiefs who were allied in some fashion. Other towns in the region also had chiefs. In a battle at Napituca, the Spaniards under de Soto killed at least nine village chiefs and perhaps hundreds of warriors, dealing the native groups a terrible blow. At that time the chief of Aguacaleyquen, who lived on the southeastern fringe of northern Utina territory, seems to have been the most important.

Once it crossed the Suwannee River, de Soto's army entered the territory of the Uzachile, a western Timucuan group whose territory encompassed Madison County. The Spaniards passed through one small village before entering the main village of Uzachile, located near modern Lake Sampala. Chief Uzachile also was affiliated with the other chiefs to the east. Indeed, the de Soto narratives make it clear that at that time he was the most important chief, even more powerful than Aguacaleyquen.

"Rites Observed at the Funeral of a Chief and of Priests." Although intended to show Timucua speakers in northeast Florida, this de Bry engraving possibly depicts a ceremony with a wider distribution. Jeffrey Mitchem's (1989b) excavation of Tatham Mound, perhaps an Ocale Indian structure, contained numerous *Busycon* cups. In addition, sixty-six small stone arrowpoints were found in the east side of the mound. The cups and points reflect burial practices similar to those described for this engraving: when a chief dies he is buried with "the bowl from which he used to drink [shown as a shell cup] with many arrows implanted round the mound" (Hulton 1977:I:152).

Those same accounts indicate that a buffer zone that took two days to march across separated Uzachile's village from his enemies, the Apalachee, whose territory began at the Aucilla River. The reports also note that the Uzachile were called Yustaga, a name that is prominent in later French and Spanish accounts.

The Ocale, a western Timucuan group south of the Potano, also were on the route taken by the de Soto expedition as it marched north from Tampa Bay. Ocale territory encompassed a portion of the Withlacoochee River, adjacent parts of the Cove of the Withlacoochee, and the higher land east of the river for ten to fifteen miles, a region in easternmost Citrus County and western Marion and Sumter counties. The archaeological assemblage in the late precolumbian and early colonial period in that area is related to the Safety Harbor culture. Freshwater shell middens and other sites are adjacent to the river and its tributaries and around the wetlands to the east. Sand mounds are present, and at least two have been found that contained large amounts of Spanish artifacts.[25]

Still another western Timucuan group, the Arapaha, lived in northernmost Hamilton and, perhaps, Madison counties in Florida, and the adjacent portion of southern Georgia. Spanish missions were established among the Arapaha, as they were among the Ocale, Potano, and northern Utina groups. The modern Alapaha River derives its name from the Arapaha Indians.

Apalachee Indians of the Eastern Panhandle

Like the Timucua-speaking groups to their east, the Apalachee Indians are well known from the archaeological and documentary records. At the time of Spanish contact the Apalachee can be correlated with a variant of the Fort Walton culture, but by the time of the establishment of the first Apalachee missions in the 1630s the Fort Walton ceramic complex had been replaced by Leon-Jefferson ceramics.[26] Colonial-period archaeological sites containing European-derived artifacts, both Fort Walton sites and Leon-Jefferson sites, are very common in the Tallahassee Hills region of the eastern panhandle, especially the area from the Aucilla River to the Ochlockonee River. This was the territory of the Apalachee Indians, the largest and most politically complex native group in colonial Florida.

Through a colossal mistake in geography, the Apalachee Indians un-
wittingly gave their name to one of the largest natural features in the
eastern United States, the Appalachian Mountains. In the 1560s,
French chroniclers in Florida, evidently not understanding their inter-
preters and eager to locate a source of gold and silver, erroneously
recorded that the Apalachee Indians lived in a mountainous region
where precious metals could be mined.[27] Indeed, the de Bry–engraved
map published in 1591, based in large part on French information,
shows the town of "Apalatci" far to the north among the mountains.
Later writers equated that group with the Appalachian Mountains,
hence the name. American Indians never mined gold or silver from the
Appalachian Mountains. But they did mine copper, a precious metal to
them, which was worked into artifacts and traded throughout the
Southeast, including to the Fort Walton culture.

Like the western Timucuan groups to the east, the Apalachee were
in contact with Spanish explorers early in the sixteenth century. When
de Soto's army marched through the region in 1539, the names of several Apalachee villages were recorded, and we can locate them approximately along the east-west line of march taken by the Spaniards.

The first major town reached west of the Aucilla River was Ivitachuco, just south of Lake Iamonia (the one in Jefferson County, not
the one in Leon County). That town was near the trail that would become the mission road in the seventeenth century. The second town to
which de Soto's army came was Calahuchi, one of a number of Fort
Walton sites just west of the Saint Marks River and south of Lake
Lafayette.

At the time of the de Soto expedition, the capitol town of the
Apalachee was Iniahica, which archaeologists have located within the
city limits of Tallahassee. These three are but a few of the many villages
that flourished in Apalachee in the early colonial period. The de Soto
expedition simply did not record the names of others, except for a village named Ochete, perhaps the same one called Aute in other accounts, which was south toward the Gulf coast and may have been
outside of Apalachee territory proper.

During the period of the Apalachee missions, beginning nearly a
century after de Soto, the names of many more mission towns were
recorded, along with the names of satellite villages located around the
individual missions.[28] Arranged roughly east to west from Ivitachuco

in the east to Cupaica in the west, some of these Apalachee mission towns were Ivitachuco, Ayubale, Aspalaga, Ocuia, Patale, Capoli, Tomole, Bacuqua, and Cupaica. Together these nine villages had nearly forty satellites villages.

Thanks to historian John Hann, we not only have the names of these mission villages and their satellites, we also have names of village headmen and names of a number of individual Apalachee Indians.[29] This extraordinary information helps to remind us that the Florida Indians, like the Europeans, were people of flesh and blood, not merely faceless names in a book.

Relative to the western and eastern Timucuan sites, as well as late-precolumbian sites elsewhere in Florida, Fort Walton village sites are larger and more densely distributed. There also are numerous small sites located all across the Apalachee landscape, presumably farmsteads where individual families lived. It could be that the bulk of the Fort Walton population lived away from the main villages.

Apalachee agriculture was much more intensive and extensive than elsewhere in Florida. Using cleared-field farming techniques, the Apalachee cultivated maize, varieties of beans and squash, and other crops. It is no wonder that the de Soto expedition opted to winter among the Apalachee. Although farmers, the Apalachee relied on fishing, collecting of wild foods, and hunting for a part of their diet.

Linguists agree that Apalachee was a Muskogean language, a family of languages that includes Choctaw, various Creek languages, Seminole, and other southeastern American Indian languages.[30] Indeed, in many ways the Fort Walton culture and the Apalachee Indians more closely resembled native groups north of Florida than they did the other Florida Indians.

Other Groups of the Panhandle

West of the Apalachee Indians lived several other native groups. Those along the coast were in contact with Spanish sailors and colonists early in the sixteenth century. In the seventeenth century a few Franciscan missions were established in the Apalachicola River drainage immediately west of Apalachee territory.

Archaeological sites containing European-derived artifacts and items made from metals salvaged from Spanish ships have been found in shell middens along and near the coast, as well as in a few other sites and in burial areas. Those late-precolumbian sites from the eastern end of Choctawhatchee Bay westward are associated with the Pensacola archaeological culture, while those more easterly sites are associated with the Fort Walton culture.[31]

The Pensacola culture bears affinities to assemblages farther west along the Gulf coast, such as in the Mobile Bay region. The Fort Walton assemblage of the western panhandle is similar to that found in the Apalachee region, though sites—both village and mound complexes— are neither as dense nor as large. The type of agriculture present in the western panhandle was not the intensive, cleared-field cultivation practiced by the eastern Fort Walton peoples and their colonial descendants, the Apalachee Indians.

One group living west of the Apalachee Indians was the Chatot, also known as Chacatos, who lived in the upper Apalachicola–Chipola River drainage in Jackson County.[32] The Waddells Mill Pond site in Jackson County, a fortified village, may have been occupied by the precolumbian ancestors of the Chatot. In the past, confusion between the names of the Chatot/Chacatos and the Choctaw Indians who lived in Mississippi apparently led to the name of the Choctawhatchee Bay.[33]

In 1639 the governor of La Florida sought to arrange an end to warfare between the Chatot and the Amacano and Apalachicola Indians.[34] The Apalachicola also lived west of the Apalachee, while the Amacano are known to have been living in the town of Chaccabi, probably on the western panhandle coast, in 1674.[35] They were said to be allies of the Chine and Pacara, two groups who spoke the same language as the Amacano and lived nearby.

South along the coast west of Apalachicola Bay were the Sawokli Indians, sometimes referred to as the Sauocola, Sabacola, or Savacola. Like the Chatot, they spoke a Muskogean language; one account says it was the same as Apalachicola. The Sawokli may correlate with the Pensacola archaeological culture rather than with the Fort Walton culture associated with the Apalachicola Indians.

Further west along the panhandle coast were the Pensacola Indians, also believed to have been associated with the Pensacola culture. In the 1680s they were related in some fashion to the Chatot, perhaps sharing a similar language. Most archaeologists agree that the Pensacola culture in the western panhandle is a late addition to the region. At many sites Pensacola materials overlie Fort Walton materials. The appearance of the Pensacola culture may be related to late-precolumbian population movements in Mississippi, Alabama, and the westernmost Florida panhandle.

In the last three chapters we have located the native Florida Indians on the modern landscape. Parts 2 and 3 will focus on the interactions between those native groups and the Spanish and French explorers and colonists who first entered their land in the sixteenth century.

The Invasion

 **PART II**

Was it an invasion, or, as my thesaurus alternatively puts it, a hostile ingress? Did armies from European countries invade Florida? Or is the use of that term simply an example of political correctness stimulated in part by the reaction of indigenous people to the Columbian Quincentenary?

There are three points of view. One is that of the Spaniards. A sixteenth-century learned Spaniard would probably argue that the exploration and colonization of Florida was certainly not an invasion, a hostile ingress, a frontier violation, or even an assailment. The entradas of Juan Ponce de León, Pánfilo de Narváez, Hernando de Soto, and Pedro Menéndez de Avilés were military and settlement initiatives duly sanctioned in writing by their respective sovereigns. They also were legal under international law. As part of the Treaty of Tordesillas between Spain and Portugal, negotiated by Pope Alexander VI in 1493 and finalized in 1494, Spain was given the right to Western Hemisphere lands west of a north-south line drawn 350 leagues (about 1,295 miles) west of the Cape Verde Islands. That line of demarcation, approximated by the forty-ninth west parallel, later was found to intersect only a small portion of easternmost South America. Nearly all of that continent, as well as all of North America, was in the Spanish sphere of influence; only the smallest part of South America went to the Portuguese. It is doubtful that those who drew up the treaty intended that

Spain receive rights to all of those lands, however. When the treaty was negotiated Europeans had almost no knowledge of the geography of the Western Hemisphere beyond easternmost coastal Canada and some of the Caribbean and Bahamian islands.

The Spanish entradas into La Florida were supported by the Catholic Church and the Spanish monarchy and were thought to reflect the will of the Spanish god. Beginning early in the sixteenth century, Spaniards were required to explain the basis of this legal/religious right to native people when they entered their lands. This was done by reading a lengthy document called the *requerimiento* (the requirement):

> On behalf of the king . . . and the queen . . . subjugators of barbarous peoples, we, their servants, notify and make known to you as best we are able, that God, Our Lord, living and eternal, created the heavens and the earth, and a man and a woman, of whom you and we and all other people of the world were, and are, the descendants. . . . Because of the great numbers of people who have come from the union of these two in the five thousand years which have run their course since the world was created, it became necessary that some should go in one direction and that others should go in another. Thus they became divided into many kingdoms and many provinces, since they could not all remain or sustain themselves in one place.
>
> Of all these people God, Our Lord, chose one, who was called Saint Peter, to be the lord and the one who was to be superior to all the other people of the world, whom all should obey. God also permitted him to be and establish himself in any other part of the world to judge and govern all peoples, whether Christian, Moors, Jew, gentiles, or those of any other sects and beliefs that there might be. He was called the Pope. . . .
>
> One of the past Popes . . . gave these islands and mainlands of the Ocean Sea [the Atlantic Ocean] to the said King and Queen and to their successors . . . with everything that there is in them. . . .
>
> In consequence, Their Highnesses are Kings and Lords of these islands and mainland by virtue of said donation [the Treaty of Tordesillas]. Certain other isles and almost all [the native peoples] to whom this summons has been read have accepted Their Highnesses as such Kings and Lords. . . . You are constrained and obliged to do the same as they. . . .
>
> [W]e beseech and demand that you understand fully this that we have

said to you . . . and that you accept the Church and Superior Organization of the whole world and recognize the Supreme Pontiff, called the Pope, and that in his name, you acknowledge the King and Queen . . . as the lords and superior authorities of these islands and mainlands by virtue of the said donation. . . .

   If you do not do this . . . we will enter your land against you with force and will make war in every place and by every means we can and are able, and we will then subject you to the yoke and authority of the Church and Their Highnesses. We will take you and your wives and children and make them slaves. . . . And we will take your property and will do to you all the harm and evil we can.[1]

So, in the view of the Spaniards who were putting up the money, effort, and, yes, lives, to explore and colonize Florida, it was not a hostile ingress, it was a God-given right. The land belonged to Spain, and the people who lived there and opposed the Spaniards did so at their own peril. To the Spanish, the exploration and colonization of Florida and the Americas was their destiny.

The second point of view is that of the native people of Florida, but they are at a distinct disadvantage in this argument because the written accounts of the time were penned by Spaniards and Frenchmen, not by American Indians. We do not have firsthand documents reflecting the native point of view. However, some contemporary observers did record what are said to be translations of native speeches or interpretations. Whether totally accurate or not, such records do provide insight into how the Spaniards thought the native people perceived them. One such secondhand oration, directed at the de Soto expedition by a native chief who had witnessed or heard about the depredations of the Narváez expedition, was recounted by a chronicler of the expedition:

I have long since learned who you castilians are . . . through others of you who came years ago to my land; and I already know very well what your customs and behavior are like. To me you are professional vagabonds who wander from place to place, gaining your livelihood by robbing, sacking, and murdering people who give you no offense.[2]

We can also try to reconstruct the native view by examining the behavior of the Florida Indians toward the de Soto expedition. The continued occurrence of skirmishes and attacks against that army leads any rational person to conclude that native groups in Florida wanted to repel what they viewed as an invasion of their lands. And in the seventeenth century, rebellions against the Spanish colonists occurred several times. Events and incidents from the colonial period lead us to conclude that the Florida Indians viewed the entradas quite differently from the Spaniards.

The third view is that of the scholar, supposedly dispassionate and aloof from politics and representing truth and science. But in reality scholars are also products of their times, reflections of their own learning and their interaction with the world around them. There is no doubt that the scholarly view of exploration and colonization of Florida and the Americas by people from Europe has changed over time. At the time of the 1893 world's fair, the Columbian Exposition in Chicago, the Spanish explorers were seen as positive forces who had brought Western civilization to the Western Hemisphere.

Today, however, with the benefit of nearly five centuries of hindsight, the colonial powers are judged in a harsher light. In the last two decades, prominent scholars have reassessed the European colonization of North America and labeled it an invasion. One of the first to do so was Francis Jennings, whose 1975 book, *The Invasion of America: Indians, Colonialism, and the Cant of Conquest,* offered a revisionist view of New England in the 1600s and of the motivation of the Puritans. Another is James Axtell's (1985) *The Invasion Within: The Conquest of Cultures in Colonial North America,* which examined the interactions among Native Americans and the French and British. One can conclude that most modern scholars would agree with Jennings and Axtell: an invasion did take place.

A tally of these three points of view shows a vote of two to one: it was an invasion. Of course this was a mock election; the outcome was obvious even before I started writing this book. Even so, this discussion makes us aware that it is important for us to consider not only the events that took place in early colonial Florida, but also how those events were viewed in the past and how they are viewed in the present. The manner in which we interpret the past can tell us as much about ourselves as it can about the past.

Having satisfied ourselves that an invasion of Florida took place, whom should we castigate for what turned out to be a catastrophe for the native population? The French? The Spanish? The Carolinian militia? Yamasee Indian slave raiders? Catholic missionaries? People who celebrate Columbus Day? Modern scholars? For my part, I find it hard to blame anyone for events that occurred hundreds of years ago. When I view the events of the sixteenth and seventeenth centuries, putting them in the contexts of their times, I cannot castigate either the European people or the native people.

On the other hand, from our vantage point we can look back on the past and say that what occurred, whatever the intent, was wrong. We can educate ourselves about the past and understand it in the context of the past and the present. We can understand how the colonization of the Americas affected native peoples, as well as the people of Europe. We can understand how the events of the past helped to shape our world today. Out of such learning comes activism to change the future.

According to the 1990 census, there are 1.5 million American Indians in the United States, a marked increase over the 250,000 native people who lived here a century ago. Today American Indians are renewing their pride in their heritage. All Americans should do the same. We cannot change the past, but we can learn from it for a better future.

The Invasion Begins

6 An error in seamanship on Christmas Eve in 1492 helped to shape the geography of the Spanish conquest of the Americas. Sailing east along the northern coast of the Caribbean Island of Hispaniola, Christopher Columbus's ship, the *Santa Maria,* struck a reef and had to be abandoned. Two and a half months earlier Columbus and his crew had landed in the Bahamas on the island called Guanahani by the native Lucayo Indians who inhabited that archipelago.[1]

In the ensuing seventy-three days the sailors had explored the Bahamas, sailing southward through those islands to the north coast of Cuba. Turning east, Columbus and his crew aboard the *Santa Maria, Pinta,* and *Niña* continued to encounter Taino Indian groups as they sailed along the western portion of Hispaniola's northern coast.

The Spanish seamen saw gold in the hands of Taino Indians in Cuba. They could not have helped but think more riches were there for the taking, if they could be found. That thought may have influenced the decision and events leading to the establishment of the first Spanish settlement on Hispaniola rather than in the Bahamas.

The *Santa Maria,* aground on a reef and apparently damaged to the extent that it could not be repaired and refloated, was salvaged. With the aid of Taino from a nearby village, the ship was off-loaded and usable timbers and hardware were taken ashore. Columbus decided to leave a portion of his crew at the native village, where they were to build a fortified encampment. In order to impress upon the Taino the military might of his expedition—an attempt to ensure the safety of the men he was leaving behind—Columbus staged a demonstration of cannon fire for Guacanacaric, the village chief. Because it was Christmastime, the small, fortified settlement was christened La Navidad. It was to be home to forty-two men while Columbus and the remainder of his crew returned to Spain.

In September 1493, accompanied by seventeen ships, Columbus sailed on his second voyage to the Americas, setting a course for La Navidad. Reaching the settlement in November, the expedition discovered that all of the crew left there were dead and the tiny outpost destroyed.[2] Columbus and his colonizing expedition departed, making their way farther eastward along the Hispaniola coast.

At a place where a better port was located (near modern Puerto Plata), a second settlement was founded. La Isabela, as the town was called, was the first of nearly twenty towns founded on Hispaniola by the Spaniards in the late fifteenth and early sixteenth centuries.[3] Those initial settlements, whose origins can be traced to the wreck of the *Santa Maria*, provided the base from which other expeditions sought to extend Spain's empire to nearby islands and the mainland regions fronting the Caribbean.

Early Voyages to La Florida

Intent on finding wealth and populated lands suitable for exploitation and settlement by conquistadores and entrepreneurs, early-sixteenth-century Spanish expeditions plied the waters of the Caribbean, exploring, mapping, and ultimately establishing settlements on islands and on the mainland of Central America and northernmost South America. Spain's colonial empire grew, fed by mineral wealth wrested from the land and the indigenous societies. The native peoples provided forced labor for mining, farming, and other activities intended to produce profits for the Spanish Crown and for the conquistadores and colonists and their backers and investors.

Geographical and navigational knowledge of the Caribbean region expanded as the empire spread. Maps and charts were drawn, informed by sea voyages that probably ranged well beyond the official versions of events and discoveries that were transmitted back to Spain. The Crown, through *asientos* (royal contracts) awarded to the leaders of

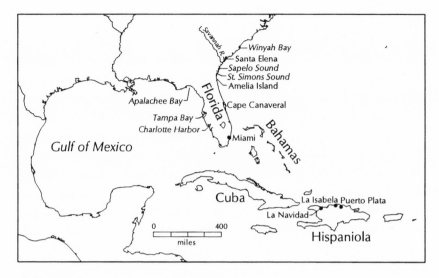

Florida, the Bahamas, and the Caribbean.

expeditions, sought to regulate these voyages and expeditions of conquest to assure the division of spoils and future earnings. Without documented permission from the Crown, exploratory and colonizing voyages could not be legally undertaken. However, unsanctioned voyages to pillage, capture native people as slaves, and locate lands for future, legal exploitation must have been ongoing. By 1530 much of the Atlantic coast of the Americas had been mapped, as had portions of the Pacific coast.

The first officially contracted Spanish exploratory voyage to what is now the mainland United States took place in 1513. One of the many early voyages that originated from Spanish Caribbean settlements, it was led by Juan Ponce de León, who previously had served as governor of the colony of San Juan on the island of Puerto Rico.[4] Ponce's contract directed him to sail northward from Puerto Rico to explore and claim for Spain an island called Bimini, thought to lie in that direction. Since the Bahamas were known to Spanish interests by that time, it is likely that what he sought was land even farther north and west that had been visited by one or more unsanctioned Spanish voyages. Knowledge of what is now eastern Canada had been recorded by the English sailor John Cabot, who had led expeditions along that coast in 1497 and 1498.[5] The results of Cabot's voyages may have been known

to Spanish sources, adding fuel to the speculation that land lay northwest of the Bahamas.

Departing port in early March, Juan Ponce's three ships sailed northwesterly through the Bahamas past the Caicos Islands, the Inaguas,
and then Mayaguana. The expedition continued past the island of Guanahani, probably San Salvador, where Columbus had first gone ashore
in 1492. After they passed what is almost certainly modern Great
Abaco Island, Ponce's pilot knew to take a more westerly route, a
heading that brought the expedition to the Atlantic coast of Florida.
Their sighting of that coast, thought at first to be a large island, coincided with Holy Week, time of the Feast of Flowers (*Pascua Florida*).
The holiday and the natural beauty of the land led Juan Ponce to name
it "La Florida." That initial landing probably took place just north of
Cape Canaveral, near 28.5 degrees north latitude.[6]

Ponce's expedition sailed down the Atlantic coast of peninsular
Florida past Cape Canaveral, at times riding the countercurrents close
to shore. Continuing southward, Ponce sailed past what is now the Key
Biscayne–Miami area before rounding the Florida Keys and traveling
up the Gulf coast to southwest Florida.

The exact location of Ponce's initial landing on the Gulf coast is uncertain. Most likely it was just below Charlotte Harbor. However, he
may have sent a ship northward to explore more of the coast, at least to
Charlotte Harbor and, perhaps, beyond. Later sixteenth-century maps
show Charlotte Harbor bearing his name, suggesting his explorations
reached at least that portion of the southwest Florida coast.[7]

A map of the Gulf of Mexico coast drawn by the 1519 Alvarez de
Pineda–led expedition has a notation written on it at about modern
Apalachee Bay stating, "Juan Ponce discovered to this point," hinting
that one of Ponce's ships had been well north of Charlotte Harbor.[8] But
the lack of detail in the account of the Juan Ponce expedition leaves
scholars confused and uncertain about the exact geography of the expedition. That account was published in 1601 in Antonio de Herrera y
Tordesillas's *Historia General de los Hechos de los Castellanos en las Islas y
Tierra Firme del Mar Océano* (History of Spain in the Americas).

Herrera tells of the first encounters between Spaniards and the
Florida natives.[9] Sailing the coast south of Cape Canaveral, Ponce and
his crew first saw native huts. Later, beset by problems caused by the
strong current, two of Ponce's ships anchored and men went ashore

(the third ship apparently was unable to anchor, and the current took it out of sight). In a brief skirmish with native peoples, two Spaniards were wounded by arrows tipped with "sharpened bones and fish spines."[10] Another skirmish took place at the same landing site before Ponce's three ships regrouped and continued their voyage. While ashore, the Spaniards collected firewood and fresh water. They also took an Indian captive as a guide.

On the Gulf coast the Spaniards entered the territory of the Calusa Indians. For more than three weeks—sufficient time for one of Ponce's ships to proceed further north to explore more of the Gulf of Mexico coast—the expedition remained in the area. Minor skirmishes took place, and the Calusa attacked with bows and arrows from canoes, some tied together as catamarans. The Spaniards retaliated, taking women and men as prisoners and damaging canoes onshore. Fatalities were suffered on both sides.

Despite the fighting, both the Spaniards and the Calusa seem to have been interested in trading and, most likely, learning more about one another. Items, including hides, were exchanged. One native man understood some Spanish words, and it was believed that he had come from Hispaniola or another island colonized by Spaniards. He also could have escaped from an earlier Spanish expedition to the region.

At one point the Calusa told the Spaniards their chief had gold and was coming to trade, but this was apparently a ruse. On May 14 the expedition departed, intent on exploring some of the islands they had passed on their incoming route and about which captive Indians had provided information.

Ponce and his men left Florida and sailed southward, making landfall on the north coast of Cuba. They then sailed northward past Chequescha, the territory of the Tequesta Indians, before returning to Puerto Rico via the Bahamas.

In 1521 Juan Ponce would return to Florida to attempt again to establish a colony.[11] Documents regarding this second expedition exist, including the royal charter granting Juan Ponce rights to the expedition and a letter by Ponce to the Crown stating his intentions, but none are clear about where Juan Ponce landed. Most scholars suggest he returned to southwest Florida, but although that is likely it is not certain.

Ponce's two ships sailed from Puerto Rico in late February, 1521. One account says the expedition included two hundred men, priests, fifty horses, seed for planting crops, and livestock, including cows, sheep, and goats. But Ponce soon discovered that his belief that the "business of colonization consisted of nothing more than to arrive and cultivate the land and pasture his livestock" was fatally wrong.[12] The chroniclers agree that a major battle with native warriors was fought and that the Spaniards suffered high fatalities, as did the Indians. Juan Ponce was himself wounded with an arrow. The expedition, facing failure, retreated to Cuba, where Juan Ponce died of his wounds.

No archaeological evidence for the locations of Juan Ponce de León's two excursions into Florida has ever been found. Because of the short duration of both, it is unlikely that the exact location of his landings will ever be pinpointed without additional documentation or definitive archaeological evidence.

Between Ponce's two voyages, several other Spaniards are known to have undertaken voyages of exploration along the Gulf coast of La Florida. Pre-1520 voyages known to have taken place include one by Diego Miruelo, who probably sailed to Tampa Bay in 1516; one by Francisco Hernández de Cordova, who sailed to the southwest Florida coast in 1517; and one by Alonzo Alvarez de Pineda, who sailed the entire Gulf coast in 1519 and provided the first map of the coastline of the Gulf of Mexico.[13] The latter voyage, sponsored by Francisco de Garay, governor of Jamaica, was intended to locate a passage from the Gulf of Mexico to the Pacific, recently discovered by Vasco Núñez de Balboa. A map drawn to show the coastline explored by Pineda shows two harbors on the Florida Gulf coast, probably Charlotte Harbor and Tampa Bay.

Except for the colonization attempts of Juan Ponce, it is likely that all of these early Gulf voyages involved only limited contact with native peoples in Florida. But unregulated slaving voyages could have infected the Florida native peoples with diseases from Europe.

While the Gulf voyages were taking place, attempts to explore the Atlantic coast also were under way. Again, the first voyages were probably illegal ones to capture slaves for labor in the Spanish Caribbean colonies. Florida's Atlantic coast, however, does not contain harbors like Tampa Bay into which large ships could sail. Landings were more likely to have taken place north of Florida along the sea islands or adjacent mainland of what is now Georgia and South Carolina. On that coast (from about St. Augustine north) ships can anchor in deep water

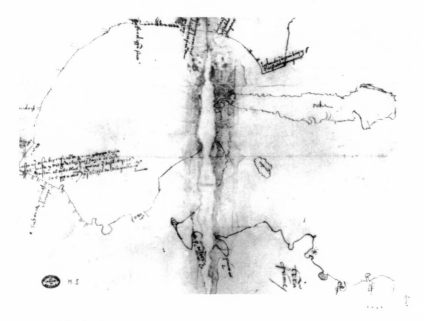

Map of the lands surrounding the Gulf of Mexico, drawn as a result of the Pineda expedition. Florida, with two Gulf harbors shown, is to the upper right, north of Cuba.

and send smaller boats up the tidal streams that drain the salt marshes, thus gaining access by water to locations on the islands and mainland.

Sometime between late summer 1514 and December 1516, the first documented voyage to the Atlantic coast (following the 1513 voyage of Juan Ponce) took place. Pedro de Salazar, a slaver representing interests in Santo Domingo, probably reached the middle latitudes of what is now the southeast United States.[14] One participant claimed that five hundred slaves were taken and that two-thirds of them died on the voyage back to Santo Domingo. The surviving Indians were tattooed and then distributed to the expedition's backers, with a few going as payment to crew members. These enslaved people soon died, also.

In 1521, Pedro de Quejo and Francisco Gordillo, on a slaving expedition and following Pedro de Salazar's lead, sailed into Winyah Bay, just north of the mouth of the South Santee River in South Carolina.[15] To secure the cooperation of the native peoples, the Spaniards gave them kerchiefs, linen shirts, red caps, four axes, "false pearls," "fine diamonds" (perhaps glass beads), and three old hammers.[16] Sixty people were lured aboard ship and taken as slaves back to Santo Domingo. The slavers were aware that the land they had found was north of Juan Ponce de León's discoveries.

That 1521 voyage would give rise to the legend of a rich land called Chicora, "abounding in timber, vines, native olive trees, Indians, pearls, and . . . perhaps gold and silver," all potential wealth to be exploited by colonial powers.[17] The legend, fueled by the contemporary written account by historian Peter Martyr, would spread through Europe, luring Spanish, French, and English explorers and colonists to the Middle Atlantic and Southeast regions in search of the fabled wealth.[18]

One of the backers of both the Pedro de Salazar and the 1521 expeditions was Lucas Vásquez de Ayllón, a judge in Santo Domingo. He used the information gathered on the two voyages to secure a royal contract to further explore and colonize the new land. In preparation for that expedition, Ayllón sent Quejo back to the coast in 1525 with two ships, a crew of sixty, and orders to reconnoiter the general region. Quejo made landfall at the Savannah River in early May and then sailed northward to Winyah Bay, where he again distributed gifts, including clothing. He also gave the native people seeds of Spanish plants and instructions on how they could be cultivated. After sailing northward toward Cape Fear, Quejo and his two ships reversed course and sailed southward, exploring the coast and searching for an inlet.

Quejo's ships put in at St. Simons Sound before sailing further south and making landfall on the northern end of Amelia Island. Below that latitude, the Spaniards apparently knew from Juan Ponce de León's previous discoveries that there was no suitable inlet. Accordingly, they again reversed course, reaching the Delmarva Peninsula and entering Chesapeake Bay in late June. Quejo then set a southerly course, sailing through the Bahamas and on to Hispaniola, where he reached port at the end of July. His remarkable 1525 voyage, unknown prior to historian Paul Hoffman's research, effectively opened the Atlantic coast to further Spanish expeditions, as it was intended to do.

These three early expeditions to the Atlantic coastal region, following on the heels of Juan Ponce's initial voyage to La Florida, all involved either slaving and/or other contact with the native peoples. Evidence of that contact—specifically, Quejo's 1525 landfall on St. Simons Sound or a similar landfall made by members of the Ayllón expedition the next

A dog with a musket ball in its ribs buried in a shallow grave in a late-precolumbian–early-sixteenth-century Native American village on St. Simons Island, Georgia.

year—may have been found in the early 1970s by archaeologists excavating in a village site and a mound on the northern end of St. Simons Island, Georgia. Charles Pearson of the University of Georgia found early Spanish beads and coins in Taylor Mound, some accompanying human interments. Subsequent University of Florida excavations in the same mound located additional metal objects. In a nearby village a dog with a musket ball in its ribs was found buried in a shallow grave. The European and native artifacts from the mound and the village suggest contact with Spaniards in the early sixteenth century.[19]

Ayllón's Attempt to Colonize La Florida

Following Quejo's second voyage, Ayllón readied his own colonizing expedition. His royal charter required him to establish settlements and bring Christianity to the native peoples, who were to be well treated and paid for work.[20] On the other hand, Ayllón was granted permission to take slaves from the native population; this was rationalized by the belief that slaves were kept by some native groups. Those individuals, because they already were slaves, could be traded for and then exported to Santo Domingo.

Ayllón's expedition left Puerto Plata, on the north coast of Hispaniola, in mid-July 1526. Six hundred or so people, including 100 to 150 sailors, women, children, African slaves, Dominican priests, and doctors, sailed on six ships. They were supplied with bread made from manioc flour, corn, olive oil, serge cloth, and live cattle, pigs, and goats, the latter to be used both for food and as stock to raise herds. A hundred head of horses also sailed with the expedition.

On August 9 the fleet reached the mouth of the South Santee River or Winyah Bay, where one ship and its cargo was lost when it ran aground. A young native man, captured from that region by the Quejo-Gordillo expedition when it landed there in 1521 and subsequently taken to Spain by Ayllón in 1523, served as a translator and guide, but as soon as he was back in his homeland he escaped.

Scouting parties were sent to reconnoiter the mainland near the landfall. At the same time, work began on building a ship to replace the one lost. It soon became obvious that the native population in the immediate locality was not very large; no native villages are mentioned. Perhaps epidemics and slaving had reduced their numbers.

Ships were sent south to look for a more suitable place for the colony. One went as far as modern Ponce de Leon Inlet, south of St. Augustine, before turning back and landing in St. Simons Sound, then sailing back to Winyah Bay. A second scouting party sailed south to Port Royal Sound and the Broad River, where the name Santa Elena was given to the point of land that is modern Tybee Island. That ship continued south to Amelia Island before returning. A third ship would essentially trace the route of the second down to Amelia Island and back.

In early September, Ayllón decided to move the colony southward to the Sapelo Sound area, which had been scouted by his ships. Most of the men and the horses were sent overland, while the women, children, and livestock went by sea, along with the men who were too sick to make the overland journey. In late September both parties had reunited and established the settlement of San Miguel de Gualdape, consisting of a church and houses. The settlement was somewhere on or very near Sapelo Sound, either on a barrier island or the adjacent mainland.[21]

During the fall the colonists suffered disease, lack of food, and cold. Scouting parties were sent inland to locate native populations from which food could be obtained, but they were not successful. Many people died, including Ayllón (on October 18). Some members of the colony moved to a nearby Indian village, but after several days their native hosts killed them. Raids took a toll on the Spaniards, and at one point some of the African slaves set fire to buildings. Defeated, the colonists abandoned the settlement in mid-November and set sail for home. Many died along the way. Ultimately, only about 150 reached Spanish settlements in the Antilles.[22] San Miguel de Gualdape was a failure.

These earliest Spanish voyages to explore and colonize La Florida were centered on the coasts, places that could be reached by ships. Ayllón had sought to learn about interior lands, but even people from his colony did not venture very far into the interior. Considerable navigational information and knowledge of the coastline was recorded on maps and in rutters, but little was known about the interior of La Florida, although rumors such as the one about Chicora probably circulated. The early voyages did, however, establish that La Florida, which Juan Ponce had thought might be a large island, was part of a huge land mass. La Florida, located on the northern edge of the Spanish empire, an empire that had expanded well beyond the initial beachhead on Hispaniola, would continue to attract Spanish conquistadores and entrepreneurs seeking wealth.

The Narváez Entrada[23]

In 1519, prior to his entrada into the heartland of the Aztec empire, Hernán Cortés had established a Spanish settlement at Villa Rica, in Veracruz on the Mexican coast. Further exploration and settlement of other portions of the Mexican Gulf coast would quickly follow.

In 1523, Francisco de Garay, asserting land claims resulting from Alvarez de Pineda's 1519 voyage, which he had sponsored, sought to place a settlement at Pánuco, on the Mexican Gulf coast north of Cortés's coastal claims. Only a few years later, in 1527, Nuño de Guzmán, the governor of Pánuco, sponsored a slave raid into the lands along the Rio de las Palmas (the modern Rio Soto de la Marina) on the upper Mexican Gulf coast. Rapidly, Spanish interests were encompassing the Gulf coast of Mexico, including Yucatán.

The next conquest was to be the lands north and east of Mexico around the Gulf, the lands leading to La Florida, the coasts of which already had been traversed by a host of Spanish sailors and adventurers. Conquest of those lands would unify and secure Spain's northern imperial frontier. To accomplish that a royal contract to explore and settle the Gulf coast from Pánuco to Florida was awarded in 1526 to Pánfilo de Narváez, a seasoned conquistador who had participated in campaigns against the native peoples of Cuba. Narváez's contract directed him to colonize the region—including establishing three forts—and to Christianize its people.[24]

Narváez's expedition of five ships, eighty horses, and as many as six hundred people, including ten women and African servants, sailed from Spain in June 1527.[25] The ships made landfall in Santo Domingo on Hispaniola, where supplies were loaded and 140 people deserted. Then the expedition sailed to Cuba, where more supplies were acquired. A storm struck the ships, drowning sixty people and twenty horses.

The star-crossed expedition, then numbering about four hundred, left Cuba in February 1528 for the upper Gulf of Mexico coast. Unfortunately, the fleet ran aground almost immediately, causing further delay. It was not until April 12 that land was sighted. The expedition, already low on supplies because of the delays, opted to seek a harbor on the coast of Florida rather than sail farther north and west to Pánuco. It would be a tragic decision.

Narváez's pilot, Diego de Miruelo, most likely sought Tampa Bay, known to Spanish sailors as Bahía Honda. But the expedition could not find that or any other harbor, choosing instead to anchor off the coast of modern Pinellas County.

Information about the activities of Narváez's army in Florida comes from a firsthand account written by Cabeza de Vaca in 1536 or 1537, at least eight years after the events took place.[26] Despite the extended gap in time before his account was written down, Cabeza de Vaca provides surprisingly detailed information about what befell the Spaniards after their landing in Florida.

Narváez formally took possession of the land on behalf of his sovereign and had himself acknowledged governor. The forty-two horses

Portion of Diego Ribero's 1529 world map showing the Americas. It reflects European geographical knowledge accumulated by that time. Both the Tiera de Garay (Land of Garay, the individual who had sponsored the Pineda voyage) and the Tiera de Ayllón are shown in what is now the southeastern United States. The original of the map is in the Vatican.

that had not died on the sea journey and most of the men who had accompanied Narváez were off-loaded from the ships. After several days, a scouting party of forty-five men, including several on horseback, went inland to explore. By evening they reached the shore of a "very large bay," probably the western side of Old Tampa Bay, where they remained for a day and two nights before returning to the landing camp.[27]

Despite finding this harbor, Narváez and his men were not convinced it was Bahía Honda, which they thought was farther north. A ship was ordered to sail along the coast to look for the northern harbor. If it were not found, the ship was to go to Havana, pick up supplies, and then return to the camp.

The ship, which did not find a second harbor because none exists, did as ordered. But when the ship returned months later the expedition

had long since moved inland, and Narváez's other ships also had departed. Four men from the returning ship went ashore to look for some
sign of Narváez, but they were captured by Indians. Seeing little hope
of rescuing the captives, the crew of the ship lifted anchor and departed. One of the captives, Juan Ortiz, would be found by Hernando
de Soto's men in 1539, eleven years later.

Soon after the first ship had been sent to search for the harbor,
Narváez and a scouting party returned to Tampa Bay to explore further. They followed the bay shore for four leagues, capturing several
Indians from whom they extracted information regarding where corn
could be found. In order to feed his army, Narváez intended to take
food from native peoples, a tactic de Soto would employ as well. The
Indians led the Spaniards to their village near the head of the bay,
where they showed the Spaniards corn that was not yet ripe. As noted
in chapter 4, it was there, probably at the village of Tocobaga, that the
Spaniards also were shown the boxes and other items salvaged from a
Spanish ship, including gold. Using "signs," the Spaniards were led to
believe that more gold could be obtained in a native province to the
north, called "Apalachen."[28]

Native guides then led the Spaniards ten to twelve leagues farther
north to another village where there was a field of corn. After exploring the area for two days, Narváez and his men returned to their
camp. Satisfied that his army could live off the land, Narváez made
plans to march northward. Because the first ship he had sent to find the
harbor had not yet returned, he ordered his remaining ships to explore
the coastline to search for the harbor, instructing his men to wait at the
harbor when they found it. The army, which would come overland,
would meet them there.

Like the ship previously sent on the same task, these ships would
also fail to find a northern harbor. As Cabeza de Vaca would later re-
alize, the harbor they were seeking was actually the one Narváez and
his scouting party already had found; de Vaca would write it was "the
one we had already discovered and where we had found the boxes
from Spain."[29]

The contention that another large harbor existed farther north on
the Gulf coast was probably based on the same erroneous latitudes that
Alonso de Chaves, the royal Spanish cosmographer, had when he compiled his *Espejo* in the late 1520s. The *Espejo*, a navigation guide to the

Americas as they were known to Spanish pilots at that time, places the mouth of Tampa Bay at 29 degrees north latitude, well north of its true location of 27.5 degrees.[30] Narváez's pilot, who would have determined the correct latitude of the harbor they had found (Tampa Bay), must have thought, based on the erroneous latitude, that a second harbor was about ninety miles—a degree and a half—north. Narváez's pilot would have known of the existence of both Charlotte Harbor and Tampa Bay, and must have reasoned, based on latitude, that the scouting party had found Charlotte Harbor; thus Bahía Honda must be north. Later, when no harbor was found, the mistake was realized.

This may be the same degree-and-a-half error that appears in the account of Juan Ponce de León's 1513 voyage to Florida, suggesting again that prior to about 1530 at least some of the Spanish latitude tables used in conjunction with sun sightings were faulty. De Soto, eleven years later, would not make the same mistake; by 1539 the correct Gulf latitudes were known.

While his ships explored the coastline, Narváez and his army left the camp and marched northward. The ships later would spend nearly a year sailing the coast searching fruitlessly for some sign of the army. The army, numbering only three hundred because some people had left on the ships, marched north according to Narváez's plan to "move along the coast" until the harbor believed to be to the north was reached.[31] There, presumably at 29 degrees latitude, the Spaniards expected to find the ships and supplies.

The army marched north for fifteen days. The plan to stay near the coast so they could intersect the nonexistent harbor was a poor one. By not moving into the interior of Florida, Narváez and his army would not encounter the agricultural Timucua-speaking Indian groups that de Soto later exploited. Without native stores of food, the daily ration of "two pounds of ship-biscuit and one-half pound of bacon" distributed to each soldier could not sustain an army on the march for very long.[32]

Perhaps also because of the coastal route they chose, Narváez and his men failed to "meet a soul, nor did we see a house or village," until they forded a large river.[33] The crossing, which took a day and was accomplished both by swimming and by using rafts, brought them face-to-face with as many as two hundred natives. Five or six were taken captive and forced to lead the Spaniards to their village a half league away, where corn was found and where the army remained for a week, recovering.

The river they had crossed was most likely the Withlacoochee. Because it was thought that the river might flow into the harbor where they were to rendezvous with the ships, men were sent to explore. The men reached the Gulf and waded through the shallow inshore waters, cutting their feet on oysters. But they could go no further south when they came to the river channel. A larger group of infantry and cavalry went back to the river, crossed it, and also followed it to its mouth, where they found the same shallow waters but no harbor.

Thwarted in their attempt to find the elusive harbor, the Spaniards continued northward, using captive natives as guides. Probably well aware of the Spaniards' penchant for taking captives, Indians often withdrew at the army's approach.

If the army continued on a northerly heading, they would have gradually traveled further and further away from the coastline, which

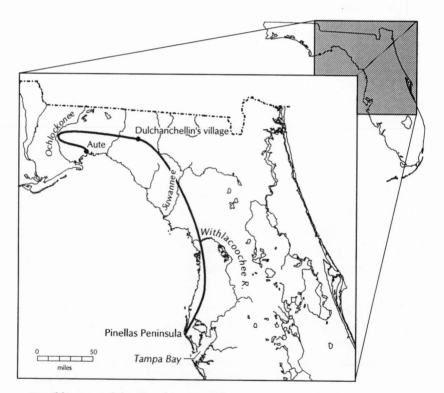

Possible route of the Narváez expedition.

curves northwesterly starting just below the mouth of the Suwannee River. Such a route would have led them into northern or northeastern Dixie County. Or, they may have continued to parallel the coast. In either case, they would have arrived in Dixie County. There they were met by a native chief who had traveled from his village to see the Spaniards.

The chief, whose name was Dulchanchellin, was carried on the shoulders of another individual, a sign of respect, and he wore a painted deerskin. He was accompanied by many villagers who played reed flutes. The Spaniards gave him bells, beads, and trinkets. The chief communicated with the Spaniards by signs, indicating he was an enemy of the Apalachee Indians. He must have recognized the Spaniards as a military force to be reckoned with and tried to enlist them against the Apalachee. He convinced his new friends to accompany him back to his village.

The journey to the chief's village took two or three days and involved

Several European accounts note that Timucua speakers carried chiefly individuals in litters, as portrayed in this 1591 de Bry engraving, "The Ceremony in Which His Chosen Wife Is Brought to the Chief" (Hulton 1977:I:150). Chief Dulchanchellin similarly may have been carried in a litter, rather than simply on the shoulders of an individual.

crossing a large river with a very strong current. This was certainly the Suwannee River. One soldier and his horse tried to ford it, but both were swept away and drowned. The dead horse was recovered, butchered, and eaten.

Beyond the river the next day, the army reached the chief's village, where the hungry Spaniards were given corn. The village was probably in Madison County, and the chief and his people were the same group of western Timucua speakers whose chief, called Uzachile, met the de Soto expedition eleven years later. Like Dulchanchellin, Chief Uzachile and his people lived just west of the Suwannee River and were enemies of the Apalachee.

After the army left Dulchanchellin's village, several Indians were captured and forced to act as guides. They led the army through a forest in which there were many fallen trees, making it difficult to travel. Most likely the Spaniards were led through the San Pedro Bay wetlands south of Madison County. De Soto's route would be just to the north of the same wetlands. Finally, the army arrived in Apalachee. Cabeza de Vaca says they "suffered greatly from hunger" on the trek from the Tampa Bay region, and many of the soldiers had wounds caused by the chafing of their armor or the loads they carried.[34]

It is difficult to reconcile the description of the native province of Apalachee given by Cabeza de Vaca with what later was found by members of the de Soto expedition.[35] The most likely explanation is that the native guides did not take Narváez's army into the heartland of Apalachee province, much less to the main town where de Soto's army would spend the winter of 1539–40. Instead, the Apalachee town where Narváez and his men were led and where they camped for twenty-five days was not near the populous towns and hamlets that typified much of inland Apalachee.

On three occasions scouting parties were sent out to explore the countryside, which Cabeza de Vaca reports was "thinly inhabited and difficult to march through, owing to swamps, forests, and wetlands."[36] Narváez additionally sought information about the land from captive Indians. According to Cabeza de Vaca, these captives said that nine days away, near the Gulf, there was a town called Aute (Ochete), which had ample corn, beans, and squash.

Abandoning any attempt to move farther into the interior of La Florida, Narváez chose to try to find Aute and the Gulf. For eight or nine days the army marched, almost constantly harassed by native archers.

It is likely that when the army had entered Apalachee territory a month earlier, the Spaniards were led on a very circuitous route through some of the roughest country their guides could find. The Apalachee similarly misled the de Soto expedition in 1539. At one point Narváez's men had reached a river, which they named Rio de la Magdalena, the later Spanish name for the Ochlockonee River.[37] If they indeed had marched to the Ochlockonee, the Spaniards had been made to travel all the way through Apalachee territory. No wonder it took nine days to reach Aute.

In Aute the army found food. Cabeza de Vaca then was sent with fifty-eight men to find the Gulf of Mexico, thought to be nearby. After a day the men came to a saltwater inlet or estuary, where they feasted on oysters. But they had not yet reached the open waters of the Gulf. Twenty men were sent to explore further. They returned to report numerous inlets and bays along the Gulf coast, an accurate assessment of the marshy Florida Gulf coast in the Big Bend area.

Back at Aute, Narváez and a third of his men had taken ill. Carrying its sick, who "became worse every day," the army left Aute and went to the estuary near the coast previously visited by the scouting party.[38] Conditions were so bad that some of the men deserted.

With the prospect of illness spreading to other members of the army, an overland march to Mexico along the coast made difficult by inlets and bays, and the presence of Apalachee archers to their rear, the Spaniards decided to build rafts to reach Mexico. Using deer hides and wooden flues to make the bellows needed to create a hot fire, the soldiers reshaped horse tack, spurs, and weapons into nails and tools. In six weeks five rafts were built and caulked with palmetto fiber and pine pitch. To sustain the army while construction took place, those soldiers who were able-bodied raided native villages for food. Horse meat supplemented the commandeered food. The horses also provided tails and manes for ropes.

Before they left on September 22, the Spaniards named the inlet where they built the rafts and butchered and ate their horses the Bay of Horses. De Soto's men would locate the exact place in late 1539.

In the short time Narváez had been in La Florida, forty of his men had died from hunger and illness and more than twelve had been killed in raids. The survivors, nearly 250 Spaniards, loaded themselves on the five rafts, "without any one . . . having the least knowledge of the art of navigation."[39]

For a week Narváez's army floated along the coast, apparently following the indented coastline of the modern St. Marks Wildlife Refuge toward Ocklockonee Bay. The rafts moved with difficulty through the shallow inshore waters, not finding a way to reach the open waters of the Gulf through the barrier islands. Near one island where they finally came to open Gulf waters, perhaps near Dog Island, they captured five dugout canoes abandoned by Indians. The canoes were used to build low sideboards on the rafts.

They continued poling westward, suffering from hunger, thirst, storms, waterlogged rafts, and Indian raids. Ultimately, as chances for ever reaching Mexico appeared slim, Narváez declared that "each one should do the best he could to save himself."[40] Most of the rafts washed ashore; the one carrying Narváez floated away never to be seen again. Some of the raft survivors tried to walk to Mexico, others opted to live among the native American Indians, and still others were captured as slaves.

By fall 1533 four members of the original army were living with native groups on the Texas coast. They were Cabeza de Vaca, Alonso de Castillo Maldonado, Andrés Dorantes de Carranza, and Esteban, a man from Morocco, who was Dorantes's servant. In September 1534 the four met when these groups came together to harvest prickly pears. Putting into effect a plan devised the previous year, the four escaped, heading toward Mexico. Nearly two years later they reached northern Mexico, where they met Spanish slavers, marking a final end to the ill-fated Narváez expedition.

Although the Narváez expedition was in Florida for only a few months, archaeologists believe they have identified archaeological sites in the Florida panhandle coast that may contain artifacts associated with the expedition.[41] Archaeologist Jeffrey Mitchem suggests that the town of Aute was near the Wakulla River, which flows into the St. Marks River just before the latter flows into Apalachee Bay, south of Tallahassee.[42] The town could have been near the Work Place archaeological site, which is located on the east bank of the river in Wakulla County. Early-sixteenth-century Spanish artifacts, including iron tools, glass beads, brass bells, and other items, have been found in the nearby Marsh Island Mound. Downriver, toward the coast, is the St. Marks Wildlife Refuge Cemetery site, also in Wakulla County, where European-derived items such as Clarksdale hawk-bells, faceted chevron beads, and other glass bead types from the early sixteenth century also have been found.[43] The St. Marks site, which is not far from the mouth of the St. Marks River, could be near Narváez's Bay of Horses.

The impact of the Ayllón and Narváez expeditions on the native people could have been immense. Accounts from both mention illnesses among the Spaniards, diseases that could have spread to the native people. Narváez's army also must have had a military impact. Cabeza de Vaca's narrative contains numerous references to skirmishes.

We can only wonder if the Florida Indian populations would have quickly recovered from the Narváez invasion. Would the damage done by the Spanish presence have been erased in a few generations? The discussion is moot because Spanish interests in La Florida did not halt with the disastrous colonization attempts of Ayllón and Narváez. As historian Robert Weddle has pointed out, the odyssey of Cabeza de Vaca and his three companions inspired rather than discouraged further exploration and attempts at settlement.[44] Indeed, the stories told by the four survivors soon prompted a Franciscan priest, Father Marcos de Niça, to lead a small expedition northward from New Galicia in northern Mexico in March 1539. His companions included Esteban, the survivor of the Narváez expedition.[45] That foray in turn led to Francisco de Vásquez de Coronado's 1542 expedition into the southwest United States.

Hernando de Soto also would hear these stories while organizing his own expedition into La Florida. It, too, would be a colossal failure. Even so, Spanish and French explorers and colonists would continue to come, bringing Christianity to the Florida Indians even while bringing diseases, the seeds of their demise.

A Tide Unchecked

7 The stories told by Cabeza de Vaca and the other survivors of the ill-fated Narváez expedition led to dreams of souls to be saved and wealth to be taken. Their embellished tales spread from Mexico across the ocean. In August 1537, Cabeza de Vaca himself arrived in Portugal and then went on to Spain, where he continued to tell stories of La Florida and his extraordinary journey. In 1538, one of the chroniclers of the de Soto expedition noted that Cabeza de Vaca, while at the Spanish court in Seville, led people "to understand that it [La Florida] was the richest country in the world."[1] De Soto, in Seville, tried to enlist Cabeza de Vaca in his planned expedition to La Florida, but failed.

The Army of Hernando de Soto

Cabeza de Vaca's stories must have been colorful. Among the people signing on or investing in de Soto's La Florida expedition were some of his relatives. A few people even sold property to finance their participation.[2]

De Soto, like Pánfilo de Narváez, was a veteran of Spain's conquests in the Americas. He was a successful conquistador who had participated in campaigns in Central America, gaining fame and wealth from the slave trade and mercenary activities. He also had served the Pizarro brothers in the sacking of the Inca empire in highland South America in the early 1530s.

De Soto's wealth and reputation allowed him to obtain a royal contract, dated November 1536, giving him permission to establish a Spanish colony in La Florida.[3] The contract, which specifically superseded the claims of Ayllón and Narváez, both of whom had died in attempting to fulfill their own contracts, required de Soto to explore, conquer, and settle both the Province of Tierra Nueva (where Ayllón had been) and the Province of Rio de las Palmas (the upper Gulf coast), essentially all the known lands north of Mexico.

The stories spread by Cabeza de Vaca could only have given more impetus to the planned expedition. Soldiers and other people were quick to sign on with de Soto, a leader who already had found success in the Americas. De Soto and his officers organized the expedition as both a military venture and a colonization effort. Participants included soldiers and the craftsmen needed to help build forts and settlements. The expedition also would be well supplied and well manned. The *caballeros* (knights) would take their servants, extra arms and armor, and spare horses. De Soto and other high-ranking officers would travel with all the tents, field furnishings, and other gear needed to live reasonably comfortably on the journey that lay ahead. The expedition would be the most ambitious Spanish initiative to date in La Florida, one that participants could only hope would meet the same Spanish-defined financial successes Cortés had experienced in Mexico and the Pizarros and de Soto had found in Peru.

Buttressed by an ideology and documents that made them representatives of God, the pope, and their sovereign, and armed with fierce weapons, de Soto and his army sailed from Spain in April 1538. The fleet arrived in Cuba, where de Soto, who had been given the governorship of the colony as a part of his contract, finalized plans for the expedition. By controlling Cuba, this conquistador would have a base of operations to supply his new La Florida colony.

Scout ships were sent ahead to reconnoiter the landing site on the Gulf coast, which was planned for Tampa Bay, the harbor known to Spanish navigators as Bahía Honda. This was the same harbor Narváez's pilot had sought in 1528 using an erroneous latitude.

On May 18, 1539, de Soto and his army sailed out of Cuba bound for the harbor on Florida's Gulf coast. Their contract with the Spanish monarch instructed them "to conquer and settle and reduce to peaceful life" the lands that lay before them.[4] As representatives of their sovereign and their church, they sought to do just that.

One week after setting sail from Cuba, de Soto's fleet of five large and four smaller ships dropped anchor just south of the mouth of Tampa Bay, probably off Longboat Key near Sarasota.[5] The pilot, who apparently had a correct latitude for the mouth of the bay, had just missed his destination. Within two days the entrance to the bay was found, and the Spaniards carefully moved their ships into it and established a camp near the mouth of the Little Manatee River in a Uzita Indian village. As many as 725 people were unloaded, including two women, tailors, shoemakers, a stocking maker, a notary, a farrier, a trumpeter, servants, priests, cavalry, and infantry. Also off-loaded were war dogs, 220 horses, a drove of pigs, and supplies for eighteen months. None of the animals and only a small amount of supplies, probably only personal arms, would leave La Florida four years later.

While camped at Tampa Bay, the Spaniards continued to encounter Uzita and Mocoso Indians and other native people. At times these encounters were peaceful, but often they involved skirmishes. The Spaniards' ability to communicate with the native peoples in Florida was enhanced by their finding Juan Ortiz. Ortiz was the Spaniard who had been abandoned at Tampa Bay in 1528 by the ship looking for Narváez. He had lived as a captive among the Uzita and then the Mocoso Indians for eleven years. When found, Ortiz was being sent to the Spaniards by the chief of the village where he had been living. He would provide translation for the army as it passed among the Timucua-speaking peoples of Florida. Later he would team with native translators as non-Timucuan languages were first translated into Timucua and then into Spanish.

The Spaniards spent six weeks reconnoitering the adjacent territory before finally beginning their march north. When the army left it was made up of about five hundred Spaniards, as well as hundreds of native people made to serve as bearers. More than one hundred people and a quantity of supplies, as well as some of the ships and boats, were left behind at the base camp as backup. The expedition would spend the summer and early fall of 1539 marching northward and then west across north Florida, searching for Apalachee, the same native province Narváez had sought.

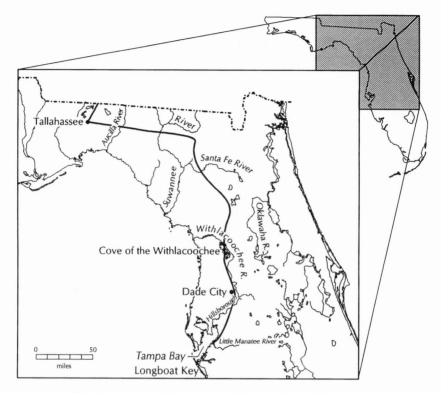

Route of the de Soto expedition in Florida (based on Milanich and Hudson 1993).

The path of the army took the Spaniards from the Uzita village, across the Alafia River, through the territory of Chief Mocoso, and then northward through Hillsborough, Pasco, and Hernando counties and into Citrus County. For much of the time they were in Florida, the army followed Indian trails, precolumbian paths that continued to be used throughout the colonial period.

While at the base camp on Tampa Bay, a contingent of soldiers had been sent into the interior of Florida to the village of Chief Urriparacoxi, the chief who demanded tribute from some of the native groups living on Tampa Bay. Urriparacoxi's villagers, like the people north of Tampa Bay, were corn agriculturists. The contingent sent to Urriparacoxi's village rendezvoused with de Soto's main army at the village called Luca, near the modern town of Lacoochee.

In Citrus County, north of Luca, the Spanish army camped at a small town, Vicela, and then arrived at Tocaste, the town located at the southern end of Lake Tsala Apopka. During this early portion of their journey in Florida the immediate objective was the town of Ocale, which the Spaniards had heard about and where they planned to winter. The information that the Spaniards had received led them to believe that sufficient food could be found there to sustain the army through the coming winter.

Ocale, however, was on the eastern side of the Cove of the Withlacoochee, while Tocaste was on the southwest side. To get to Ocale the army needed to find a way through the swamps and ponds of the cove. Eventually an advance party did find such a passage, probably following a trail approximated by modern Turner Fish Camp Road, which leads easterly from Inverness across the cove to the Withlacoochee River. After a difficult crossing of the Withlacoochee, the advance force passed through a small settlement and then arrived at the main village of Ocale in southeastern Marion County or northwestern Sumter County. Following the same track several days later, the rest of the army made a very difficult multiday journey across the wetlands and reached Ocale.

While they marched northward, scouting parties were sent out to explore and to seek food. The plan de Soto implemented was the same as Narváez's: to feed his army by moving from native village to native village, taking stored corn and other food as needed. The army also took native women as consorts and captured men and boys for use as guides and bearers.

If the army intended to stay any length of time in one place, then the demand for food increased proportionally, and the place where the Spaniards were going to winter had to have even larger food supplies. De Soto did not wish to repeat the errors of earlier expeditions into La Florida.

Unfortunately for the Spaniards, Ocale was not able to provide the food the army would require for a winter stay of several months. The natural bounty around the town was nothing like what de Soto had been led to believe. Indeed, after they raided the countryside it became obvious there was not even enough food to sustain the expedition's members for more than a few days. It also was obvious that the army needed to rest and recuperate from its trek north from Tampa Bay and the difficult crossing of the Cove of the Withlacoochee, when some of the people on foot were forced to forage for edible roots to sustain themselves.

The immediate need for food was satisfied by sending a raiding party eastward to take corn from the Acuera, the eastern Timucuan group believed lived near or on the headwaters of the Oklawaha River. A longer-term solution to the problem also was sought. De Soto and an advance party of fifty cavalry and sixty infantry marched northward to explore, looking for Apalachee or another town or province where sufficient food supplies could be gathered for the upcoming winter. At that point—it was early August—de Soto must have realized that winter was a relatively long way off and that he had time to locate Apalachee and assess its food supplies before entering winter camp.

De Soto and the advance party moved rapidly north from Ocale through Marion and Alachua counties, following established trails. They marched through the territory of the Potano Indians, crossed the Santa Fe River, and marched on to the village of Aguacaleyquen, the northern Utina group in southern Columbia County.

In Aguacaleyquen, de Soto and the advance party quickly became aware that they had entered a region with a denser native population. Chiefs controlled more people and villages than had the chiefs the Spaniards had encountered thus far. Although the Spaniards maintained a great military advantage over the Indians in terms of weaponry and tactics, the sheer number of native people presented a threat.

To counter the threat, de Soto first took Chief Aguacaleyquen's daughter as hostage. Then he sent eight horsemen back to Ocale with orders for the remainder of the army to join him at Aguacaleyquen, which they did. During the time the bulk of the army had been camped at Ocale, they must have continually raided the region for food, devastating the countryside.

Reinforced, de Soto and his army marched westward from Aguacaleyquen. Before breaking camp, de Soto used the chief's daughter to entice the chief to enter the Spanish camp, where he, too, was taken hostage. De Soto used the chief and his daughter to dissuade the northern Utina from attacking his army.

De Soto's goal was Apalachee, which native guides told him was to the west. Even if Apalachee were not the bountiful province he hoped it was, de Soto had time before winter to march his army back to Tampa Bay, where he had deliberately left supplies just in case such a withdrawal was necessary. At least some of the soldiers thought this plan

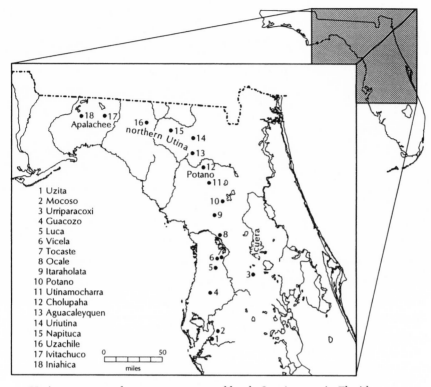

Native groups and towns encountered by de Soto's army in Florida.

should be implemented immediately. The Aguacaleyquen painted a dismal picture of Narváez's experience in Apalachee, and the Spaniards were well aware of the fate of that expedition.

De Soto and his army marched across Columbia and Suwannee counties, through northern Utina territory. At Napituca in western Suwannee County, the Spaniards fought two battles with Indians, resulting in huge native fatalities, including the execution-style slaying of chiefs and several hundred other warriors. The Spaniards would not tolerate any opposition and employed especially cruel retaliation when it occurred.

The army crossed the Suwannee River into Madison County. Emissaries from Chief Uzachile, perhaps the successor to Chief Dulchanchellin, brought venison as a sign of friendship. Representatives of the chief, the most powerful in the northern Utina region, had previously made contact with the expedition as it marched across Columbia and Suwannee counties. Those emissaries had played flutes, a sign that they were coming in peace. Flute players similarly had accompanied Chief Dulchanchellin when he had met the Narváez expedition in 1528.

De Soto and his men entered Chief Uzachile's main town, which had been abandoned by its inhabitants. If these were the same people who had met Narváez in 1528, they already were well aware of the behavior of the invading Spaniards.

From Uzachile's town the army marched through the forest that was the buffer between Uzachile's territory and the territory of the Apalachee, which began at the Aucilla River. At the river the Apalachee battled to contest the army's attempts to cross, but the Spaniards finally were successful and de Soto and his men marched on to Ivitachuco, a major Apalachee town. For the next several days they made their way westward, moving from town to town. The agricultural bounty encountered along the route was ample evidence that Apalachee could provide sufficient food to sustain the Spaniards. But the army practically had to fight its way across Apalachee as they attempted to locate the main town, which the Apalachee called Ini-

Nueva Cadiz glass beads like these from the early sixteenth century, excavated from the Weeki Wachee Mound in Hernando County, are thought to have been brought to Florida by the de Soto expedition (Mitchem et al. 1985). The largest is about 1 inch long. Strings of Nueva Cadiz beads may have been used to suspend crosses (courtesy of Robert Allen).

ahica. Worse, Apalachee guides deliberately misled the army, trying to prevent them from reaching Iniahica, just as they had misguided Narváez eleven years earlier.

In early October the army reached Iniahica and established their winter camp. The location of that town has been established by B. Calvin Jones of the Florida Bureau of Archaeological Research as being at the Governor Martin archaeological site in Tallahassee. The Martin site has since been investigated by bureau archaeologists.[6] At that site, as well as other locations along de Soto's route, artifacts—beads, bells, mirrors, scissors, and pieces of chain mail—believed left behind or discarded by the army or given to native people have been found by archaeologists.[7] At one site, Tatham Mound in the Cove of the Withlacoochee River in Citrus County, native burials exhibiting cuts and wounds from edged weapons, possibly Spanish swords, have been excavated.[8]

In spring 1540, de Soto's army broke camp and headed northeast across Georgia toward the Carolinas and the mythical land of Chicora.

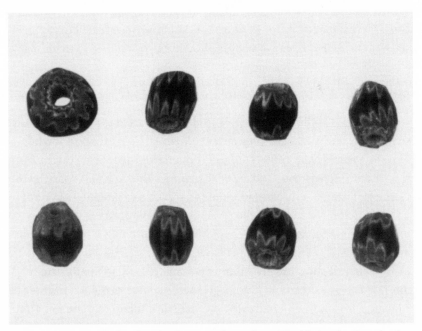

Faceted chevron glass beads also were brought to Florida by the Spaniards in the early and mid-sixteenth century. These were excavated from the Tatham Mound by Jeffrey Mitchem (1989b; Mitchem and Leader 1988; courtesy of Jeffrey Mitchem).

They then turned north, crossing the Appalachian Mountains into Tennessee. Across the Appalachians the army traced the Tennessee River Valley southwest through the large native province of Coosa, reaching well into eastern Alabama. Farther south, in Mobila, a town in the chiefdom of Tuscaluza, a bloody battle against native peoples was fought. Afterward the army turned northwest, marching across Alabama and into Mississippi, where another major battle was fought and where the expedition again wintered (1540–41).

Their march brought the Spaniards to the Mississippi River in May 1541, two years after landing. De Soto's third year was spent in Arkansas, moving from one native village to another, searching for wealth, before returning to the Mississippi River, where he died June 20, 1542.

A new leader attempted to march the army across Texas to Mexico, but after traveling many miles the Spaniards realized it was futile to continue. The army returned to the Mississippi River, reaching it in December 1542. The first six months of the next year were spent constructing boats to float downriver to the Gulf and then to Mexico. Twenty days after setting out, in late June 1543, the army reached the Gulf. Two and a half months later, the 311 survivors reached a Spanish settlement near present-day Tampico, Mexico, ending their odyssey.

More Failed Attempts—Luna and Villafañe

Although the Ayllón, Narváez, and de Soto expeditions all were unsuccessful, one might say tragically so, Spanish interest in colonizing La Florida was revived in the 1550s. An overland route was sought from New Spain across the Gulf coastal plain to the Atlantic coast in the vicinity of the Point of Santa Elena, the place associated with Ayllón in 1526.[9] Such a road would allow goods to be transported from Mexico to the Atlantic coast by land, avoiding the more dangerous sea route around Florida. From the port at Santa Elena, the goods could be loaded aboard ships for the Atlantic Ocean crossing to Spain. The road, intended to pass through Coosa, the large native province in interior Alabama through which the de Soto expedition had marched in 1540, would be protected and maintained by Spanish settlements placed along it.

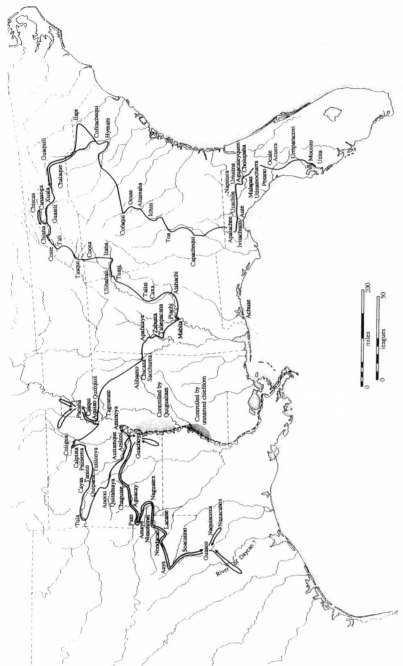

De Soto's route through the southern United States (as reconstructed by Charles Hudson and Associates; courtesy of Charles Hudson).

Priests urged that settlements be placed in lands fronting the northern Gulf coast, where they could serve as centers for missionary activities among native peoples.[10] Christian Indians would be more favorably disposed toward shipwrecked Spaniards than, for example, had been the native peoples who dealt with the survivors of the Narváez expedition. Coastal settlements could provide a base for the salvage of cargoes from ships sunk or run aground by storms or navigation error, and they could offer protection for Spanish sea lanes. Such settlements also would thwart the interest of other colonial powers in the region, lands claimed by Spain.

Lastly, despite the realities found in La Florida by early Spanish expeditions, there persisted the belief that wealth and agricultural bounty existed in that region. Chicora still loomed large in many minds. Paul Hoffman cites a 1547 letter written to the king of Spain that describes La Florida as "a big land, populated, and filled with many of the things of Spain, including vines, trees that give nuts like chestnuts, fields full of cattle (bison?), and forests of all sorts."[11] The settlements urged for La Florida, in addition to filling strategic and religious needs, could be financial successes as well.

For all of these reasons, various of which were urged by government and religious officials, La Florida again would become the focus of an attempt to found a Spanish colony. The plan was for several initial settlements. One was to be at Ochuse at modern Pensacola Bay. Others were to be at Coosa (north of Ochuse) and Cofitachequi, the latter another province de Soto had visited, which was in interior South Carolina, near the legendary Chicora. Still another was to be at the Point of Santa Elena on the coast nearby.[12]

Ochuse would be first. The harbor at Ochuse had been visited by boats sent by de Soto while his army was at Apalachee during the winter of 1539–40. Spanish brigantines, previously anchored at the Tampa Bay camp, had sailed to Apalachee Bay once de Soto was ensconced in this winter camp and had sent word back to Tampa Bay for the people and supplies left there to break camp and join him. Some of those people marched overland; others came by sea. The small fleet anchored in Apalachee Bay, perhaps near Narváez's Bay of Horses. Once the ships were unloaded, they were free to explore the coast. Ochuse had originally been found as a result of those explorations.

To establish the colony at Ochuse, an expedition supported by the

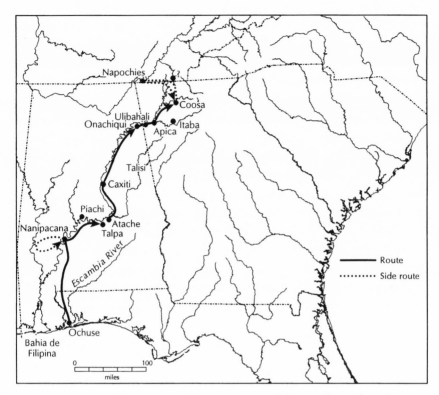

The Luna expedition's route into the interior of the Southeast (based on Hudson et al. 1989a, 1989b).

viceroy of Mexico, Luís de Velasco, and led by Tristán de Luna y Arellano set sail from the coast of Mexico in June 1559.[13] Fifteen hundred people, including Mexican Indians, a Native American woman taken from Coosa by de Soto's army, five hundred soldiers (some of whom had marched with de Soto twenty years earlier), and craftsmen, settlers, and clergy, sailed aboard thirteen ships. As Ayllón and de Soto had done earlier, a scout ship had been sent ahead in the fall of 1558 to explore the La Florida coast and find a landing site. But that ship had only gone as far as the port of Filipina, modern Mobile Bay.

Sailing eastward along the northern Gulf coast, the Luna expedition in 1559 apparently missed the entrances to both Mobile Bay and Pensacola Bay and made landfall just west of Apalachee Bay. Luna's ships sailed back westward, looking for Ochuse. But the pilot again missed the entrance and the fleet continued on to Mobile Bay. Although some modern sailors might scoff at the trouble early navigators had in finding the entrances to bays on the Gulf coast, those passages, un-marked and hidden by islands, often were difficult to find.

Knowing that Ochuse was back to the east, Luna sent a frigate in that direction. After finally locating Ochuse, the ship returned to Mobile Bay to report. Luna off-loaded his horses and some of the soldiers and instructed them to march overland to Pensacola Bay. Then the main fleet of ships, with the remainder of the expedition's members, went by sea to Ochuse, arriving in early August. The bay was renamed the Bahía Filipina del Puerto de Santa María, usually shortened to Bahía de Santa María. Soon the colonists began to refer to the settlement as Polonza, perhaps a local American Indian name and possibly related to the name Pensacola. It had taken the expedition just over two long months to reach its destination in La Florida, a relatively short distance from Mexico.

The journey aboard ships must have been difficult, but more hard-ships would soon follow. Five days after the expedition arrived at Pen-sacola a hurricane struck, sinking nine ships, ruining food and other supplies, and drowning some colonists. If the colonists were going to avoid starvation, they would have to obtain food from native groups, but that would not be an easy task. Luna had taken a large number of people with him, and feeding such a multitude would be difficult even if the food supplies of native peoples could be commandeered. The sit-uation would grow more desperate when it was realized that the seem-ingly large native populations observed by the de Soto expedition in the interior of Alabama north of Polonza apparently no longer existed, or at least could not be found. Luna's colony would end up paying for the sins of de Soto's army.

When it was clear that the small local native population could not supply sufficient food, Luna sent out two expeditions to reconnoiter the area around the new settlement. Like Narváez's army, Luna's colonists were incapable of providing food for themselves by fishing or hunting. The first scouting expedition went north thirty miles or so but failed to find any native towns or food. The second traveled by boat up the Escambia River, but also failed to find villages with stored food sup-plies. If the colony was to survive, the members would have to go even farther inland to find food.

Based on firsthand information provided by men who had marched through Alabama with de Soto in 1540, Luna sent a third detachment—150 to 200 people—northward from Ochuse to find the native town of Piachi, which was expected to have stored food. The town was probably located on the Alabama River.[14] De Soto's army had marched through Piachi nearly twenty years earlier.

Luna's men marched more than one hundred miles cross-country in search of Piachi. After arriving at the Alabama River, the Spaniards began to search its southern bank for the town. Piachi was not found; it was farther north. The Spaniards did locate several small towns and a larger one, Nanipacana, said to have eighty houses. Seemingly with no alternative, Luna ordered that the colony be moved from the coast to Nanipacana. One group of people traveled in two small boats that first sailed to Mobile Bay and then navigated the Alabama River to the native town. The remaining colonists, except about fifty people left at Pensacola, went overland.

Luna and the colonists would not find enough food to sustain them in Nanipacana. The native residents, who had experienced firsthand the depredations of de Soto's army a decade before, abandoned their village, taking their stored food. And rather than leaving crops in the field for Luna's colonists, they burned the fields, destroying the produce. Scouting the river valley north and south of Nanipacana, Luna's scouts learned that the native peoples in both directions had also withdrawn. Even on the Tombigbee River, where another detachment was sent, the native peoples had abandoned their villages, denying Luna's colonists food.

To locate another town, Luna sent still another detachment northward on the Alabama River in two boats. But a place suitable for the colony was not found. Large portions of the river valley were depopulated, presumably a result of the devastating impact of the de Soto expedition (or the people had simply abandoned their homes to avoid Luna's men). In April 1560, on the verge of starvation, the colony made another attempt to find food. One hundred forty cavalry and infantry marched northward, hoping to locate the native province of Coosa visited by de Soto. Ultimately they reached the province of Coosa and the Tennessee River, traveling as far as southern Tennessee and northwest Georgia.

In the meanwhile, Luna had withdrawn the colonists from Nanipacana and returned to Pensacola. The detachment sent to Coosa returned and joined the rest of the colonists on the coast. The failure to

establish a settlement and find reliable sources of food had led to disagreements among the colonists. Lawsuits were filed, a means of
wresting power from Luna, and dissension racked the colony.

The attempt to found a settlement at Ochuse was a failure. In April
1561, Angel de Villafañe arrived with orders from the viceroy of
Mexico to move the colony to the Point of Santa Elena on the Atlantic
coast. The starving colonists, reduced to eating shellfish and grass,
readily agreed to be rescued. Taking on many of the survivors, Angel de
Villafañe sailed to Havana, where he allowed those colonists who
wished to leave to do so. Nearly 150 did. He then sailed northward to
the Atlantic coast, exploring from Santa Elena northward to near Cape
Hatteras. There a storm hit and Villafañe lost some of his ships. His own
attempt at colonization thwarted almost before it began, he returned to
the Caribbean.[15]

In the half century following 1513 and the initial voyage of Juan
Ponce de León, Spanish soldiers and sailors, often accompanied by
craftsmen and clergy, learned a great deal about La Florida and its
people. Those same Spaniards also had an impact on the land and its
people. Although the details of that impact are debated, it is certain that
where Spaniards and American Indians came face-to-face, the outcome was often disastrous for the latter. Where archival information is
present, such as that provided by the Luna expedition when its members revisited towns and places in Alabama where the de Soto expedition had been twenty years earlier, the scope of the disaster seems
clear. Large sections of the Alabama River Valley were greatly reduced
in population, and others were abandoned.

The best explanation is that the de Soto expedition, known to have
fought battles with the native people in that region, also had brought
diseases that resulted in localized epidemics. As suggested in chapter 4,
the double-edged sword of battle fatalities and disease had also been
thrust into sixteenth-century Florida, devastating native populations
such as those around south and east Tampa Bay. Ultimately, that same
sword would annihilate all the indigenous societies of Florida.

Despite the failures of Luna and Villafañe, the Spanish Crown could
not ignore La Florida. Other colonial powers, notably France, were
making efforts to gain control of the land and its resources. As we shall
see in the next chapter, Spain would try several more times to colonize
La Florida before finally achieving success.

Colonization and First Settlement

8 Spain was not alone in wanting to establish a colony in La Florida. One of her rivals, France, also had designs on the Americas, La Florida included. In 1524 the Florentine explorer Giovanni da Verrazano, sailing under the flag of France, had reconnoitered the Atlantic coast from Florida to Cape Breton, providing some basis for French claims of ownership. The expeditions of Luna and Villafañe were in part responses to actual and rumored French excursions. France and Spain both realized that to control La Florida, settlements were needed.

In late 1561 rumors of a French expedition to La Florida reached the Spanish Crown. Jean Ribault was said to have sailed for the Americas to establish a colony.[1] Although his actual sailing date was not until early 1562, news of Ribault's expedition and stories of other planned French initiatives prompted the Spanish Crown to approve a new attempt to place a colony in La Florida even as Luna and Villafañe met with failure. Lucas Vázquez de Ayllón, son of the leader of the unsuccessful San Miguel de Gualdape colony, was contracted to found a settlement in the Bahía de Santa María, the Spanish name for Chesapeake Bay.

Ayllón had considerable trouble organizing his expedition, and did not sail from Spain until October 1563. But he got no further than Santo Domingo on Hispaniola. Disgruntled participants and financial problems caused Ayllón to abandon the attempt and to flee during the night, reportedly for Peru.[2]

In the meanwhile, Ribault and a crew of 150 had sailed from France, bound for North America, where he was to explore "a certen long coaste . . . from the hed of the lande called la Florida . . . 900 leages, or therabout [to the north]."[3] Making landfall at about St. Augustine, Ribault sailed north to the mouth of the St. Johns River, which he named the River of May and where he placed a stone marker inscribed with the arms of France.[4]

Exploring the coasts of Georgia and South Carolina as they sailed further northward, the Frenchmen reached the Point of Santa Elena, where they entered Port Royal Sound, a name given by Ribault. After raising another stone marker, work was begun on a fort. Leaving thirty soldiers behind to man Charlesfort, as the fort was called, Ribault returned to France.

Learning of Charlesfort, the Spanish Crown ordered its destruction. In the summer of 1564 a Spanish ship reached the site and destroyed what was left of the already abandoned French settlement. The soldiers left by Ribault had not fared well and had decided to sail back to France in a small boat. They reached France, but only after having to resort to cannibalism, having been ill supplied for the voyage. When the Spanish destroyed Charlesfort they also found and removed the stone marker and sent it to Spain.[5]

In the meanwhile the French were planning new voyages. René de Laudonnière had sailed for the Americas in April 1564 with three ships and three hundred people, including settlers, soldiers, and craftsmen. Laudonnière, who would be in charge of the La Florida colony for fifteen months, had been second in command to Ribault on the first voyage.

Accompanying Laudonnière on the second voyage was Jacques Le Moyne, who served as cartographer and artist. Le Moyne later returned to France and painted a series of pictures depicting scenes from La Florida. After Le Moyne's death his widow allowed a German engraver and publisher, Theodor de Bry, to publish a book of etchings and an accompanying narrative based on the paintings and French accounts. De Bry's book, with an accompanying map, was published in 1591 in Frankfurt in Latin and German editions.[6] The illustrations, narrative, and map are often-cited sources on the Florida Indians. How-

"The Floridians Worship the Column Set Up by the Captain [Ribault] on the First Voyage." The text with de Bry's 1591 engraving states that the Timucua Indians lived near the mouth of the St. Johns River, where the French erected a stone column and placed in front of it "fruits . . . and roots that were either good to eat or medicinally useful, dishes full of fragrant oils, and bows and arrows" (Hulton 1977:I:141).

ever, de Bry borrowed liberally from other illustrations of native peoples in the Americas, and the map draws heavily on Spanish sources, as well as some imagination. Today only one original set of Le Moyne's watercolors still exists.[7]

Laudonnière and his expedition, which included women and children, made landfall on the Atlantic coast of Florida in July 1564.[8] The French sailed north, reaching the St. Johns River two days later. There they found the first stone marker Ribault had raised. The next day Laudonnière sailed three leagues (about eleven miles) up the St. Johns River to a high bluff on the south bank, certainly the high point of land today known as St. Johns Bluff. They explored the area around the bluff briefly before returning to the coast to explore further.

Several days later they went back to the bluff, then walked overland a short way to a flat plain on the riverbank. There in late July work began on a fort, named Fort Caroline. The ships were unloaded and the supplies stored in a storage barn roofed with palm thatch and built for

that purpose. Sheep and chickens had been brought as breeding stock.[9]
Laudonnière described the fort:

> Our fort was built in a triangular shape. The west side, which was the
> landward side, was bounded by a little ditch and built with turfs [sod]
> making a parapet nine feet high. The other side [north], which was to-
> ward the river, was bounded by a timber palisade. . . . On the south side
> there was a kind of bastion, inside which I had a supply shed built. The
> whole thing was built of stakes and sand, except for about two or three
> feet of turf, of which the parapets were made. I had a large area eighteen
> paces square made in the middle. In the center of that, facing the southern
> side, I had a guardhouse built, and a house on the other, northern side. I
> built it a bit too high, for not long afterwards the wind blew it down. . . . I
> had an oven [for baking] built at some distance from the fort to avoid the
> risk of fire, since the houses were covered with palm leaves.[10]

The supply problems that had beset Ayllón and Luna also vexed the
French. By November 1564, suffering from a lack of food and other
hardships, some of Laudonnière's men stole a ship and headed for the
Caribbean. This incident was soon followed by a full-blown mutiny,
and for a time Laudonnière was imprisoned by his own men. In December sixty more men deserted, taking two small boats and sailing
south.

The next year brought no relief. Throughout the winter and spring
and into the summer the French suffered from hunger while they tried
to make alliances with eastern Timucuan groups to obtain food. The
colonists survived only because native peoples occasionally brought
them maize, beans, acorns, fish, deer, turkeys, "leopards," and little
bears they traded for axes, knives, glass beads, combs, and mirrors.[11]
Some native people came from far away to trade, and all struck hard
bargains. They knew the French were at their mercy.

In early August spirits lifted when an Englishman, John Hawkins,
was sighted off the coast with four ships. The French traded arms and
artillery for one of Hawkins's ships and for supplies, including flour,
beans, salt, oil, vinegar, olives, rice, biscuit (hardtack), candle wax, and
shoes. As soon as Hawkins sailed out of sight the French set in motion
plans to use the ship, along with another they still retained, to return
to France.

By mid-August they had stored water and loaded supplies and were

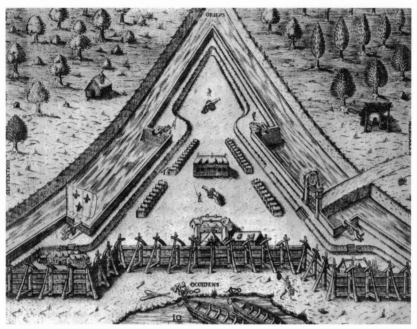

"Plan of Fort Caroline." The text with this de Bry engraving says the River of May (the St. Johns River) was selected for the fort because the French had found gold and silver there (Hulton 1977:I:142). If true, the metals were certainly salvaged from Spanish ships, not mined in La Florida.

waiting only for favorable winds. Laudonnière planned to capture native men and women to take to France, reasoning that the captives could be taught French and returned to La Florida, where they would be important ambassadors, promoting French interests.

Finally, on August 28, the tides and winds were both favorable and the two ships prepared to leave. As luck would have it, a small fleet was sighted. It turned out to be commanded by Jean Ribault, who came with orders giving him command of the colony. The return to France was put on hold.

In the meanwhile, the Frenchmen who had earlier deserted had sailed to the Caribbean and were raiding Spanish interests. Their actions drew the attention of Spanish officials, who viewed the French as outlaws and pirates. To get rid of this menace and to oust the French from La Florida, Pedro Menéndez de Avilés, commander of Spain's Caribbean fleet, was dispatched from Spain on orders from Philip II.

Menéndez's fleet arrived at mouth of the St. Johns River on September 4, 1565, only a week after Ribault's fleet had landed. The French and the Spanish were well informed about one another. From their ships Menéndez's men called out the first and last names of the French leaders. Laudonnière notes that "before they left Spain they must have been told of the [French] expedition and of the people who were to carry it out."[12] And Ribault's deputy carried a letter from the French admiral who commanded Ribault and Laudonnière, which read in part: "Captain Jean Ribault, as I was sealing this letter I had certain information that Don Pedro Menéndez is leaving Spain to go to the coast of New France [La Florida]. You will take care not to allow him to trespass on us."[13] Spies at the royal courts of Spain and France had done their jobs.

When Menéndez arrived, Ribault's anchored ships were undermanned because many of the crew were ashore. Facing superior numbers, the French still on board cut their anchor cables and made their escape. The Spaniards pursued but soon gave up the chase and sailed to St. Augustine, where Menéndez had set up camp among the Seloy Indians. Seeing the Spaniards' camp, the French ships returned to Fort Caroline to report that Menéndez had off-loaded supplies, infantry, and munitions. One of Chief Seloy's men also told the French that a large number of Spaniards had landed and were fortifying the native village. The Spaniards were accompanied by Africans, who had been brought as laborers.

Ribault decided to attack, taking his ships and crews and a number of Laudonnière's men from the fort (as well as some of the supplies Laudonnière had set aside for the return to France). On September 10 the French fleet, with six hundred soldiers and sailors, set sail for St. Augustine. As luck would have it a tropical storm struck, which, according to Laudonnière, was "the worse weather ever seen on this coast."[14] The storm scattered the French fleet, and four large vessels were blown ashore, three near Ponce de Leon Inlet and the fourth, the *Trinité*, with Jean Ribault aboard, near Cape Canaveral.

Menéndez, in St. Augustine, decided to use the occasion to attack Fort Caroline—not by sea, but by land. On September 18 he marched on the fort. In a driving rain at dawn two days later, Menéndez and his five hundred harquebusiers attacked. The French lookouts had been withdrawn by their squadron leader, who had thought the weather too foul for the Spaniards to initiate military action. By the time Menéndez and his men were sighted, they were practically inside the fort.

The fort was taken quickly. One hundred thirty-two French colonists, some in their nightclothes, were killed, and fifty or so women and children were captured. Laudonnière and forty-four of his men, including Jacques Le Moyne, managed to escape and make their way to their ships anchored nearby. Others of the French, including Ribault's son, also escaped. The fleeing French sank one of the three French ships to prevent it from falling into Spanish hands and sailed the other two to France.

Menéndez began rounding up the French colonists who had escaped into the nearby woods. He offered gifts to the Indians, probably the Saturiwa or allied groups, to entice them to bring the French refugees to him.

At this time, the survivors of Ribault's fleet who had been shipwrecked began to walk north toward Fort Caroline, not knowing it had been taken by Menéndez, who had renamed it San Mateo. One group of Frenchmen walked to an inlet eighteen miles south of St. Augustine, where their presence was observed by natives and reported to the Spaniards. Menéndez and a company of soldiers arrived at the inlet on the morning of September 29. There they confronted the French, who agreed to surrender if their lives were spared. But Menéndez would make no such promise, telling them he was "bound to pursue them with a fire and blood war to extermination."[15] In his view they were both outlaws and heretics (most of the French were Protestants).

The French, numbering between 111 and 200 people—the documents disagree—chose to surrender. Menéndez ordered their hands tied. Then they were taken behind a nearby dune and killed. A dozen or so were spared because they were Catholics. After the executions, which remain controversial after more than four centuries, the small inlet received the name Matanzas (Massacres), a name it still bears.

Two weeks later a second group of shipwreck victims, including Jean Ribault, arrived at the same inlet. Menéndez and 150 soldiers confronted them on October 11, agreeing to accept their surrender if they would put themselves at the mercy of the Spaniards. The next day about half did so. Again nearly all those who surrendered were executed in the same fashion as their countrymen, Ribault among them. Those who had not surrendered withdrew south.

Later that month Menéndez learned that a third group of ship-wrecked French, perhaps including some of the people who had refused to surrender at Matanzas, were living near Cape Canaveral, close to where the *Trinité* had wrecked. A sand-walled fort they had built was protected by six bronze cannons salvaged from the ship.[16] They were a threat Menéndez immediately sought to blunt. He sailed southward and put 150 infantry ashore, who marched overland to the French fortification. One hundred soldiers on board three small ships approached by the sea. Seeing what they were up against, seventy-five of the French surrendered. Others chose to flee inland. The fort was taken and destroyed.

A possible location for the French encampment and fortification was noted in the nineteenth century by Robert Hanson of St. Augustine:

About ten miles due north of the lighthouse [at Cape Canaveral], near De Soto Grove, Captain Clinton P. Honeywell, the present lighthouse keeper discovered what he took to be the remains of ramparts of fortification. It was reported that the few Huguenots who escaped from Menéndez at Matanzas, left in small boats and were last heard of near Canaveral.[17]

In 1934 it was reported that

about 45 years ago old earthworks were discovered some five miles north-east [sic] of the present lighthouse at Cape Canaveral and . . . are probably still to be seen, grown over with thick scrub. It has always been the belief of the settlers that this may mark the site of the fort built by (Ribault's) fleeing Frenchmen.[18]

In the 1960s a local resident reported having found the remains of the fort—subsequently obliterated by construction of the Canaveral missile facility, now Kennedy Space Center.[19] The resident's directions suggest the fortification was located near the beach on the stretch of coast known as False Cape, quite close to one of the launch complexes used for the space shuttle. Timbers from a ship's hull and four cannons were found eroding out of the sand several miles north of this location. Artifacts—a square mallet, part of a carved chair back, the sole from a wooden shoe, spikes, hinges, metal hardware—were also found, but it has never been determined if these items were from a French ship.

Recently National Park Service archaeologists have excavated an archaeological site on the coast of Volusia County, several miles north of the possible fortification location. Iron spikes, nails, coins, and personal articles of gold and silver, some identified as French from the sixteenth century, were recovered.[20] Perhaps these were items obtained from the French by Timucuan or Ais people, or perhaps the site was occupied by some of the Frenchmen who chose not to surrender to Menéndez.

The French and the Florida Indians

On his first voyage to La Florida, Ribault had made landfall on the south bank of the St. Johns River. There he met Florida Indians, most likely Saturiwa, who brought him "presents of chamois skin" (tanned hides) as a show of respect and friendship.[21] On the opposite side of the river there was another group of Timucua, whose chief, seated on boughs of green laurel and palm fronds, refused to stand to greet the French, a gesture to emphasize his importance. That chief also presented Ribault with gifts, including "an egret plume died red and an Indian-style basket constructed very skillfully of palm leaves and cloth, also a large animal skin painted and decorated all over with various wild animals so vividly represented and depicted that they seemed alive." In return Ribault gave him "little bracelets of silver-plated tin, a billhook, a mirror, and some knives."[22] Such ritualized gift giving was common in Florida; chiefs often presented hides, mantles, and other gifts to one another and to the French and Spanish, who reciprocated.[23]

Ribault met still a third chief, who also feigned indifference, choosing to remain in an arbor of boughs rather than greet the French. Ribault gave him bracelets that looked liked gold and silver (but were not), and other trinkets.

During the fifteen months in 1564 and 1565 that the French were at Fort Caroline, they had numerous interactions with native groups, most of whom were eastern Timucuans. There were many occasions for European-made goods, trinkets as well as tools, to reach native hands. Face-to-face interaction also provided opportunities for diseases to be spread to the native populations, but if epidemics did occur they are not documented in the French accounts.

The realm of French interaction encompassed a wide region, including the entire lower (northern) St. Johns River Valley above Lake

George and much of northern Florida east of the Aucilla River, largely the region of the Timucua speakers. Laudonnière also gathered information about south Florida from the two shipwrecked Spaniards he had ransomed. They apparently had been wrecked in the Florida Keys and had been taken north to the Calusa Indians, where they had lived for a time.[24]

Perhaps the groups with whom the French had the most dealings were the Saturiwa and their allies and the Utina. Because of Chief Utina's importance, the French sought to befriend and manipulate him. From his village in northwestern Putnam County, Utina controlled the main trail into the interior of north Florida.

Laudonnière first learned of Chief Utina from one of his men, Captain Le Vasseur, who had gone up (south) the St. Johns River to explore. On that journey Le Vasseur met Chief Molona, a vassal of Chief Utina, who spoke of the chief. In September 1564, Le Vasseur and ten to twelve French soldiers went to Utina's village. Utina, who attempted to use the French for his own purposes just as they sought to use him, was able to convince the French to allow six or seven of their soldiers to go with him and two hundred of his warriors to raid Chief Potano's village. Utina saw that French weapons would provide a massive military advantage.

The native warriors and French soldiers attacked the village. As Utina had supposed, French firepower carried the day. A number of Potano's villagers, including men, women, and children, were taken prisoner, and others were killed.[25]

Early the following year, Chief Utina again convinced the French to send him twelve to fourteen soldiers to raid Potano's village. In return he promised to help the French reach the "mountains," where the French were led to believe gold and silver could be mined and which they equated with the Apalachee Indians. Utina, a shrewd leader, had quickly learned how to maneuver the French to his designs.

Not fully trusting Utina, Laudonnière instead sent thirty soldiers, a force thought too strong for any treachery Utina might have in mind. A war party of three hundred of Utina's warriors, in addition to women, children, *berdaches* (who carried supplies),[26] and French soldiers set out for Potano's village. About ten miles from the village scouts were sent to reconnoiter. Surprising three of Potano's villagers fishing from a canoe, the scouts attempted to kill them to prevent them from giving advance warning to Potano. One was captured, killed, scalped, and dismembered, but the other two escaped.

Losing the element of surprise, Chief Utina made camp while he consulted his *jarva* (a diviner), who could foretell the outcome of the approaching battle. The diviner reported that Potano had two thousand warriors and that many of Utina's warriors would be taken prisoner if Utina attacked. Based on this information Utina wanted to call off the raid, but the French soldiers, irate at having traveled so far only to be turned back, convinced him to attack.

In a three-hour battle, French firearms again routed Potano's warriors, killing a large number. But Utina elected to withdraw. The French, who recognized an easy victory when they saw one, were disgusted.[27]

These raids probably had a severe impact on the Potano Indian population. The raids also point up differences between French and Florida Indian warfare. The French wanted to destroy the enemy given the chance; the Utina were content to raid, do some damage, and withdraw, leaving the enemy embarrassed and insulted.

By late spring 1565, the French colonists at Fort Caroline were suffering from a lack of food. They had not been resupplied from France, and the maize fields of the nearby Timucua Indians were not yet ripe. The maize and beans they had been receiving in trade were exhausted; those still in native hands were being kept for seed. To survive, the French traded for fish and acorns. The natives, seeing the plight of the French and realizing they had the upper hand, "sold them . . . at such a high price that in no time at all they got . . . all . . . [the] remaining merchandise."[28] Once the French trade goods were expended, no more food appeared, except for an occasional fish for which the French even traded their clothes.

To remedy the worsening situation, Laudonnière ordered Chief Utina taken hostage and held for a ransom of food. But because the field crops were not yet ripe, or so the Utina said, they had nothing to ransom. The standoff between the French and Indians lasted several weeks. During that time the French traveled up the St. Johns River in search of ripe maize, but found little.

The ransom negotiations often were tense, and on several occasions the natives tried to trick the French, setting them up for an attack. Eventually Utina was released, but the French never received the food they needed. At one point Utina's warriors staged an all-day attack on the French. It ended only when the French began to break the arrows shot at them, preventing them from being retrieved and reused. Once the villagers exhausted their supply, the attack halted.

The French came to know the route from Fort Caroline to Utina's village quite well, making the journey up the St. Johns River and then overland to the village a number of times. They also explored other portions of north Florida well beyond Utina's village and the lower St. Johns River. Shortly after establishing Fort Caroline, Laudonnière had sent expeditions north along the coast. He also sent two boats south to explore the St. Johns River. According to Roberto Meleneche, a Spaniard who had signed on with Laudonnière's expedition, the voyage the French made up river from Fort Caroline took ten days and covered sixty to seventy leagues. The French apparently went all the way to Lake George before they halted. Or they heard about the lake ahead and turned back. On the return trip, with the current, the journey was only five days.[29]

On that return journey the Frenchmen went to Utina's village, where they left six Frenchmen who were to explore northern Florida. Two of the soldiers traveled west to the territory of the Yustaga Indians, the western Timucuan group also known as the Uzachile. They reported that the chief of Yustaga had three to four thousand warriors.[30]

Earlier, in November 1564, another one of Laudonnière's men, La Roche–Ferrière, also had visited the Yustaga during the five or six months he and another Frenchman were engaged in exploring the interior of northern Florida. The Yustaga chief had sent Laudonnière a lynx-skin quiver filled with arrows, two bows, four or five skins "painted in their style," and a silver chain. Laudonnière sent back two suits of clothes and some billhooks and axes, indicating a third French expedition marched across northern Florida.

In the end these widespread encounters with the Florida Indians did the French little good. They were unable to fend for themselves, unable to produce food to assure the survival of the colony. Like the early Spanish colonization attempts, supply problems assured the failure of Fort Caroline. That failure was hastened by the appearance of Pedro Menéndez. But if nothing else, the time the French spent in Florida produced a superb documentary record, one more valuable than gold to modern scholarship.

With the fall of Fort Caroline and the subsequent executions, the French colony was routed. Pedro Menéndez de Avilés had won. About fifty of the French captives were kept at a fortified encampment manned by two hundred Spaniards and located just south of Cape Canaveral. Other of the French soldiers were taken to Cuba, and the captured French women and children were taken by ship to Puerto Rico.

La Florida was in Spanish hands, and it would remain a Spanish colony for the next two centuries. In those two hundred years, all of the indigenous groups would disappear.

Menéndez and the Colonization of Florida

In 1563, when confirmation of France's exploits in La Florida had reached King Philip II of Spain, Pedro Menéndez already was preparing to return to Seville from the Americas. The king needed this Asturian sea captain to help plan his response. Menéndez was one of his sovereign's most important naval officers, serving as captain-general of both the New Spain (out of Veracruz, Mexico) fleet and the Tierra Firme (out of Cartegena, Colombia) fleet. Yearly, huge fleets of Spanish ships were organized at each of these ports and sailed to Spain, often being joined by other ships along the way. By sailing en masse and with naval protection, the ships and the wealth they carried were afforded protection against pirates and privateers.

Once in Seville, Menéndez became embroiled in disagreements with officials who charged him with smuggling. The disputes dragged on through 1564 and into early 1565 while Menéndez was held under house arrest. Finally, in February, the claims were settled and Menéndez was free to negotiate a royal contract to found a colony in La Florida. His contract followed on the heels of the contract in 1563 to the namesake of Lucas Vásquez de Ayllón. But, as we have seen, Ayllón (the younger) was unable to mount an expedition. Menéndez's contract was dated March 15, 1565.[31]

Menéndez's fleet left Spain in late June, aware that Ribault was heading from France to Fort Caroline with supplies and reinforcements. Sailing first to Hispaniola and then through the Bahamas, Menéndez and his fleet, which included eight hundred men, sighted Cape Canaveral in late August and immediately sailed northward, investigating each inlet to find Fort Caroline. On September 4, as Ribault was unloading supplies, Menéndez's ships anchored at the mouth of the St. Johns River, and the events recounted above were played out.

Menéndez's contract stated that he should explore the coast of La Florida, a region from the Gulf of Mexico northeast of Mexico around to Florida and up the Atlantic coast to Newfoundland. He was required to establish and occupy two or three towns and to provide for the conversion of the native peoples. The latter was to be accomplished by missionary priests, including Jesuits.[32]

Although his initial settlement was St. Augustine, where he took possession of La Florida on September 8, 1565, Menéndez planned his main town farther north, at Santa Elena, the same location where Ribault had build Charlesfort. Menéndez would control the coasts of La Florida and the surrounding waters of the Gulf and Atlantic, especially the Bahama Channel, to protect his fledgling colony and Spanish shipping. He thought the rivers of La Florida would provide him with entry into the interior of the continent. Menéndez also would seek a "northwest" passage from the Atlantic to the Pacific. Another goal was the establishment of the overland route from Santa Elena to New Spain.

But before he could put his ambitious plans on line, Menéndez had to follow up his victory at Fort Caroline and secure the coast against other French initiatives. Following his voyage to Cape Canaveral to destroy the threat posed by Ribault's shipwrecked men, he sailed south along the coast to the Santaluces Indians, where he established Fort Santa Luciá.

In February 1566 he sailed to southwest Florida to the Calusa Indians, among whom Juan Ponce de León had landed. From the Calusa Menéndez rescued five shipwrecked Spanish men, five mestizo women from Peru, and an African woman.[33] These people had been shipwrecked in about 1545 along with a number of other Spaniards, forty-two of whom had been sacrificed by the Calusa. The survivors included Hernando d'Escalante Fontaneda.[34] At least two of the survivors chose to remain among the Calusa.

The Spaniards' entrance into the Calusa village of Calos on Mound Key was calculated to impress the local populace. With weapons drawn and harquebusier matchcords lit, the Spaniards marched to the accompaniment of fife, drum, and trumpet. In addition to the two hundred

Menéndez's settlements and forts in Florida.

harquebusiers, the entourage included a flag, fife and drum, three trumpets, one harp, one violin, one psaltery, and a dwarf who could sing and dance.[35]

Menéndez later sent a second expedition to the Calusa village with orders to establish a garrison and a small settlement named San Antonio. He would return to the Calusa in March 1567 accompanied by Father Juan Rogel, a Jesuit priest who began to missionize the native people. On that same 1567 voyage, he would sail north to the native town of Tocobaga, on Old Tampa Bay. There a second garrison would be left, manned by Spanish soldiers. Father Rogel would later travel to Tocobaga to minister to the soldiers and the native people.[36]

After returning to St. Augustine from the first (1566) southwest Florida voyage, Menéndez was greeted with news that some of his men had mutinied and deserted. He also learned that Fort Santa Lucía had been abandoned. After restoring order in St. Augustine, Menéndez set sail up the Georgia coast to Santa Elena, where, at Easter time 1566, his second Spanish town was established. Led by Stanley South and more recently by South and Chester DePratter, archaeologists from the University of South Carolina are excavating large portions of sixteenth-century Spanish Santa Elena and its forts, producing important information on the nature of the colony and the adjustments the Spanish colonists made to the Americas.[37]

Later in 1566 a Spanish expedition was dispatched north to Jacán, modern Chesapeake Bay, called Bahía de Santa María by the Spanish. The expedition reached the Delmarva peninsula, but a storm forced them to anchor farther south in the outer banks region of the Carolinian coast before abandoning their mission and sailing for Spain. In the meanwhile, some of the deserters from St. Augustine who had sailed southward were apprehended. On their way to the Caribbean, the deserters had gone ashore near modern Miami to get fresh water. Most of the men then left, leaving twenty of their number behind, all of whom were later found by other of Menéndez's men. To avoid punishment, the twenty agreed to remain and man a garrison at Tequesta, the native town near the mouth of the Miami River. They would be joined by a Jesuit brother, Francisco Villareal, who founded a mission to serve the Tequesta Indians. Brother Villareal arrived in Tequesta with the same 1567 expedition that had delivered Father Rogel to the Calusa.[38]

In addition to exploring the coast and establishing garrisons, block-houses, and forts at select locations, Menéndez sought to explore the waterways of Florida. He erroneously thought that the various rivers—the St. Johns, Caloosahatchee, Miami, and perhaps the Hillsborough—connected with one another and the Atlantic inland waterway. Once he found the connections, he would have water transportation to tie together the small settlements he had put at Tocobaga, among the Calusa, and at Miami with the forts at San Mateo (at the mouth of the St. Johns River), on Cumberland Island, Georgia, and at St. Augustine.

In the summer of 1566 Menéndez led an expedition up the St. Johns River to explore. He met a number of eastern Timucuan chiefs, many of them subject to Chief Utina, and distributed gifts, establishing friendly relations even while making clear the military power he represented. This journey took the Spanish beyond Lake George to the territory of the Mayaca Indians.

Menéndez's plan for using the rivers of Florida.

Later in 1566 Menéndez sent another expedition down the coast from St. Augustine to Mosquito Inlet (modern Ponce de Leon Inlet). The soldiers were then to march west—inland—to reach Mayaca territory; however, the attempt failed because the overland route was too difficult. The expedition, led by Gonzalo Gayón, did stop at villages in the Ponce de Leon Inlet area and ransom several Frenchmen, more survivors of Ribault's wrecked ships.[39]

By 1566, just over a year after first landing at St. Augustine, Menéndez had accomplished a great deal. In a letter to the Crown dated October 15, the governor of Spanish Florida wrote of his future.[40] He was going to use small, fast ships to control the fisheries off Newfoundland, charging fees to non-Spaniards who wished to fish there. Instead of using the dangerous coastal sea lanes around Florida to ship goods to and from Cuba and New Spain, he planned to utilize

Florida's rivers. It was only a short sea journey from his south Florida garrison settlements to Cuba and Mexico.

He also sought a Jesuit school in Havana to educate the sons of native leaders, ensuring future generations of Hispanicized native chiefs loyal to Spain. Additionally, Menéndez sought to put into action his original plan for an overland route from Santa Elena to New Spain. The information the Spaniards were accumulating on La Florida would provide them with a foundation on which to implement his plans.

The scope of Spanish efforts was immense. Menéndez's nephew, Pedro Menéndez Marquéz, one of several trusted kinsmen to whom Menéndez assigned duties, later wrote:

> In 1565–1569 I went by order of Pedro Menéndez de Avilés . . . to reconnoitre and sound, see and discover the coast, shoals, rivers and ports, bays and coves which are in the said coast of [La] Florida. . . . In compliance with which, I have run the length of the coast from the Bay of Saint Joseph, which is eighty leagues from the River of Pánuco [on the northern Gulf coast of Mexico], to Tocobaga once, and from Tocobaga to Santa Elena and Santa Elena to Tocobaga many times, and from Santa Elena to Jacán and from there to Newfoundland.[41]

But Spanish perceptions of the geography of La Florida were flawed. At Menéndez's time it was thought that the Appalachian Mountains extended to northern Mexico to the silver mines of Zacatecas. That distance also was thought to be much less than it actually is, leading the Spaniards to miscalculate the effort required to establish the overland route from Santa Elena to New Spain. Another misconception was that an arm of the Pacific Ocean extended far eastward, perhaps to the Atlantic Ocean. That such a "northwest passage" existed would continue to draw Spanish sailors to the Chesapeake Bay and other coastal locations in search of the passage, a shortcut to the Orient.

To establish the overland route to Mexico and to gather intelligence about the native populations of the interior Southeast, Menéndez sent an expedition under Juan Pardo inland from Santa Elena. Between December 1566 and 1568, Pardo twice marched into the interior with an army. His orders were to find a suitable route to New Spain and fortify it with a string of forts.

On his first journey, Pardo and more than one hundred soldiers marched into western North Carolina. On the second he traced that

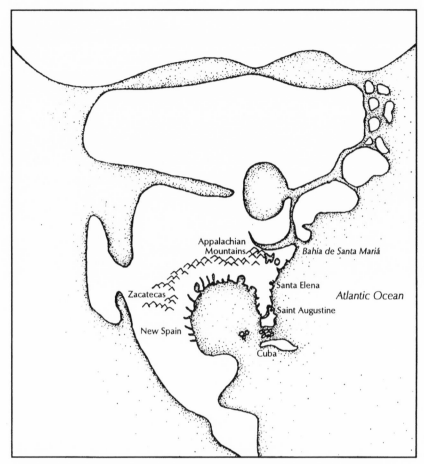

Spanish conception of the geography of North America at the time of
Menéndez (adapted from Lewis and Loomie 1953; also see Hudson 1990).
Bahía de Santa María is Chesapeake Bay. Zacatecas was the location of silver
mines thought to be at the southwestern end of the Appalachian Mountains.

route into North Carolina and then continued farther, crossing the Appalachian Mountains and reaching Tennessee in the general vicinity of
modern Newport.[42] But Pardo never found the route to Mexico, in
large part because the Spaniards had greatly underestimated the distance. Pardo did establish several forts, but they lasted only a few
months.

La Florida did not contain exportable mineral wealth, and many of
the native populations in peninsular Florida were not farmers whose
produce could be used to support the Spanish colonists. Maintaining

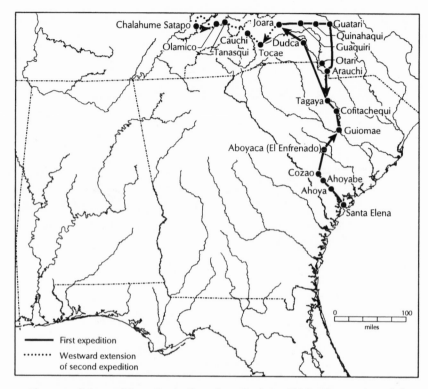

The expeditions of Juan Pardo (based on Hudson 1990). The portion of the second expedition that went beyond the farthest point reached on the first is dotted.

the Florida colony was a financial drain on the Spanish Crown. The garrisons outside St. Augustine were not well supplied, in part because of financial and logistic problems, but also because of the failure of the missions to build support among the native peoples. At times this lack of support took the form of open aggression, such as at Tocobaga, where the entire Spanish garrison was slain.

Menéndez's plans for an intra-Florida river system never materialized because no such system existed, as least not one that could be used by Spanish ships. Even today the establishment of a cross-state shipping canal—Menéndez's sixteenth-century dream—has proven unfeasible.

The plans harbored by Menéndez for La Florida began to unravel with the abandonment or failure of the Florida coastal garrisons. San Mateo was abandoned in 1569, as both the Spaniards and the Jesuits looked away from peninsular Florida to the coast north of St. Augustine, toward Santa Elena.

Jesuit missions soon were established along the Georgia and South Carolina coasts, and Fort San Pedro was established on Cumberland Island. But the Jesuit missionary priests were never able to garner any significant numbers of native converts. Several Jesuits were killed by native people, and there were frequent disagreements between soldiers and friars. The successes the Jesuits would enjoy in Brazil and elsewhere in the Americas would not be duplicated in La Florida. In 1572 they withdrew from La Florida.[43]

With Menéndez's death in 1574, what had become a greatly reduced colonial effort was scaled back even further. Raids by native peoples and supply problems led to the abandonment of Santa Elena in 1587. St. Augustine was once again the only Spanish town in La Florida.

The Aftermath

PART III

The withdrawal of the Jesuit missions from La Florida in 1572 left a void in Menéndez's colony, one he soon would fill by inviting the Franciscan order to La Florida. His contract made him responsible for the conversion of the native inhabitants to Catholicism, and missions were one way to accomplish that.

Besides saving souls, missions serving the native population benefited the colony in other ways. The conversion of native peoples transformed possible military opponents into Spanish subjects who displayed allegiance to the Spanish Crown. It was more expedient to use missionaries to control native groups than to establish forts and use military might. That rebellions did occur indicates that conversion did not always make lifelong allies.

A mission system also provided a means to organize a free, or at least inexpensive, labor force. Native villagers drafted through the missions and used as laborers could produce profits for the colony. Conscripted labor, mainly adult males, could be used in many tasks.

Was use of native labor legal? It was. The contract awarded Pedro Menéndez made reference to the *Ordenanzas* of 1563, which allowed colony founders like Menéndez to use Indian labor and to make grants of land and native labor to colonists. Menéndez was allowed two *repartimientos* for himself and his heirs in each town he founded, and he could grant three *encomiendas*.[1] Repartimientos were divisions of land among Spanish colonists. Encomiendas granted the right to native labor in exchange for the holder of the encomienda promising to protect the native peoples, including assuming responsibility for their religious nurturing. Once the native people pledged their obedience, they were considered legal subjects of the Crown.

Although slavery was technically forbidden, native people were frequently not paid for their labor. Instead, mission villagers were conscripted for periods of time to work at various tasks. Consequently, it was in the Spaniards' best interest to maintain friendly relations with mission villagers and their leaders and to keep the mission towns populated with Christian Indians.

For these reasons, the Franciscan missions would be a primary focus of Hispanic/Native American interaction in La Florida from the late sixteenth century throughout the seventeenth. The missions, an integral part of Spain's La Florida colony, are the focus of chapter 9. Chapter 10 tells what the missions were like and how they changed the lives of the native people.

When the mission system began to fall apart in the late seventeenth century under the brunt of raids inspired by the government of the English colony centered at Charleston, Spain's hold on La Florida was weakened. The destruction of the La Florida missions in 1702 through 1704 by Carolinian militia, aided by Indian allies, effectively reduced the Spanish colony to St. Augustine and the region immediately surrounding it (although the fort at San Marcos de Apalachee was established in 1717). Spanish influence in the lands north of Florida ended. The Carolinian raids and subsequent raids in the later eighteenth century, recounted in chapter 11, were the major reasons why Florida did not remain a Spanish colony.

It is important to remember that the individual Jesuit and Franciscan missionary priests sought to better the lives of the Florida Indians. Yet one cannot forget that the mission system was a part of an insidious colonial empire, an empire that ultimately destroyed the very people the Franciscans sought to save.

The Franciscan Frontier

9 In 1573, one year after the last of the Jesuits had left Florida, the first Franciscan priest in the New World, Father Francisco del Castillo, reached Santa Elena. By 1578 another Franciscan, Father Alonso Cavezas, had been assigned to St. Augustine, where, like his counterpart at Santa Elena, he served as chaplain to the garrisoned soldiers.[1] The activities of these and future Franciscans were supported in large part by royal subsidies.

Once it was arranged for Franciscan priests to enter the La Florida mission field, the next task was to establish *doctrinas,* missions with churches and resident priests who instructed the native people in religious matters. Church and governmental officials collaborated on the geographical organization of the missions. First, missions were put along or near the coast between Santa Elena and St. Augustine. A Spanish presence and cooperative native peoples would assure safe travel and communication by Spaniards moving between the towns. Missions were on both barrier islands and the adjacent mainland in places that could be reached by ship or boat. Because of the abandonment of Santa Elena in 1587, the Franciscan mission chain never extended into present-day South Carolina; the northernmost mainland missions were San Diego de Chatuache on the Ogeechee River and San Phelipe de Alave on the Midway River.[2] On the barrier islands the northernmost mission was on St. Catherines Island.

A group of eight Franciscan priests sailed from Spain in May 1584, led by Father Alonso de Reinoso and bound for St. Augustine. Father Reinoso earlier had been at Santa Elena and had returned to Spain specifically to recruit priests for the colony. The trip to Florida was not without incident. One priest was deliberately left behind in the Canary Islands. Two more stayed in Hispaniola, where their ship had docked, and a fourth deserted. A fifth priest left for Havana and then Mexico shortly after arriving in Florida.

Evidently Father Reinoso was a difficult leader, one who did not feel constrained to account to officials for his behavior, including his handling of funds allotted by the royal treasury for the priests' support. He was accused of using some of the money to buy beads, hatchets, and knives to use as gifts for the native people, an action one detractor labeled fraud, since the money was earmarked for the support of priests. He also was accused of excessive cardplaying. In his wake across the Atlantic and Caribbean, Father Reinoso left a trail of outraged officials.

He was not daunted. In 1587 Father Reinoso brought twelve additional Franciscan friars to La Florida, and in 1590 another eight. But life in the La Florida colony was a challenge, and in 1592 only two priests and one lay brother remained. Three years later another group of twelve friars arrived in La Florida, and Franciscan missionary efforts among the native peoples finally began in earnest. Father Francisco Marrón, the superior of the Florida Franciscans, assigned the priests to their missions in consultation with the governor of La Florida, Domingo Martínez de Avendaño. At least some priests took up their new posts accompanied by the governor and a detachment of infantry, a show of pomp and force meant, no doubt, to impress the native people and show them the priests were protected by the Spanish military government.

History of the Missions

For administrative purposes and for reference, the Spaniards divided the region of mission activity into provinces or districts that roughly correlated with geographical areas and/or native linguistic groups. These provinces became entities as the mission system grew. There also were flexibility and changes in nomenclature over time as the mission

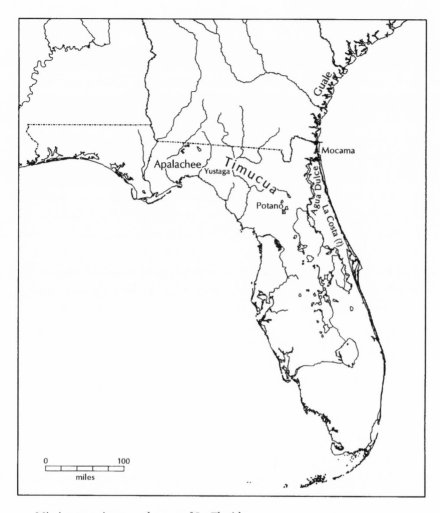

Mission provinces and areas of La Florida.

system expanded in some areas and contracted in others. Names of the districts were used differently by different people at different times.

The Georgia coast north of the mouth of the Altamaha River would be called Guale, derived from the name of the native people who lived there. From St. Simons Island south to St. Augustine, an area occupied by Timucua-speaking groups, the coastal region and adjacent mainland would sometimes be considered a separate maritime district called San Pedro. After mid-seventeenth century it was known as Mocama, a Timucuan word meaning salt water and the term used most commonly by modern scholars. During the seventeenth century that region would frequently be included in Guale.

The coastal region south of St. Augustine for an unknown distance was sometimes referred to as La Costa (the coast), while the St. Johns River drainage south to Lake George was the Agua Dulce (fresh water) district, in reference to the eastern Timucua living along the river. Timucua province was the interior of northern Florida east of the Aucilla River. The part of that large region between the Aucilla and Suwannee rivers was often called Yustaga. Another name for Yustaga was Cotocochonee; Uzachile seems not to have been used in the mission period.[3] Potano was also a part of Timucua. The upper Oklawaha River region was spoken of as Acuera, named for the eastern Timucuan group. The Spaniards sometimes called the area Diminiyuti or Ibiniuti.[4]

Apalachee province coincided with the territory of the Apalachee Indians. Like Guale, Apalachee would remain a specific region throughout the mission period. A few missions also were established west and north of Apalachee in the lower Flint River and Apalachicola–Flint River drainages.

From the late 1670s to the 1690s, as the native populations of Timucua and Guale continued to dwindle as the result of epidemics, the Spaniards would look southward in Florida to establish new missions among non-Christian groups. Four new missions—San Salvador, San Antonio, La Concepción, and San Joseph—would be established among the Mayaca and Jororo Indians in central Florida.[5] Still later in the 1690s an attempt would be made to establish missions among the Calusa Indians.

Missions were located elsewhere in Florida, but, with a few exceptions, they never lasted more than a short time, several years or less. The provinces of Timucua and Apalachee, roughly the northern third of the state, from Marion County north and northwest into the eastern panhandle, and the provinces of Guale and Mocama would be the major arena of Spanish–Native American interaction throughout the seventeenth century.

Due to the efforts of Father Reinoso and Father Marrón, the mission system in Guale and Mocama grew rapidly in the late sixteenth century. By 1596 the Guale-Mocama mission chain north of St. Augustine was in operation, and nine doctrinas had been established.[6] Near the southern end of the chain were Nombre de Dios, a mission serving

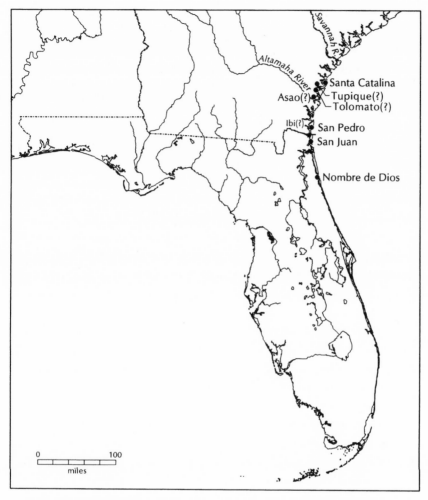

Missions of La Florida in 1596. The locations of Ibi, Asao, Tolomato, and Tupique are approximate.

Timucua speakers that was on the north side of St. Augustine just north of the old city gates, and mission San Sebastian, located nearby. San Juan del Puerto, also serving Timucua speakers, was on Fort George Island, and San Pedro, sometimes called San Pedro de Mocama, was on the southern end of Cumberland Island, Georgia. On the mainland in southeast Georgia there was a mission among the Ibi, probably inland on the eastern fringes of the Okeefenokee Swamp.

The northernmost coastal mission serving Timucua speakers was San Buenaventura de Guadalquini, probably established early in the seventeenth century. Although it was long thought to have been on Jekyll Island, recent research indicates the mission was on the southern end of St. Simons Island.[7] Artifacts associated with a mission have been found on the southern end of that island.

More missions were farther north on the Georgia coast in Guale. Asao was on the Altamaha River, probably near its mouth; later it was moved to one of the sea islands. Tolomato was on the mainland north of the Altamaha River; Tupique also was on the mainland, north of Tolomato. The mission at Ospo was still further north, and Santa Catalina de Guale was on St. Catherines Island.

Especially after the 1650s, Spanish soldiers were stationed at or near some of the Guale and Mocama missions, such as Santa Catalina and San Pedro. The garrisons were there to keep order and to offer the missions some protection against raids by nonmission Indians or by pirates or privateers.

The presence of soldiers, an arm of the secular government in St. Augustine, caused almost constant friction between the missionary priests and military officials. Soldiers often used native villagers as personal servants and as unequal trading partners, activities the Franciscans viewed as corrupting influences in conflict with the goals of the church. Acrimony over such issues was made worse by the Franciscans' contention that the military was well funded, while their missionary efforts were not.[8] In 1602 Father Francisco Pareja wrote what many of the priests must have been feeling:

> Often it appears that they [Spanish officials in St. Augustine] throw it [supplies and other support] to the dogs, since it seems to them that the soldiers are the necessary ones [in La Florida] and that we are of no use; but we are the ones who bear the burden and heat and we are the ones who are subduing and conquering the land.[9]

In September 1597 a revolt was set in motion by the Guale Indians living at missions on the Georgia coast. Most scholars have stated that the rebellion was in direct response to Franciscan missionary activities seeking to change aspects of Guale culture, such as native marriage and inheritance patterns. But it also is likely that the Guale leaders who fostered the rebellion were reacting to labor tribute demands by the

Spanish government that threatened the native leaders' power and status.

During the rebellion five Franciscans were killed and most of the Guale missions were destroyed or abandoned.[10] In October and early November, Spanish soldiers sailed from St. Augustine to put down the rebellion and restore order. The soldiers burned aboriginal villages and stored crops, preventing the Guale from congregating at villages and, perhaps, from carrying out further raids against Spaniards.

The documentary record for the Guale missions in the first years following the rebellion is sketchy. At least some of the Tacatacuru villagers from San Pedro were withdrawn to San Juan del Puerto for protection, or, perhaps, to prevent the rebellion from being taken up by those Timucua speakers. Quantities of the distinctive pottery made by the Tacatacuru who lived at San Pedro in the late sixteenth century have been found at the site of the San Juan mission, possible evidence of such a population movement.[11]

Guale was too important to Spanish efforts to be left in disarray for long. During the two decades following the rebellion, missions were rebuilt and new ones established in the region, often on the sea islands where they were easily reached by boat.[12] One such mission was San Joseph de Zapala, from which Sapelo Island gets its name. The chain from St. Catherines Island to St. Augustine was reestablished.

Even as the Guale and Mocama missions were being established, Franciscans began visiting interior north Florida to lay the groundwork for missions there. Father Baltasar López made several trips in the late 1590s, traveling fifty leagues from his mission on Cumberland Island to north Florida. He visited a major village he called Timucua, a town near (or the same as) Aguacaleyquen, where Hernando de Soto's expedition had been in the summer of 1539.

The same town is thought to be the location of the seventeenth-century mission of San Martín, established by Father Martín Prieto in 1608 on the Ichetucknee River in Columbia County. Archaeologists have known of the general location of the mission since the late 1940s, but it was not until the late 1980s and early 1990s that the site representing the remains of the mission was pinpointed and excavated.[13]

López, who spoke Timucua, established one *visita* at the town and two additional ones among the Potano Indians to the south.[14] Visitas were mission stations that did not have a resident priest but were

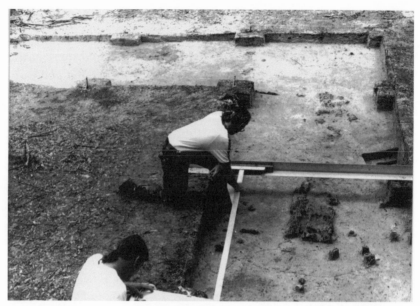

Archaeologists map a burned sill plate and door threshold unearthed at the presumed first church or chapel at mission San Martín (courtesy of the Florida Bureau of Archaeological Research; photograph by Brent Weisman).

served by friars like Father López, who only visited the settlements. Each visita had a small church or chapel where Mass and other rites were conducted.

The church at Timucua was built with tools given to the village chief in 1597 when he visited St. Augustine to request that a priest be sent to serve his people. The chief was instructed to build a church and a house for a priest, who, as it turned out, was Father López. A small church or chapel at the archaeological site that represents San Martín has been excavated by Brent Weisman.[15] That structure could well have been the small church built in 1597.

The first doctrina west of the St. Johns River in the province of Timucua was the mission of San Francisco de Potano, founded by Father Martín Prieto in 1606. The name of the mission reflects both the name of the saint on whose feast day the mission's first Mass was performed—in this case Saint Francis, or San Francisco—and the name of the existing native town where the mission was located, Potano. This was the case with the names of nearly all of the La Florida missions. Besides San Francisco, Father Prieto and a second priest, Father Alonso

Archaeologist Brent Weisman at the San Martín mission site in 1989 (courtesy of Brent Weisman).

Serrano, served several other nearby Potano villages. They named the towns Santa Ana, San Miguel, and Santa Buenaventura.[16]

San Francisco is almost certainly the archaeological site known as Fox Pond, west of the Devil's Millhopper in Alachua County.[17] As noted in chapter 5, the village of Potano probably had originally been located on the west shore of Orange Lake when an advance party of the de Soto's army stayed there in 1539. It was also at that location when the French and Utina Indians raided the village in 1564. The town was moved to the Millhopper location following a 1585 Spanish raid on the Potano Indians. That raid was in retaliation for the Potano's earlier (1567) attack on Capt. Pedro de Andrade and a detachment of Spanish soldiers.

San Francisco de Potano would continue to exist for nearly a century. The location of the mission was well known even in the eighteenth century, when Creek Indians from Georgia began to repopulate northern Florida after the demise of the Franciscan missions. The Creeks pronounced San Francisco as San Felasco, the name today given today to the hammock just north of the mission site.

San Francisco was quickly followed by other inland missions, as the Franciscans established more doctrinas and visitas in the first two and a half decades of the seventeenth century, first in the general Potano area, then among the northern Utina (Columbia and Suwannee counties), and then in Yustaga (Madison and Hamilton counties) and the Arapaha area. One of the interior north Florida missions was Santa Fé, located between San Francisco and San Martín in northwest Alachua County. The archaeological site representing that mission has been found and partially excavated.[18] The site is adjacent to a second site, one that may be the town of Cholupaha, where de Soto and a portion of his army stayed in 1539. The mission has given its name to the modern Santa Fe River.

Another mission was established at Cofa, at the mouth of the Suwannee River to the southwest.[19] Still another, Santa Isabela de Utinahica, was founded north on the Altamaha River in eastern Georgia, perhaps near its confluence with the Oconee River.[20] The presence of Santa Isabela is good evidence that the distribution of Timucuan speakers encompassed much of southeastern and southern Georgia, all the way to the Altamaha River.

Other missions founded in western Timucua during the first two decades of the seventeenth century were San Juan (by 1612), probably the archaeological site at Baptizing Spring in southern Suwannee County north of the Suwannee River, and Santa Cruz de Tarihica (also by 1612), probably the Indian Pond site in Columbia County west of Lake City.[21] By 1623 the mission frontier had moved farther west and northwest into the Yustaga and Arapaha area, where more missions were established: San Pedro y San Pablo de Potohiriba (which gave its name to Lake Sampala in Madison County), Santa Helena de Machaba, San Miguel de Asile (which gave its name to the Aucilla River), San Matheo de Tolapatafi, San Augustín de Urihica, Santa Cruz de Cachipili, San Ildefonso de Chamile, San Francisco de Chuaquin, and Santa María de los Angeles de Arapaha.[22]

Two missions were among the Acuera Indians in Marion County, near or on the Oklawaha River (San Luís de Acuera and Santa Lucia de Acuera), and a third was near the Withlacoochee River among the Ocale Indians (San Luís de Eloquale [Ocale]).[23]

San Antonio de Enecape (Antonico) was established by at least the early seventeenth century among the eastern Timucua on the St. Johns River, possibly at the Mount Royal site just north of Lake George. Several other villages in that region also were served by Franciscans.[24]

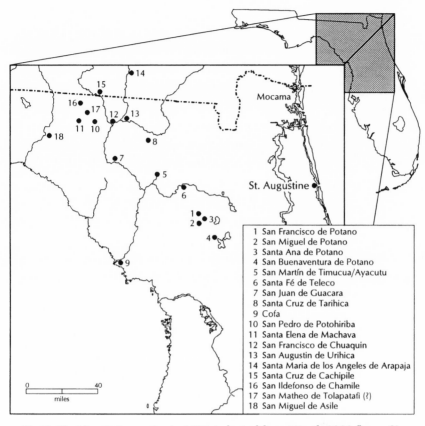

North Florida missions prior to 1633 (adapted from Worth 1992:figure 2).

South of Lake George, among the Mayaca Indians—perhaps in the vicinity of the Thursby and Hontoon Island archaeological sites west of Deland—was another mission, San Salvador de Mayaca.[25] At least one mission was placed near Surroque on the Atlantic coast in Volusia County, possibly near Spruce Creek.

The expansion of the Franciscan mission chain across northern Florida proceeded systematically. After Timucua, Yustaga, and Arapaha, Apalachee would be next. Following a number of visitations by missionary priests, the first Apalachee doctrinas were started in 1633, and over the next few years nearly a dozen missions were built.[26] Others would follow later. Missions present at various times after 1633 included San Lorenzo de Ivitachuco, San Francisco de Ocone, San Luís de Xinayca, San Cosme y San Damián de Cupaica, San Martín de Tomole, San Joseph de Ocuia, San Juan de Aspalaga, San Pedro y San

Pablo de Patale, San Antonio de Bacuqua, Santa María de Ayubale, and Santa Cruz de Capoli.[27] The names of some Apalachee province missions, such as Nuestra Señora de Candelaria de Tama and San Carlos de los Chacatos, indicate those missions were established to serve native peoples that moved into Apalachee from elsewhere. Tama was a region in northern Georgia, while the Chacato (Chatot) Indians, as we saw in chapter 5, lived west of the Apalachicola River.

In the last half of the seventeenth century, missions also were established west of Apalachee in the Apalachicola, Chattahoochee, and lower Flint River drainages.[28] As noted above, missions also were sent to the Mayaca and the Jororo in the last quarter of the seventeenth century, and one unsuccessful mission was sent from Cuba to the Calusa Indians in the late 1690s.[29]

Nearly all of the doctrinas in La Florida, whether in Apalachee, Timucua, or Guale, served not only the people living at the mission proper but those in outlying villages as well. In 1620 the thirty-two doctrinas of Guale and Timucua, administered by twenty-seven Franciscan priests, "served more than 200 places and congregated villages."[30]

The names of the satellite villages surrounding doctrinas are often recounted by Spanish officials who were required to visit the mission provinces periodically and report on their condition. Each satellite village probably was inhabited by a group of people who shared a common village identity and did not wish (or were not allowed) to live at the village located at the mission proper. This arrangement was inconvenient for the priests, who complained of having difficulty reaching some individuals at times of crisis, such as when one of the villagers was dying and last rites were warranted.

Archaeological evidence emerging from investigations in Apalachee suggests that there most of the native peoples served by a specific mission did not live at the mission complex itself, or even in the outlying villages.[31] The native people residing at a doctrina seem to have been chiefs, their families, and, perhaps, natives who served the Spanish residents. Thus the buildings found at any one Apalachee doctrina might include a church, the priests' residence and kitchen, houses for the Apalachee chief and his family, a communal building or council house where the people affiliated with that particular native village met to handle their affairs, and servants' quarters. The bulk of the Apalachee populace lived at farmsteads scattered across the landscape. Even so, these farmsteads were affiliated with specific villages and doctrinas.

This settlement arrangement mirrored that of the Fort Walton ancestors of the Apalachee. That pattern featured a village where a paramount chief and other officials and their families resided, other villages governed by village chiefs who were vassals to the paramount chief, and outlying farmsteads affiliated with a specific village. Such a pattern reinforced the power and status of the chiefs and maximized agricultural production.

The same was true of the mission Apalachee settlement system, except in the latter the Spaniards injected themselves for their own benefit. By placing missions at major villages and influencing and controlling the Apalachee leaders who lived there, the Spaniards effectively controlled the population of the outlying farmsteads. In this fashion the Spaniards also could control labor and agricultural products from the farmsteads, providing food for St. Augustine and goods and produce for export. The missionary priests sought to bring a better life to the Apalachee; the mission system, on the other hand, was an arm of the colonial government.

The Aftermath of the 1656 Timucuan Rebellion

A list of missions made in 1655 and two lists compiled in 1675 give the names of thirty-eight, thirty-seven, and thirty-eight missions, respectively, for the provinces of Guale (and Mocama), Timucua, and Apalachee.[32] The two 1675 lists provide data on distances between the missions, important clues to the location of those missions, especially those in Timucua. Several generations of researchers have used these data to locate and identify Apalachee and Timucuan missions.[33]

The documents associated with the 1675 mission lists make it clear that the Timucuan missions west of the St. Johns River and east of the Aucilla River were located on or near the major east-west trail that led from St. Augustine to Apalachee. That trail, at various times referred to in the literature as the royal road, mission trail, or king's highway, was mapped by the British in 1778 during the twenty-year period when they held St. Augustine and the La Florida colony. The resulting map has been a major source of information about the geography of the

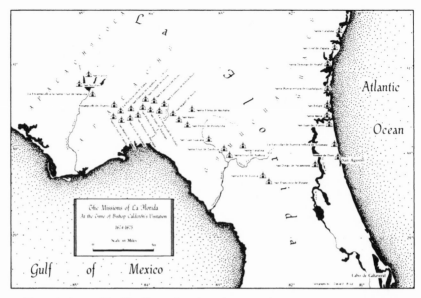

The missions of La Florida at the time the 1675 lists were made (from Gannon 1965:64ff.). Note the linear arrangement of the Timucuan missions.

Timucuan missions.[34] Indeed, the general locations of several missions—San Luís (in Leon County), San Pedro (in Madison County), and Santa Fé (in Alachua County)—are noted on it, as are intersecting trails that have been shown to lead to other missions. Interpretation of the documents and map pointed out the east-west linear arrangement of the Timucuan missions on or near the main mission trail.

But recent research has shown that the history and geographical arrangement of the Timucuan missions is more complicated than this linear model. New archival and archaeological information has brought new perspectives on mission locations and the impact of the Spanish colonial system on the Indians of northern Florida.[35]

That the accepted model of mission settlement in Timucua might not be correct first became evident in 1976 with the excavation of the Baptizing Spring archaeological site in southern Suwannee County, discovered earlier that year by two University of Florida archaeology students, Thomas DesJean and Arthur Rountree. Investigations revealed a horseshoe-shaped native village located around a plaza beside a small, clay-floored church. Also found was a second, earthen-floored building, thought to be the *convento*, the residence of the Franciscan priests who lived at the mission. Additional investigations later located several satellite settlements, some only several hundred yards away.[36]

At some point, perhaps at the time of the 1656 rebellion, the church had burned to the ground. The fire, fueled by the wooden wall posts and the roof beams and thatch, baked the clay floor and turned it a deep orange-red. When the site was unknowingly plowed for planting pine seedlings, a common commercial venture in Florida, the burned rubble of the church was exposed. Spanish pottery from the site dated from early in the seventeenth century, and two radiocarbon dates indicated the site was occupied at least during the period from 1595 to 1621.[37]

But what mission was it? Using the 1675 accounts, Calvin Jones of the Florida Bureau of Archaeological Research had found and identified the mission of San Juan de Guacara several leagues to the west, at Charles Spring on the Suwannee River. Those same accounts indicated that another mission, Santa Cruz de Tarihica, was several leagues east of Baptizing Spring. But there was no information on a mission located between San Juan and Santa Cruz at Baptizing Spring.

In the late 1980s, additional archaeological investigations in northern Columbia and Suwannee counties produced more information that disagreed with the model of mission settlement patterning based on the 1675 accounts.[38] Kenneth Johnson and his field team found two probable Spanish mission sites, one at Indian Pond and one near Peacock Lake, about twelve miles apart along an old east-west trail that ran roughly parallel to the more southerly and better known mission trail. Neither of these two missions, both of which contain Spanish pottery dating from the early seventeenth century, was mentioned on either 1675 list.

What did the evidence mean? Why were three early-seventeenth-century Timucuan missions not accounted for in the archival record, and why were two of them well north of the 1675 mission trail? The answer emerged from research carried out by John Worth in the Spanish archives in Seville, Spain. Worth found documents indicating that the missions were geographically reorganized following the 1656 rebellion.[39] Prior to that rebellion, missions had indeed been located in Columbia, Suwannee, and Madison counties well north of the trail that later would become the main mission road.

As a result of the rebellion, many of these missions were abandoned.

Later, Governor Rebolledo ordered that rather than reestablishing the missions at their present locations, some of them would be moved to what would be the main mission trail.[40] They would be placed roughly a day's travel apart along the trail, as well as at river crossings where ferries were needed. The missions of Timucua would become way stations supporting the major route, the mission road, between Apalachee province and St. Augustine through Timucua. Food from Spanish-owned farms and ranches in Timucua and Apalachee could be transported along this trail to St. Augustine. Native people from the missions would provide labor to transport the goods, keep the road in repair, and man the ferries on the Aucilla, Suwannee, and St. Johns rivers. Travelers along the trail could stay at mission villages a day's travel apart. Even some of the southern missions already on the mission trail were moved east or west so their new locations fit with the spacing dictated by Governor Rebolledo's reorganization plan.

The existence of essentially two mission systems in Timucua—a pre-1656 pattern and a post-1656 one—explains the archaeological evidence. Mission sites such as the Indian Pond and Peacock Lake sites, which are north of what became the main mission road after the 1656 rebellion, should date prior to that time; after the rebellion they were abandoned. The Indian Pond mission, perhaps the mission of Santa Cruz, may have been moved south to the main mission road in southern Suwannee County. The fate of the Peacock Lake mission is uncertain. Both sites contain only early-seventeenth-century Spanish ceramics because they were occupied only during that period. Documents have been found indicating that other missions were moved, but archaeological sites corresponding to those missions have not yet been located.[41]

At the time of the rebellion, the mission at the Baptizing Spring archaeological site, probably the original mission of San Juan, was abandoned (and possibly burned) and moved west along the southern mission road to the Suwannee River.[42] There it was known as San Juan de Guacara, Guacara being the Timucuan word for the Suwannee River. Later, San Juan would give its name, San-Juanee, to the Suwannee. The Christian Indians at San Juan de Guacara operated a ferry, perhaps simply two canoes lashed together, across the river.

Other prerebellion southern missions abandoned during the rebellion were reestablished at their same locations or at locations near the old ones. Missions San Francisco de Potano and Santa Fé, both in Alachua County, may be two such examples. Artifacts from the site of San Francisco suggest what has been found is the postrebellion manifestation of San Francisco de Potano. Several hundred yards west of the site, however, early-seventeenth-century artifacts have been found, perhaps debris from the prerebellion mission. On the other hand, the artifacts from Santa Fé appear to be from the prerebellion mission.

The mission reorganization resulted in the well-known linear arrangement of Timucuan missions across northern Florida along the mission trail. Each mission probably had a small resident population that provided the needed labor for manning ferries, hosting crews transporting goods to St. Augustine, repairing the road, and whatever else was required. Apalachee continued to be the location of numerous doctrinas, with their associated satellite villages and agricultural farmsteads. In both Apalachee and Timucua, Spanish ranches, supported in large part by native workers, provided produce and goods for the Spanish colonists.

In chapter 10 we will examine other ways in which the missions and the colonial system changed the lives of the Florida Indians. Chapter 11 recounts the documentary and archaeological evidence for the demise of the mission system and the final destruction of the indigenous people of Florida.

New Lives for Old: Life in the Mission Provinces

10   Within the provinces of Apalachee and Timucua, the mission system was a major agent of change affecting the native people. The Spanish Crown and its representatives sought to transform the people into a population that not only was *not* detrimental to the La Florida colony, but one that contributed to Spanish colonial interests. An expedient way to do this was to work to make the people Catholic Spanish subjects who participated in and were dependent on the Spanish empire.

How were the Spaniards able to accomplish this transformation? How did they replace traditional lifeways with aspects of Spanish lifeways?

The Franciscans entered the La Florida mission field more than seventy years after Juan Ponce de León's 1513 voyage. The first inland Timucuan mission was founded nearly seventy years after Hernando de Soto's army had marched through the province. By the time of these first mission efforts, depopulation and cultural changes resulting from disease had been ongoing for more than two generations. As anthropologist Henry Dobyns has noted, epidemics "made inoperative many conventional understandings evolved by large populations" and led to many native groups questioning "their respective visions of the fundamental postulate of ethnic superiority."[1] A way of life that had served so well for generations suddenly did not provide the security it had in the past. The missions offered a new way to think and be, a way of life that might well have seemed superior to the old one.

A New Way of Living

As we saw in the previous chapter, the missions were not randomly situated across Florida. They were placed where there were relatively large agricultural populations within a reasonable distance from St. Augustine. Sedentary farming societies fit better into the colonial mission system than did groups that were not sedentary agriculturists. Attempts to establish missions among nonagriculturists never succeeded.

Missions also were not established among the many agricultural populations in the Southeast that lived north of the Timucua and Apalachee Indians and west of Guale. The Spaniards never founded missions in the piedmont of South Carolina or Georgia, where there were large agricultural populations, despite such regions being viewed as fertile ground for missions. Indeed, as early as 1597 a Spanish expedition that included two Franciscan missionaries visited Tama, one such native province in the Georgia piedmont. Although they described it as a good place for missions and for a Spanish settlement, missions were never established there.[2] One possible reason was financial; the Spanish Crown could not afford to establish missions in the interior of La Florida. When Governor Canzo of La Florida asked to put a settlement in Tama, the Crown refused.

Another reason for not placing missions among piedmont native groups was their relative remoteness and the lack of military protection for the Spaniards who would live there. The distance from St. Augustine to Tama, for example, was eight long days by foot. Without a nearby Spanish settlement or garrison, priests would have been far from supply lines and soldiers. The risks became evident when one of the priests on the Tama expedition barely escaped being scalped. Successful missions in Tama or elsewhere in the piedmont would require a chain of missions—and a supply line—to the location. And garrisons would be needed also.

In 1608, when the Franciscans were considering moving into Apalachee, they noted that they would not have any nearby support and, because of the distance from St. Augustine, supplies (mainly food) could not easily reach them. It was not until 1633, when the chain of missions led from St. Augustine across Timucua and Yustaga, that Franciscans first established doctrinas in Apalachee.

But the Spaniards' awareness of the large agricultural populations in Tama did not go for naught. In the seventeenth century, as the population of the Mocama missions declined, people from Tama, called Yamasee, moved to the Georgia coast and settled at missions there.[3] This movement may have been in part because of raids by Westo Indians, which forced the Yamasee out of their traditional territory.

The earliest missions in interior north Florida, those in Timucua, seem to have been established adjacent to existing native villages. Many of these early locations correlate with villages visited by the Hernando de Soto expedition in 1539.[4] For instance, the seventeenth-century mission village of Santa Ana, just west of modern Gainesville and associated with the San Francisco doctrina, was probably at the location of the village of Utinamocharra, where de Soto had camped. When Father Martín Prieto served Santa Ana in 1606, he was told of the cruelties inflicted on the chief of the village by Hernando de Soto's army when the chief was a boy.[5]

Other early missions in Timucua, as well as some in Apalachee, are thought to have been located at or near towns through which de Soto's army marched: Santa Fé was at or very near Cholupaha, San Martín at Aguacaleyquen, the pre-1656 Santa Cruz mission at Uriutina, San Miguel de Asile at Asile, and San Lorenzo de Ivitachuco at or near Ivitachuco. Apparently, major villages at the time of the de Soto entrada retained that status in the early seventeenth century.

As time went on, especially after the 1656 rebellion, missions were moved or abandoned and new ones were established. Missions also were moved because the inhabitants had used up the nearby easily obtainable wood supplies for fuel and construction or because nearby fields had lost fertility.[6]

Ideally, each mission had a resident priest who served the villagers who lived there. At times, however, a single priest might serve more than one mission. The people living at a mission village were only a portion of the total number of people served by that mission. As noted in chapter 9, surrounding each doctrina were satellite villages. The people of those villages (and in Apalachee the people living on adjacent farmsteads) attended the mission church, participated in mission life, and were served by the mission priest. For instance, in 1602 it was reported that the mission of San Juan del Puerto on Fort George Island served the following satellite villages: Vera Cruz (0.5 leagues away), Arratobo (2.5 leagues), Niojo (5 leagues), Potaya (4 leagues), San Mateo (2 leagues), San Pablo (1.5 leagues), Hicacharico (1 league), Chinisca (1.5 leagues), and Caraby (0.25 leagues).[7] If this is the official league of 2.6 miles, these villages ranged from a little more than a half mile to thirteen miles away from the doctrina. No wonder a priest complained that a person could die before he arrived to administer last rites.

Satellite villages also are documented for Apalachee and Timucua.[8] Over time the number of satellite villages in Timucua gradually declined, but this was not true in Apalachee. Numbers of satellite villages thus may reflect demographic trends. In Timucua the native population continued to decline, while the larger population in Apalachee stabilized during the last half of the seventeenth century.[9]

Kenneth Johnson's surveys to locate satellite villages around the Santa Fé mission in Timucua have shown that roughly circular clusters of villages, several square miles in area, were present in the late precolumbian era. But this arrangement was subtly altered in the mission period when the villages were arranged linearly, probably along a trail. The change was probably an artifact of the mission system, a way to provide priests with easier access to the satellite village near the missions.

What did the missions look like? No single detailed, written description of a doctrina/mission complex exists. However, there is a 1691 drawing showing the layout of buildings at a mission. The plan was sent by the governor of Florida to the king of Spain. The caption reads:

> Palisade made on the island of Santa Maria and place of Santa Catalina in the Province of Guale; three varas of height with bastions to fire arms; the bastions have earth ramps to half their height; there is a moat; and within it are the church, the Convento of the Doctrina, barracks for the infantry, and a small house for cooking.[10]

The map purportedly shows the Santa Catalina mission and garrison complex built at Santa María, the Spanish name for Amelia Island. However, from other documents and from archaeological research carried out at the site, it is known that the full palisade and the moat were never built.[11] Thus, instead of being a plan of an actual site, the

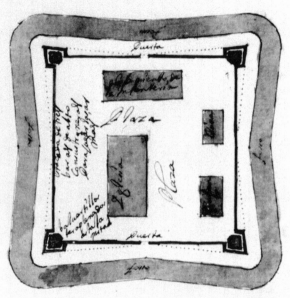

Drawing made in 1691 of a mission and garrison compound said to have been built on Amelia Island. Depicted within a moated palisade are a church (lower left), convento (lower right), kitchen (upper right), and garrison house (top), all situated around plazas (courtesy of the P. K. Yonge Library of Florida History, University of Florida).

drawing represents a template, depicting what the mission, garrison house, and moated palisade were supposed to look like.

The arrangement of the church, convento, and *cocina* (kitchen), the latter perhaps to serve the priests and soldiers, does correlate with the arrangement of similar buildings excavated at mission Santa Catalina on St. Catherines Island, Georgia.[12] At that site, however, no garrison building has been identified.

Although the 1691 drawing does not show an actual mission, the drawing is important because it identifies by name and relative size the buildings at a doctrina. The rectangular church is shown with plazas on two sides, separating it from the other buildings. Across one plaza were two smaller, rectangular buildings, the larger of which was the convento and the smaller the cocina. Both of the latter are oriented in the same direction as the church, with the cocina in line with the convento. The garrison house is perpendicular to the other three buildings and separated from the church by a second plaza.

Numerous documents mention conventos and churches at the La Florida missions; it is certain that at every doctrina both were present. Those scraps of information and the Santa Catalina/Santa María drawing have allowed archaeologists excavating at mission sites in Apalachee, Guale, and Timucua to assign names and functions to the buildings found at those sites.

The identification of buildings, however, is not as easy as simply matching the shapes and orientation of mission buildings reconstructed from archaeological evidence to the Santa Catalina/Santa María template. Variations in size, shape, and orientation of doctrina buildings exist.[13] Generally, however, the church is the largest rectangular building found at each mission site, averaging about sixty by thirty-five feet. Most of the churches contain few artifacts beyond building materials, such as iron spikes and clay daub. In a few churches, and in some convents, grains of wheat have been found, perhaps from wheat ground into flour for the communion host.

Rarely are artifacts found in any quantities immediately around the church. Evidently the religious precincts at the missions were kept clean. Many more artifacts are present in and around other mission buildings, especially the cocinas.

Materials and methods used in building churches varied. Some had vertical board walls, while others had walls of wattle (lathing) and daub (clay), which could be plastered and even painted. Still others apparently had no walls at all, but were open, pavilionlike structures. One possibility is that at the founding of a doctrina, an open, pavilionlike structure was built first to serve as the church. Later, that pavilion could be rebuilt and turned into a walled church, or a new, more substantial church would be built nearby. The small, open church found by Brent Weisman at mission San Martín was apparently replaced by a much larger and more substantial structure, although, as suggested above, the smaller church may have been associated originally with a visita served by Father Baltasar López.[14] The later, larger church evidently first had an earth floor, which was later replaced by a clay floor, perhaps again an example of construction elaboration over time or an indication that the church was rebuilt at a future date.

Some walled churches had clay or, in the case of one northeast Florida mission church, shell packed along the base of the outer walls to help anchor them. Shells or clay also were packed around post bottoms anchored in large pits, some more than three feet deep. The large posts were the supporting members for the roof beams. Smaller, vertical posts were placed between the large posts to help support the walls.

Church roofs probably all were thatched with palmetto fronds. Unfortunately for mission villagers, the dried thatch could be easily ignited with flaming arrows or torches. Accidental fires and fires deliberately set by raiding parties charred many mission churches.[15] In his San Martín excavations, Brent Weisman even found several fire-hardened mud-dauber nests, which probably had been under the eaves of the buildings when they were burned.

At some mission sites hundreds of small and large wrought-iron nails and spikes have been recovered, hardware used in the construction of the exterior and interior of the churches. Presumably they were brought to the missions from St. Augustine, although San Luís in Apalachee, a thriving Spanish-Indian town in the late seventeenth century, had a visiting smith operating at the site on at least one occasion, and a small anvil has been found at another Apalachee mission.[16]

Church and convento carpentry and construction were done with a variety of tools, which sometimes were in short supply. In 1630 one friar begged the king to order St. Augustine officials to increase his allotment of nails so more churches could be built. The king also was asked to authorize the loan of carpentry tools from St. Augustine so they could be used in the construction of the mission.[17] In 1695 the king similarly was requested to provide tools to the four new missions in Mayaca and Jororo:

> For the four areas [missions] that they mention, they may be sent two hundred double mattocks, six large saws and six small ones, fifty [scythes] or large [sickles] for cutting . . . four large augers . . . four medium ones, and four of the thinnest ones . . . these are the most necessary ones [tools] that they need for the . . . building of the temples and houses for the villages that they are to establish.[18]

Individual churches apparently were built by native parishioners working under the supervision of the Spanish priests and were funded by the royal treasury. The royal treasury could certainly afford to support the missions, but the procedure of having to ask the Crown for nails—a process involving sending a letter to Spain by ship and waiting for a reply—must have been awkward at best.

At several sites, fences or walls were used to delineate areas within the mission complexes, surrounding, for instance, the church and/or the convento. Some of these walls were daubed in the same fashion as buildings.

The church at Santa María, a seventeenth-century mission on Amelia Island, appears to have had some type of elaborate wooden construction at one end, perhaps a wooden facade at the entry.[19] Rites such as marriage ceremonies, baptisms, and funerals were performed at least in part in the church doorway, which led from outside into the nave.[20] The sanctuary at the early San Martín church on the Ichetucknee River was constructed with board walls enclosing a raised wooden floor, although the rest of the small church was open.[21] Within churches, saints and other images were displayed in the sanctuary, which also contained the altar. Although the floors of church naves might be earth or clay, the floors of sanctuaries were made of boards and were raised.

Each church also had a sacristy, a separate room off the sanctuary, where items used in services were kept. At the San Martín chapel excavated by Weisman, the sacristy might have been the closet-sized room on the east end of the sanctuary, which apparently had full-height board walls chinked with clay. The door whose wooden threshold was found would have led into the sacristy.[22]

John Hann has translated and studied two documents listing the contents of mission churches.[23] The first, written in 1681, recorded the furnishings and vestments of thirty-four doctrinas. The second lists items brought to St. Augustine in 1704 from the Apalachee missions at the time of the Spanish withdrawal from that province. Working from these lists, Hann has identified the items the typical doctrina in La Florida would have contained in the late seventeenth century and has offered a description of the churches:

> However primitive the church buildings themselves might have been with their walls of wattle and daub (or, in a few cases of planking), and thatched roofs, and their floors of packed clay, and, however simple the altars themselves may have been, these churches had an amply supply of diverse vestments and valuable and ornate sacred vessels and other altar furnishings that must have lent a certain splendor to the religious services. . . . And some of the churches at least were painted and embellished within with drawings executed by the natives.[24]

Furnishings and Ornaments for a Typical Late-Seventeenth-Century Doctrina (based on Hann 1986a)

1 monstrance, either of silver or gilded (to hold the Host)

2 silver chalices

2 missals, including one used for Requiem Mass (books containing the Mass, prayers, devotions, etc.)

1 wooden missal stand and coverlet

9 or 10 sets of chasuble, stole, and maniple in various colors (vestments worn by priests at Mass)

7 or 8 antependiums in various colors (cloth hung down the front of the altar)

6 albs of white linen (outer garment worn by priests when saying Mass)

7 handbells

8 brass candlesticks

1 or 2 choir-copes (robes)

5 or 6 altar cloths

7 amices (part of the priests' vestments)

7 or 8 palls (linen cloth for covering the chalice)

11 coporals of starched linen (cloth on which the bread and wine to be consecrated are placed)

5 burses (cloth pocket used to store the folded corporals)

11 or 12 chalice veils

2 surplices (a vestment)

3 or 4 rochets (a vestment)

5 cinctures (rope-like belt)

1 long decorated stole (a vestment)

1 coverlet for the altar

1 silver lunet for the Viaticum (to hold it upright in the monstrance)

   ceramic or glass cruets (for communion and for washing the priest's fingers during the Offertory section of the Mass)

1 or 2 silver chrism vials (for Holy oils)

1 altar lamp of silver or brass

1 silver procession cross

1 thurible and incense boat and spoon of silver or brass

2 religious banners (which could be mounted for use in processions)

2 engravings each depicting some religious motif

5 or 6 statues (of Our Lady, Infant Jesus, and various saints)

13 picture or painting depicting religious motifs

4 cornialtares (possibly altar cards displayed during Mass)

1 cedar chest for storing vestments (a few missions had more than one)

1 silver crown or halo

1 procession lantern

1 cloth communion paten

1 silver communion paten

1 silk humeral cloth (a vestment)

1 or more linen hand cloths

1 ritual (a book of prayers)

1 veil or curtain

1 host press

1 mirror

Note: The procession lantern, silver communion paten, humeral cloth, ritual, host press, and mirror were not present at all missions.

Though simple in construction, the mission churches contained more than sufficient accoutrements to bring the beauty and splendor of Catholic ritual to the native peoples. But the churches may not always have been so well furnished, nor were the lives of the missions priests easy. In the early seventeenth century, Father Francisco Pareja testified that

> Fray Pedro Ruiz and I have made chalices of lead, which we have used at Mass many times; that for weeks it was necessary for one to use the vestments and the other to remain without saying Mass until we provided ourselves with the necessities of the sacred ministry by the sacrifice of our meals.[25]

Money for vestments, wax, lamp oil, and wine—all of which were needed for services—did not always reach the missions in timely fashion.

In addition to the vestments and furnishings used within the church, many of the missions had bells that were rung to summon villagers to services and to communicate information. Bells carried the voice of religious authority, calling villagers to work and worship.

When Carolinian militia were approaching Santa Catalina on Amelia Island just after midnight on November 4, 1702, the bells were rung to alert the villagers, causing the priests and villagers to flee, taking with them the church statues and ornaments.[26] Some bells, too large to be easily carried, were buried at the Apalachee missions when the Spanish retreated from that province.[27] During at least one native revolt, mission villagers destroyed these symbols of Spanish authority.

At some missions archaeologists have found the *campo santo* (cemetery) in which the Christian natives were interred, nearly always extended on their backs in individual shallow graves with arms folded on chests or hands clasped. Similar interments are found inside churches, where the Christian natives were buried in shallow graves dug into the

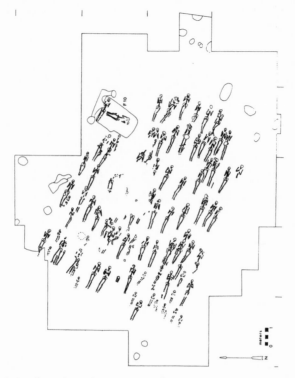

Christian burials in the Santa Catalina mission, Amelia Island (courtesy of Rebecca Saunders).

floor.[28] Some burials were wrapped in cloth shrouds pinned with brass straight pins.

It is possible that most burials in areas originally interpreted as cemeteries are actually interments made through the floor of open, pavilionlike churches, as seems likely at the mission of Santa Catalina on Amelia Island.[29] On the other hand, at San Martín in Timucua, the small, open church at the site definitely had burials placed around (outside) the building; none were found inside of the area covered by the church roof. At the same site, however, the nearby, large church contained hundreds of burials interred through its floor. Based on the evidence on hand, interment within a church seems to have been the most common burial form in both Timucua and Apalachee.

Recent excavations by Bonnie McEwan and Clark Larsen at San Luís revealed that a number of natives were interred in Christian-style pine coffins. At mission Santa Catalina on Amelia Island, two native men were buried in a single wooden coffin. Investigations at mission Santa

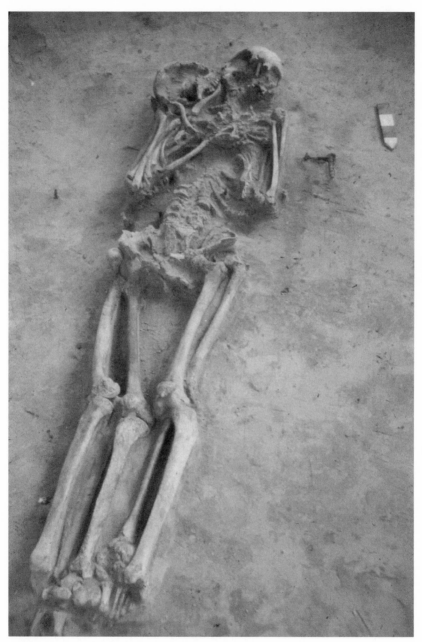

These two individuals were buried one on top of the other in a single wooden coffin at the Santa Catalina mission. Nails from the coffin can be seen just to the right of their left shoulders.

Fé in Timucua suggest that a wall or fence surrounded the cemetery there, if indeed this feature was not a church wall.

The orientation of burials within both cemeteries and churches is the same as the church with which the interments are associated. Rarely is this orientation north-south.[30] Most often it is well off north, at times as many as 45 degrees east of north. This orientation, which might be called the "Spanish slant," is also reflected in the positioning of the Spanish colonial land grants demarcated on maps of northern Florida. Those grants were laid out at angles to true north.

Each mission had one or more native villages located at the mission proper. At the Baptizing Spring site, thought to be the prerebellion early-seventeenth-century mission of San Juan, and at missions Santa Fé and San Martín, all in Timucua, the villages were crescent-shaped, as were some precolumbian villages in northern Florida. Although the mission system brought much that was new, some of the old ways persisted.

A New Way of Being

What was life like for the native peoples who were served by the missions? Documentary descriptions and emerging archaeological information suggest several ways in which aboriginal life was changed as the native peoples of Timucua and Apalachee were brought to Christianity. The Franciscan missionary priests sought to instruct the villagers in the Catholic faith and to bring them a better way of life, one embracing aspects of Hispanic culture, such as crops, the Spanish language, metal tools and other European items, and new ways of thinking and behaving. To do this it was necessary to convince the villagers to change old patterns, especially things the priests deemed in conflict with Christian teachings.

Initially the priests worked to make first-generation converts. The children of those first converts were born into Christian families and grew up within the mission system. Father Pareja at San Juan on Fort George Island wrote in 1620 that Catholicism had vanquished many of the native, "pagan" superstitions so effectively that the mission Indians "do not even remember them; so much so that the younger generation [who grew up under the missions] derides and laughs" at those of the older generation, who occasionally still practice the old ways.[31]

To gain the attention of potential converts and assure friendship, Spanish officials in St. Augustine gave presents to visiting native chiefs. During a two-week visit to St. Augustine in the summer of 1597, the chief of the town of Timucua—then the site of a Franciscan visita—and his entourage of nineteen people were given thirty pounds of flour per day, a hoe, axes, and complete outfits. The outfits were tailored during their visit. The chief and his heir accessorized their new clothes with red hats, shirts, doublets, and shoes.[32] Other native visitors to that town received similar gifts or such items as blankets, buttons, or tools.

Priests and government officials knew that European goods were an important stimulus prompting native peoples to request that they be served by missions. The Indians who were a part of the Spanish expedition to Tama in the Georgia piedmont in 1597 had been given Spanish blankets, knives, fishhooks, scissors, glass beads, hatchets, and sickles before leaving St. Augustine. The message to be conveyed to the native population of Tama was, "Live as Christians under our aegis and you, too, could have access to such items." Creating a desire for and a reliance on goods controlled by the Spanish was a not-so-subtle way to exert power over native populations.[33]

Gift giving was practiced in the mission provinces as well.[34] Cattle and hogs were given to native leaders by the owners of Spanish ranches who needed their permission to use lands controlled by those chiefs.

Mission priests worked diligently to convince native leaders to become Christians and to influence their followers to do likewise. Throughout the seventeenth century, the friars and Spanish officials continued to work through the indigenous political system, with its chiefs and hierarchy of social positions.[35] The Spaniards understood that native leaders could be used to obtain the labor and cooperation of their people. Governors regularly sent officials to visit the missions and to adjudicate disputes relating to native inheritance and chiefly succession (as well as disputes between natives and Spaniards). The St. Augustine officials usually supported the native system, except where it was in their best interest to interfere with or override it.[36]

But while the Spanish church and government officials supported village chiefs, their presence undermined the authority of the paramount chiefs and the intervillage alliances that had existed prior to the presence of the Spaniards. The king of Spain, through his representatives in

St. Augustine, replaced the traditional intervillage chiefs. If respect and tribute were to be paid, they were to be paid to the Spaniards. But even so, the villagers themselves still recognized that some village chiefs were more important than others because of traditional status.[37] The voices of the past were never completely obliterated.

Loyal native chiefs could be rewarded with special gifts. One such leader, Don Juan of mission San Pedro on Cumberland Island, served the Spanish so well he was given two hundred ducats. This was no small amount, since it was estimated that the upkeep of each mission priest cost about 140 ducats per annum.[38]

The education of mission Indians included religious teachings and, in many instances, instruction in learning to read and write Spanish. As early as 1595, individuals at the mission of San Pedro on Cumberland Island could speak Spanish.[39] Mission villagers, including children, also were taught to read and write Timucua. In 1630 a priest noted that primers and devotional books translated from Spanish into Timucua were in use. That same priest recognized that literacy was a very efficient way "for imprinting the Christian discipline and doctrine . . . in those hearts and lands."[40]

As *catecumenos,* the religious students learned the catechism and other information from their study of books before attending their baptism and becoming *cristianos.* As Christians they received a Christian name, and some adult males were awarded the honorific title "Don."[41]

As Christians, the mission Indians knew how to sing Mass and participate in morning and evening prayers. Some aided the priests at Mass. The Christian Indians also celebrated the appropriate festivals and feast days. At some missions the villagers became so *muy españolados* (Spanish-like) that they participated in religious confraternities or associations like those present in Catholic communities elsewhere.[42] Baptisms, marriage ceremonies, and burial rites were conducted at the door of the church according to Catholic doctrine. The Indians living at the missions *were* Catholics. In about 1602, one Spanish soldier commented that the Christian Indians served by a mission on Cumberland Island practiced flagellation during the Holy Thursday procession.[43]

Just how Hispanicized the mission villagers were remains an active topic of research. As more and more archival sources are being found, this topic will continue to be examined. Today the picture we can develop of life at the missions is much more vivid than that found in the writings of Father Maynard Geiger (1937) published more than a half century ago. For instance, we now have numerous references to native people being taught to speak Spanish. Were some or many mission villagers bilingual? In the seventeenth century, after several generations of living in missions, did native leaders converse with Spaniards in Spanish?

At the missions the pageantry, color, and meaning of Catholic ceremonies replaced similar elements of indigenous ceremonial life. John Hann has described what one aspect of life at the missions may have been like:

> Equally impressive [as the furnishing and ornamentation of churches] were the religious processions that coursed through the surrounding village with the priest arrayed in a rochet and silk cape, walking under an embroidered canopy, swinging a polished silver censer, preceded by one of the Indian church officials holding a silver processional cross and one or more others carrying religious banners, and followed by the images or portrait of one or more saints wearing a silver crown or halo and carried on a flower-decked platform.[44]

The Spanish presence also altered the lives of mission Indians in other ways. Plants brought from Spain were grown in mission gardens and found their way into the diet of the mission villagers. Watermelons, peaches, figs, hazelnuts, oranges, and garbanzos, all of which have been identified from mission sites, supplemented traditional diets.[45] Many other plants were brought by the Spanish to St. Augustine, including European greens, aromatic herbs, peas, sugarcane, garlic, melons, barley, pomegranates, cucumbers, European grapes, cabbages, lettuce, and sweet potatoes.[46] Any or all of these could also have been grown in mission gardens.

New foods and new ways of preparing them resulted in the native people making ceramic vessels in the shape of Spanish tableware, perhaps for their own use as well as the use of the Spaniards living at the missions. Native-made copies of Spanish plates, pitchers, and other dishware are present at all of the mission sites investigated by archaeologists thus far.[47]

Something old and something new. The small size of the charred corncobs contrast with the relatively huge size of modern ears of corn. Also shown are a charred peach pit and a modern one. The charred examples are from mission San Juan in Suwannee County.

Wheat, identified from several mission sites, was grown at Spanish ranches. It could be ground into flour to make bread, a valued commodity, or used to make the host for communion. The unleavened flour was shaped into round wafers with a metal, tonglike press device.

At each mission, crops were cultivated for the support of the mission priests. Corn was also grown at farms and in native fields in the mission provinces for export to St. Augustine or was transported to the Gulf of Mexico coast and shipped out. It was also grown by native people for profit. In 1592 a chief sold 263 arrobas of maize—about three tons—to the Spaniards for "fifty silver ducats, six axes, three hoes, fifty varas [about forty-three yards] of burlap cloth, and some thread."[48]

It may have been the kernels, removed from the cobs, that were transported from the mission village fields to St. Augustine. Archaeologists have found hundreds of charred corncobs at mission sites in Apalachee and Timucua. The cobs, shorn of the kernels, made a readily available source of fuel.[49] Smudge-fire pits filled with charred corncobs have been found at every mission site excavated to date. The kernelless cobs evidently served as a long-burning and smoke-producing fuel, one just right for helping to keep insects away.

This native-made bowl from the convento at mission San Juan in southern Suwannee County was fashioned in the shape of a Spanish bowl.

That native populations be agriculturists was important to the Spaniards. When new missions were established among the Mayaca and Jororo Indians in the late seventeenth century, a priest requested that the Crown provide funds for hoes so that the people could be turned into farmers and live as "rational beings."[50] If native people were to be brought to Christianity, they should live as sedentary agriculturists. Hoes have been found at several mission sites, including in native houses.[51]

Livestock, including chickens, pigs, cattle, and, occasionally, horses, were kept at the missions.[52] In Apalachee, livestock products—tallow, pork, cowhides, and beef—provided income for Spaniards and the Apalachee Indians alike. The Apalachee were participants in the economic life of the colony. They took part in trade and commerce, and they understood the use and significance of money. Indeed, in 1695 two Apalachee Indians living near St. Augustine were arrested for counterfeiting Spanish coins out of tin.[53]

Although new foods and tools were introduced to the missions, the native people continued to build houses in the old ways and to hunt, fish (with both spears and weirs), and gather wild plants. At San Martín and the Baptizing Spring mission site, both in Timucua, a variety of traditional stone, bone, and antler tools were found in the native villages, along with some iron tools, scraps of brass, and the like.[54] Even though iron tools are found associated with native houses, those same houses contain little or no iron construction hardware, such as nails, unlike the nearby mission churches and conventos, where such items are common.

The process of altering the cultures of the native people of Apalachee and Timucua may have been all-encompassing. As Maynard Geiger has noted, "spiritual ideas were conveyed by . . . architecture, painting, statuary, [and] the symbolism of the liturgy."[55] Similarly, ideas about Hispanic culture were conveyed to the mission populations, including ideas about food, clothing, material items, and acceptable behavior. Indigenous cultural elements that were viewed by the friars as "morally dangerous and detrimental [were] discarded."[56] Those aboriginal beliefs and practices that were viewed as superstitions or that involved prayers to powers other than those associated with Christianity (and thus were viewed by the priests as associated with the "Devil's arts") were to be ignored. "Signs of birds and animals, none of it is to be believed."[57] Abortion, certain sexual practices, and polygamy were to be eradicated.

Native symbols were also destroyed when they were thought to conflict with Christian ones. When Father Martín Prieto began his missionary work in Timucua, he burned twelve wooden "idols" in the plaza of the main town (later the site of San Martín) and then traveled to four other towns, where he destroyed six more carved images in each.[58] In their place Christian symbols were introduced. Crosses have been found stamped on native pottery, and at a number of mission sites religious medallions, rosary beads, and reliquaries have been discovered.

One controversial indigenous practice was the Southeast Indian stick ball game, which priests in Apalachee and Timucua sought to ban because of its association with non-Christian elements.[59] Although some Christian Apalachee Indians admitted that it should be banned, others were not so sure, and neither were some Spaniards. The native peoples did not always agree with the friars on what was to be deemed "morally dangerous and detrimental." One of the leaders of the 1597 Guale revolt noted, "They [the friars] prohibit us . . . our dances, banquets, feasts, celebrations, games and war. . . . [They] prosecute our old men, calling them wizards."[60] But at the missions, old ways had to give way to new, or so the missionaries wished.

Ceramics from mission San Juan in Suwannee County. The top potsherd was malleated with a wooden paddle decorated with a cross motif. The most common paddle-malleated Jefferson ware pottery has a bull's-eye, or concentric circle, motif. The two bottom potsherds are Spanish majolica decorated with a blue and white floral design.

Among the people of Apalachee and Timucua prior to Spanish contact, the demand by chiefs for tribute, both goods and labor, was an accepted practice. Working through village chiefs in the mission period, Spanish officials regularly sought similar favors, especially labor. Chiefs, who received payment from the Spaniards, provided their villagers to fill the labor quotas of the military government.[61] Most often it was unmarried adult males who were used to service the colony, but it is clear that other males, and occasionally women, also provided labor.

Adult males were required to serve as burden bearers to transport corn and, at times, other foodstuffs from Apalachee and Timucua to the Gulf coast, where they could be shipped. Or they were required to carry loads overland to St. Augustine. Another route to St. Augustine was by canoe along the Wacissa/Aucilla River out into the Gulf of Mexico to the Suwannee River and then up the Suwannee to near mission Santa Fé. There the water route intersected with the overland mission road. At times, the chief of Santa Fé provided horses to transport the goods to St. Augustine, or goods were loaded on the backs of native people for the trek.[62]

Mission Indians from the provinces also were conscripted for work at St. Augustine, or they were retained after transporting supplies to the town. They tended the fields that provided food for the garrison, worked on construction projects (such as building forts), timbered, and cut stone (coquina) in the mine on Anastasia Island. Historian Amy Bushnell notes that as many as three hundred Indians were involved in the construction of the stone castillo in the 1670s.[63] Other native people worked as house servants for Spanish families in St. Augustine. All of these activities, for which some minimal payment was supposed to be made, caused the Indians to be away from their home villages for months at a time.

Mission Indians also were required to maintain the road to St. Augustine, clearing brush, repairing creek crossings, and even building bridges. Where the mission trail crossed larger rivers, mission natives maintained ferry services. People from the village at Salamototo complained about having to provide ferry service across the St. Johns River, a task that often kept them away from home for several days in bad weather. Ferries were maintained elsewhere in Timucua, and in Guale ferries allowed passage between the barrier islands.

Christian Indians were servants for the priests and the Spanish soldiers stationed at missions. They cooked, tended gardens, did household chores, and provided maize, fish, and other food. Villagers provided soldiers stationed at the garrison at mission Santa Catalina in Guale with food, cassina (a tea), and fishing lines.[64] At San Luís in Apalachee, villagers constructed a palisaded wooden fort and houses for Spanish settlers.[65]

Additionally, in the mission provinces some natives were organized into a militia.[66] They were drilled and armed to serve as a reserve military force for the Spanish infantry stationed in St. Augustine. In the late 1620s and again in the 1650s, the governor of the colony called up the native militia when it was thought St. Augustine might be attacked by the English.

Mission villagers interacted with the Spaniards in other ways, such as bartering foodstuffs or labor to soldiers stationed at the mission garrisons or to Spanish traders in exchange for goods. Occasionally they were paid for their produce and labor.[67] Sometimes the Spaniards took advantage of the native entrepreneurs. In 1677 the villagers of San Juan de Aspalaga in Apalachee complained to Spanish officials that seven or eight years earlier their chief, since deceased, had traded one hundred arrobas of beans and maize to a Spaniard for half their worth in money plus a horse, but no payment had been made. On another occasion mission villagers had traded maize for blankets, but again they complained they had not received the payment due them.[68]

Deerskins were another commodity furnished by the Indians to the Spaniards. A government official decreed that any villager who allowed a nonlocal Indian to stay at his village for more than a few days without Spanish permission would be required to pay a twelve-deerskin fine to the provincial garrison head, who was to use it for "pious works."[69] Quite likely these hides entered the Spanish trade network.

In June 1677, raiders—perhaps pirates—entered the port of St. Marks, which served the interior Apalachee missions and farms. The raiders stole a frigate and goods belonging to soldiers, including a quantity of deerskins and "amber," probably ambergris.[70] Apparently, Spanish soldiers stationed at the inland garrisons had been trading with the Apalachee Indians for items they then exported through the port. Smuggling—taking items out without paying required duties—was common.

The picture that emerges from Apalachee in the second half of the seventeenth century is one of a province in which food production, trade, and the exporting of goods and foodstuffs was common. Native Americans were participants in a system of commerce that stretched well beyond Florida.

The Spanish-owned *haciendas* (cattle ranches and farms) located in Timucua and Apalachee were another Spanish endeavor in which mission villagers were used as laborers.[71] Ranches and farms produced wheat, corn, cattle, and hides for use in St. Augustine and for export. One of the earliest was in Timucua, where by 1630 the royal treasurer, Francisco Menéndez Márquez, a relative of Pedro Menéndez de Avilés, had established a cattle ranch. Called La Chua (*chua* in Timucua means "sinkhole"), the ranch was on the north side of Paynes Prairie, near

Gainesville.[72] Modern-day Alachua County receives it name from the ranch, which in turn may have received its name from the Alachua Sink on nearby Paynes Prairie.

La Chua was twenty-five square leagues, as many as seventeen miles on a side. Archaeologist Henry Baker has located the area of the main buildings associated with the ranch and found artifacts associated with the ranching operation.[73] The Zetrouer archaeological site several miles to the north also may have been associated with the ranch in the late seventeenth century, although it may have been a separate ranch.

In order to maintain the La Chua ranch, Menéndez Márquez needed permission of the chief of Timucua, a northern Utinan man. At the time the ranch was established, the Potano population in whose territory the ranch was established had probably been effectively wiped out due to disease and the impact of the French and Spanish raids of the sixteenth century. What had been Potano territory was under the control of a northern Utina chief.

Menéndez Márquez befriended the chief, providing him with gifts, perhaps including beef and hogs for feasts, and even serving as his godfather, an event that led to the chief's adopting Menéndez as his own surname.[74] Menéndez Márquez later was found to have embezzled 16,165 pesos from the treasury in St. Augustine, some of which may have helped to finance the ranch.[75] After Menéndez Márquez's death in 1649, the chief complained that things were not as they used to be. The support of Menéndez Márquez must have been important in the chief's maintaining his status in the region.

An inventory of the ranch made after Menéndez Márquez's death lists cattle, pigs, and slaves among the assets. Two African slaves worked there, along with two native laborers.[76] Other Indians probably worked at the ranch intermittently.

The ranch remained in operation throughout the seventeenth century and was a major source of beef for St. Augustine. Cattle were driven to that town, slaughtered, the meat sold, and the hides and tallow exported. Tómas Menéndez Márquez, Francisco's son and owner of the ranch after Francisco's death, carried on a lively commerce, trading cattle products to Havana in exchange for rum.[77]

La Chua and its cattle were a tempting target for raiders who wanted to steal cattle and damage the resource base of St. Augustine. In 1682, French buccaneers camping on Anclote Key just off the Gulf coast north of Tampa Bay used the Suwannee–Santa Fe river system to travel into Timucua and raid the ranch. They returned two years later, this time using the Withlacoochee River and then marching north through Marion County.[78] Rustlers and cattle thieves also occasionally helped themselves to La Chua's stock.

Between 1703 and 1706, when English-inspired raids were devastating the missions in Apalachee and Timucua, several raids were made on the ranch. A blockhouse was built for protection, but it was soon abandoned and the residents of the ranch moved northward to San Francisco for protection.

A second hacienda in Timucua was established about 1645 by Gov. Benito Ruíz de Salazar Vallecilla near the mission of San Miguel de Asile on the Madison County side of the Aucilla River.[79] The archaeological site corresponding to the mission was found in the late 1940s by Hale Smith near U.S. highway 27 and the river.[80]

The Aucilla hacienda, originally intended to be a cattle ranch, developed into a farm that produced corn and wheat; pigs also were raised. The hacienda was a major operation that used large numbers of native people as laborers. It, too, operated with the consent of the local chief, the chief of Asile, who controlled the land.

The Aucilla farm had six square leagues planted in crops and included buildings, granaries, and a corral. Horses and teams of oxen were used to cultivate the land.[81] When Governor Salazar died, the farm was sold by the acting governor. The ranch was closed down about 1651 or 1652.

Inventory of the Farm at Asile, 1650s (based on Cumbaa [1975:205–6])

22 oxen

8 horses

45 head of swine

1 whetstone (used)

1 auger

4 auger bits

1 lance

4 spades or hoes (used)

7 hatchets (used)

8 sickles

3 hand adzes

2 saws and 1 handsaw

6 carpenter's planes

4 ell-hooks

3 machetes

8 iron goads (used)

2 iron chains

2 posts (? *mastillos*)

1 wooden table

6 wooden benches

1 oil lamp

3 wooden beds

1 old bottle case

2 used table-cloths

1 pewter dish

2 bricks of chocolate

Note: This inventory was prepared by Spanish officials when there were plans to sell the ranch following the death of Governor Benito Ruíz de Salazar Vallecilla. Included in the inventory were an African slave from Angola named Ambrosio and the mulatto overseer, Francisco Galindo. The inventory also listed a large wooden house, a separate wooden kitchen with oven and two foot-mills, a thatched building for storing flour, a new house with daub walls and thatched roof, pasture, and six square leagues of land.

Following the Timucuan rebellion, land in Timucua became easier for Spaniards to obtain title to. This was in large part because the native population had been greatly reduced in number and much uncontrolled land existed. Land grants were common, and taxing them provided funds for the coffers of St. Augustine. Ranches established in Timucua after the rebellion included one owned by Juan de Hita, who was married to Antonia, a daughter of Tómas Menéndez Márquez. The Hita ranch was near San Francisco, perhaps at San Felasco Hammock. A second ranch, named Chicharro and owned by Francisco Romo de Uriza, was on the south side of Paynes Prairie, where it could be seen from La Chua.[82] De Uriza, too, was married to one of Tómas Menéndez Márquez's daughters. Hann notes there is documentary evidence for twenty-five (not counting Asile) cattle ranches in northern or east Florida in the region of Timucua speakers.[83]

Ranches in east Florida were distributed southward to Surruque just north of Cape Canaveral and down the St. Johns River drainage into Mayaca territory.[84] Hann found that the reason many ranches were mentioned in documents was that native villagers complained to Spanish officials that the cattle from the ranches were running loose and destroying crops.

Apalachee, with its good soil, also was the focus of farms and ranches, especially in the 1670s, when Spanish settlers moved into the province.[85] Prior to that time hogs and chickens were raised for export to Cuba. In 1675 a number of land grants for ranches or farms were made, and by 1698 or 1699 there were nine ranches in Apalachee province engaged in farming wheat and/or raising cattle, hogs, and horses. Some of these ranches were owned by high-ranking Apalachee Indians.[86]

Artist's reconstruction of daily life in the Spanish quarter at mission San Luís in Tallahassee (courtesy of the Florida Bureau of Archaeological Research, Division of Historical Resources).

The Floréncia family, members of which lived in Apalachee, including at the town of San Luís, and some of whom owned ranches, was especially engaged in entrepreneurial endeavors in Apalachee, often "treating the province as a private fief."[87] Other ranch-owning Spaniards included Diego Ximénez and Marcos Delgado. The latter's ranch, named Our Lady of the Rosary, was established in 1677.[88]

Livestock and crops from Apalachee were sent to St. Augustine as well as to Cuba. The latter journey was by boat from Apalachee along the St. Marks River to the coast and then to Cuba. In 1685 a ship was loaded at the St. Marks port with 100 chickens, 110 hams, 35 jars of lard, 300 deerskins, 44 bushels of corn, and 60 arrobas (approximately 25 pounds) of pine tar.[89] Apalachee carried on a vigorous trade with destinations outside Florida, making profits for the Spanish settlers who lived there and who were supported in large part by Apalachee Indian labor.

These profits are reflected in the artifacts excavated by Bonnie McEwan from the Spanish portion of San Luís. She notes: "The natural fertility [of the province], successful agricultural endeavors, surplus economy, and active shipping . . . afforded at least some of the Spanish residents of San Luís economic affluence and access to an exceptional range of imported materials."[90] They lived as well as, if not better than, some of their compatriots residing in St. Augustine.

In a colony as poor as La Florida, the mission Indians represented one of the few resources that could help the Spaniards derive a profit from the land. Certainly the missions sought to better the life of the native inhabitants, but the system also provided a means of support for Spanish economic initiatives.

Despite the best intentions of the Franciscan missionary priests, the native peoples of Timucua province were not able to survive the epidemics that depleted the population. And although for a time the Apalachee Indians apparently were able to successfully adjust to the Spanish presence and maintain a stable population level, in the end they, too, did not survive. Caught up in the power struggles between England and Spain, the remaining Timucua speakers and the Apalachee would be forced off their traditional lands.

The End of Time

11

Although direct documentary evidence is lacking, it is certain that disease epidemics had an impact on the Florida native Indians prior to the late 1590s, when missions were established. Bioanthropological evidence from Tatham Mound, a site in eastern Citrus County near the route of Hernando de Soto, supports the contention that epidemics began almost as soon as the first Spaniard stepped ashore.[1] The mound contained good evidence for an outbreak that killed as many as seventy people, probably Ocale Indians, who were buried in the mound together.

More certain is the fact that the native people who lived at the Spanish missions in Florida suffered the ravages of diseases brought from Europe. Epidemics mentioned in Spanish documents tell of the devastating effects of smallpox, measles, and other afflictions.

In the past, scholars have thought that as the indigenous population of the Timucuan missions declined in the second half of the seventeenth century, native people from elsewhere were moved to those missions to repopulate them. When they came, these outsiders brought their own styles of pottery and other artifacts, accounting for the presence of the nonlocal types of native ceramics found at late-seventeenth-century mission sites. One of the major groups involved in this repopulation was thought to be the Apalachee. This model helped to explain the archaeological evidence found at Timucuan missions, especially the presence of large amounts of Leon-Jefferson ware, the same pottery found at the Apalachee missions.

Similar evidence thought to reflect the movement of nonindigenous people into Timucua—in this case Guale and/or Yamasee Indians from the Georgia coast—also has been found. Altamaha and San Marcos pottery, known to have been associated with the native people of the Mocama and Guale missions, has been found both at Timucuan missions and in the town of St. Augustine. Still other styles of nonlocal ceramics, again reflecting the movement of other native people from the north into Timucua, have been excavated from mission sites.

But recent archival research by John Hann has called into question the view that Leon-Jefferson ceramics at Timucuan missions resulted from the movement of Apalachee Indians to those villages. Hann notes there is not a single shred of documentary evidence that Apalachee Indians were resettled in Timucua. Nor is there evidence for large-scale movements of other groups to the western Timucuan missions, although several documents mention the need to move Timucua speakers from one mission or area to another mission within the province.

Is the archaeological evidence correct, or is it the archival record that holds the truth? Let us look at this puzzle and see if it can be at least partially resolved. In the discussion we also will look at the documentary evidence for severe disease epidemics at the missions across northern Florida.

Epidemics and Repopulation: A Timucuan Puzzle

Archaeologists have long felt that the presence of Leon-Jefferson pottery and other nonindigenous ceramics at Timucuan missions could be explained by the movement of Apalachee and other non-Timucuan Indians into Timucua in the seventeenth century. Leon-Jefferson pottery is also called Lamaroid ware because of its resemblance to Lamar pottery from Georgia, a type of pottery quite distinct from the locally made pottery found at late-precolumbian and early-colonial-period Suwannee Valley (northern Utina) and Alachua (Potano) culture sites. The styles of pottery appear so different from one another that it seemed very unlikely that they were made by the same people.

Today this model is being questioned—at least the part that holds that Timucuan missions were repopulated in part by Apalachee Indians in the late seventeenth century. For one thing, it has become evident that Leon-Jefferson ware is present in large quantities at early-seventeenth-century, prerebellion (pre-1656) mission sites in Timucua, as well as at late-seventeenth-century sites. In other words, what was thought to be Apalachee pottery may occur at Timucuan missions as early as—or even earlier than—it appears in the Apalachee missions. The mission sites at Fig Springs, Baptizing Spring, and Indian Pond—all prerebellion missions in Suwannee and Columbia counties—contain large amounts of Leon-Jefferson pottery. At those sites, as the frequency of Leon-Jefferson pottery increases over time, the frequency of locally made types decrease.

Some of our best data for the presence of Leon-Jefferson ware in Timucua comes from Brent Weisman's excavations at Fig Spring, the mission of San Martín. Those investigations revealed that more than half of the aboriginal pottery in the portion of the mission village that was sampled is the Lamaroid Leon-Jefferson ware.[2] Other types of nonlocal native pottery, like those found at archaeological sites well to the north or northwest in Georgia or even Alabama, also were excavated at Fig Springs. It was data such as these that led archaeologists to suggest that as the indigenous population of Timucua declined, Apalachee Indians were moved eastward to repopulate mission villages east of the Aucilla River.

Another example of archaeological evidence supporting the possibility that Timucua was being repopulated with nonlocal native people comes from the late-seventeenth-century Zetrouer site in eastern Alachua County, probably a village associated with a Spanish hacienda.[3] There the majority of aboriginal pottery is a Yamasee/Guale Indian type (Altamaha or San Marcos ware) probably made by native people who came from Georgia. At that site the Yamasee/Guale occupation could date from the very early eighteenth century, when Yamasee are known to have entered northern Florida.

So the archaeological evidence does suggest that new populations replaced the old. But was repopulation of the Timucuan missions necessary? Certainly the archival record leaves no doubt that the indigenous population of Timucua suffered severe reductions in the seventeenth

San Marcos ceramic vessel, probably made by Yamasee Indians. The 14-inch-tall container came from Amelia Island (courtesy of Florida Museum of Natural History).

century. Hann's research indicates that by the 1650s populations at the north Florida missions were being annihilated by disease. During that decade alone epidemics "killed uncounted thousands" of natives.[4] Writing in 1657, Governor Rebolledo noted that the Indians of Guale and Timucua were few in number "because they have been wiped out with the sickness of the plague (*peste*) and smallpox which have overtaken them in the past years."[5] The mission of Nombre de Dios, near St. Augustine, was devastated by the epidemic that also halved the population of San Martín in Timucua. But more was yet to come. In 1659, the incoming governor of Spanish Florida alleged that ten thousand Indians had died in a measles epidemic.[6]

Hann also has found documentary evidence of even earlier epidemics affecting mission populations.[7] A severe epidemic struck the coastal missions in 1595. Between 1612 and late 1616 there were a number of "great plagues and contagious diseases" that affected half of the mission Florida Indians, as well as Spanish soldiers.[8] This is within a decade after the first missions were established in western Timucua. One missionary priest observed that a very large number of Indians had died as a result of the epidemics.[9]

Another epidemic is documented for St. Augustine in 1649 and 1650. At that time one priest stated that several of his colleagues had died, suggesting the epidemic also reached the missions.[10] Then in 1655 a severe smallpox epidemic ravaged Guale and Timucua as well as St. Augustine (one of the epidemics referred to by Governor Rebolledo).

That epidemics had a severe effect on the Timucuan missions early in the 1600s is certain. They were so extensive that in the early seventeenth century some of the Timucuan missions, especially those in Potano, could not provide sufficient adult males to meet the labor quotas demanded by authorities in St. Augustine.[11] Within a century after the de Soto expedition marched through the heart of what would become the mission province of Timucua, the indigenous population was greatly reduced.

Potano, as well as parts of the lower St. Johns drainage, may have been severely depopulated by 1620. Indeed, the mission system itself, which brought native peoples together in villages, may have hastened the impact of diseases by providing more opportunities for infections to be transmitted within and between villages. John Hann notes that this is implied in the remarks of a Franciscan priest, who, following the epidemics of 1612 through 1616, noted: "a very great harvest of souls has been made in these mortalities."[12] Mission villages and villages sending laborers to St. Augustine apparently suffered most in those epidemics.

The scope of the devastation of the Timucua-speaking population is graphically illustration by a 1689 survey probably commissioned by the bishop of Cuba. A detailed, village-by-village count of Christian Indians served by the missions lists a total of only 646 families of Timucua speakers.[13] If average family size was five people—doubtful given the effects of the epidemics—the total Timucuan mission population would be only 3,230 people. This is about 2 percent of the 150,000 total Florida Timucua speakers estimated for 1492 prior to first Spanish contact.

Historians, archaeologists, and other anthropologists continue to argue over the exact nature of these disease epidemics that raged through La Florida and the entire Americas. Were there pandemics that swept through the native populations in North and South America in the first decades after Columbus's initial voyage, decimating "virgin soil" populations who had no resistance to foreign germs? Did such pandemics precede Europeans into most regions of the Western Hemisphere, spreading from native group to native group after first being introduced by Spaniards when they landed in Central America or Mexico? The jury is still out, although those involved in the debate agree that epidemics in the Americas were devastating.[14] What is certain is that in the seventeenth century, numerous epidemics struck the Florida missions provinces and that at least some were restricted in geographical extent.

Diseases brought to the Americas from the Eastern Hemisphere in the sixteenth and seventeenth centuries are thought to include smallpox, measles, chicken pox, scarlet fever, typhus, malaria, bubonic plague, pneumonic plague, influenza, typhoid, dysentery, diphtheria, and yellow fever.[15] Whatever the exact vectors of disease that ravaged the native populations were, in Florida the result was catastrophic.

Governor Rebolledo's mid-seventeenth-century decision to reorganize the Timucuan missions may have been necessitated in part by this population reduction. Sufficient labor could not be found in Timucua for Spanish needs, so it was necessary to focus on Apalachee, which still had a sufficient population (most likely the result of having a larger and denser precolumbian population than Timucua). The reorganization enhanced travel to Apalachee and to the Spanish farms and ranches in Timucua.

These two observations—archaeological evidence of ceramic changes and documentation of severe epidemics in Timucua—make the explanation that Apalachee and other Indians were brought to the Timucuan missions to repopulate them an attractive one. But, as John Hann has pointed out, the archival record provides no information about repopulation ever taking place. Known archival sources all make it clear that the Timucua language continued to be the language spoken at the missions in Timucua. Timucua was inhabited by Timucua Indians.

On the other hand, there are several documents expressing the need to shift Timucua speakers around within the province to maintain populations at specific missions, but there is no confirmation this was actually done or that, if it were done, the people who were moved remained at their new location for long.[16] One example is a 1645 account that tells of the need to move Timucua-speaking Oconi Indians to the site of San Diego de Elaca on the St. Johns River, located where the mission road reached that river. But that move apparently never took place.[17] Another example comes from Santa Fé in Alachua County. Attempts were made in 1657 to move Arapaha Indians to the mission and, in 1659, people from Yustaga. The geographical source of these native people may have been northernmost Madison and Hamilton counties and the adjacent portion of south-central Georgia.[18]

Could Timucua speakers from the northern fringes of the mission province of Timucua—perhaps from the Arapaha area, Oconi, or other inland locales in Georgia—be the source of the Leon-Jefferson pottery found at sites such as Fig Springs and Baptizing Spring? Perhaps, but we do not know enough about the ceramic assemblages of the late-precolumbian and early-colonial-period inhabitants of southern Georgia to determine if the Leon-Jefferson ceramic assemblage was present there prior to the time of the missions.

Even if repopulation of Timucua did occur by moving other Timucua speakers with Leon-Jefferson pottery into the region, it is doubtful that this immigration alone was sufficient to account for the ceramic change so evident in the archaeological record.

At this time, depopulation and repopulation of the northern Florida Timucuan missions cannot explain the appearance of new ceramic inventories at those missions. Although population movements may have been occurring within the region of Timucua speakers, they apparently were too limited to have been related to the appearance of Leon-Jefferson ceramics. And ceramic changes certainly cannot be tied to movements of Apalachee Indians into Timucua.

Can another explanation be formulated to explain the ceramic assemblage changes found at northern Florida Timucuan sites in the colonial period? Are there other explanations for the presence of Leon-Jefferson pottery at sites like Fig Springs, Baptizing Spring, and Indian Pond, all locations of Spanish Franciscan doctrinas? Unfortunately, there is not as yet a single explanation that can be shown to be correct and supported by both archival and archaeological evidence. But we can begin to approach the problem.

First, let us accept the contention that the explanation is not related to depopulation and repopulation of the Timucuan missions. Supporting this is the presence of Leon-Jefferson ware at mission villages in Timucua in the early seventeenth century, before the first missions were established in Apalachee. In other words, what is usually characterized as pottery associated with Apalachee mission Indians may actually be found at Timucuan missions that are as early as, if not earlier than, those in Apalachee, the latter dating after 1633. Another often-overlooked fact is that in the province of Apalachee, Leon-Jefferson ware, which appears at the time of the missions, itself is quite distinct from and replaces the Fort Walton pottery found there in late-precolumbian times and at early-colonial-period sites such as the Governor Martin site, the location of Iniahica where de Soto's army camped in 1539.

Thus it is possible that the appearance of Leon-Jefferson pottery in Apalachee and Timucua occurred at approximately the same time, a time that correlates with the period when the first Franciscan missionaries were entering those regions to establish visitas and doctrinas. Perhaps the adoption of Leon-Jefferson ware in Apalachee and Timucua is somehow related to the spread of Catholicism through the mission system. Did priests encourage the process, urging the native potters to fashion new styles of ceramics that were not decorated with traditional symbols and were associated with new food habits? At Baptizing Spring, aboriginal ceramics were excavated that were stamped with cross motifs.

This explanation leaves much to be desired, especially because the situation with Leon-Jefferson pottery is actually more complicated than I have presented. Leon-Jefferson pottery is closely related to Lamar ceramics, an aboriginal ware associated with cultures found in Georgia. Why would priests urge adoption of Georgia aboriginal pottery by Florida mission Indians? Perhaps they did not. Perhaps it is only by chance that Leon-Jefferson ceramics were becoming popular in north Florida at or near the same time that Franciscan missionaries entered the region. Such widespread ceramic shifts are known to have occurred in north Florida in the precolumbian period.

The puzzle remains unsolved. A detailed technological analysis of late-precolumbian and mission-period ceramics will shed some light, and more information will come from archaeological investigations in southern Georgia. Ultimately, however, the question of repopulation of the Timucuan missions may lie in genetic analysis of the mission villagers themselves.

Apalachee Demography

The situation regarding population levels in Apalachee during the post-1633 period of mission activity was different than in Timucua. John Hann has carefully documented the growth and history of the Apalachee mission system from its beginning in 1633 to its destruction in 1703 and 1704.[19] During that seventy-year period a number of missions were established to serve the Apalachee, and most had satellite villages. Together, mission and satellite villages at any one time totaled about forty. Although the Apalachee, like the Timucua speakers to the east, suffered severe population reductions from the time of first contact with Spaniards in the early sixteenth century to the time of the first missions in 1633, after about 1675 the population appears to have remained relatively stable.[20]

Hann estimates a precolumbian population of 50,000 for the region of Apalachee province. In 1608, according to an estimate by a visiting Franciscan, the population was 36,000, a figure close to estimates of 30,000 given by other Franciscans prior to the establishment of the missions, including one from 1617. A 1638 census taken just after the founding of the missions gave the figure as 16,000; still another from the 1640 said 26,000. A priest writing about 1648 put Apalachee's population at 20,000. Although the figures vary, until the last quarter of the seventeenth century the population continued to decline. It reached about 10,000 by 1675 and stabilized at that or a slightly lower level until the English raids of the early eighteenth century destroyed the Apalachee missions.

The Apalachee population appears to have more successfully adjusted to the Spanish presence than did the populations of the various Timucuan groups. Some of the epidemics of the 1650s that were so devastating in Timucua may not have reached the Apalachee or were not as severe. On the other hand, it may be that what appears to be a stable Apalachee population actually is in part a reflection the presence of non-Apalachee Indians, such as Chatot Indians or people from Tama, moving into the province.

For the colonial Spanish, Governor Rebolledo's mission reorganization could be viewed as a success. The number of missions in La Florida in 1675 was the same as the number that had existed in 1655 prior to the rebellion, due in large part to the founding of new missions. But behind those numbers lies the demographic catastrophe in Timucua. Consolidating populations from satellite villages and founding new Apalachee missions with people from outside the province may have resulted in the number of missions remaining the same. After 1675 the efforts to put missions in central Florida among the Mayaca, Jororo, and Ais Indians and among the Calusa may have been a response to the severe decline in the native population in Timucua.

Raids of 1680 to 1707

In the end, the fact that the native population of Apalachee may have successfully adapted to colonial life would not matter. The mission system did not last. La Florida became a pawn in the conflicts involving colonial powers, especially England's colonial expansion down the Atlantic seaboard. To successfully reap the full benefits of her southeastern colonies, England needed to push Spain off the Georgia coast and out of Florida.

The English had founded Charleston in 1670, the same year the Treaty of Madrid was signed by England and Spain, giving each country the right to lands in America that it controlled at the time. The Georgia coast, largely the mission province of Guale, clearly was a portion of Spain's La Florida colony, but England would choose to ignore the treaty provisions, setting the stage for military conflict between these two colonial powers. That conflict was played out across La Florida, ultimately leading to the destruction of the Spanish missions.[21]

In 1680 a raiding party of Indians, abetted by Carolinian or English soldiers, attacked the mission of Guadalquini on St. Simons Island, then hit Santa Catalina to the north in Guale. These raids were followed by more attacks in 1684 on the coastal missions of Mocama and Guale.[22]

After the next raid, against the Timucuan mission of Santa Catalina (near Ichetucknee Springs) by Carolinian-abetted Yamasee Indian slavers, the Spaniards decided to retaliate, sailing northward to attack the Carolina colony. Although Charleston itself was not assaulted, nearby Stuarts Town was attacked and plantations belonging to Charleston colonists were raided. The Spaniards, expecting retaliation, continued construction of the stone fortress at St. Augustine, a project begun in the mid-1670s to replace an older, wooden fort.[23] Built of coquina mined from Anastasia Island, it is that stone fort, the Castillo de San Marcos, that still stands today.

These raids signaled the start of an "undeclared war" between Spain and its mission populations and the Carolinians and their American Indian allies.[24] But the warfare was decidedly one-sided; the warriors fighting with the Carolinians had firearms, while most Guale and Timucuan villagers did not. Because it was futile to try to defend the Spanish missions and garrison outposts without adequate military support, all of the Guale missions were withdrawn by early 1685. Spain essentially had relinquished the Georgia coast. The northernmost Spanish garrisons and missions were only fifty miles north of St. Augustine, on Amelia Island.

Some of the Native Americans who had lived at the abandoned missions, including Yamasee Indians who had moved to the missions from northern Georgia, fled the coast. Others sought refuge among the English colonists in the Carolinas, were taken as slaves, or were moved by the Spaniards to old and new missions between Amelia Island and St. Augustine. Some were moved as far south as Mayaca.[25] Mission sites on Cumberland, Amelia, and Fort George islands all contain aboriginal pottery thought to be associated with the Guale and/or Yamasee Indians, perhaps reflecting the shift of mission populations down the coast.

The Yamasee Indians living in the Carolina colony quickly learned that slaving paid well. Native people captured from the poorly defended Florida missions could be taken back to Charleston and sold for labor to be used in the Carolinas or the West Indies. For instance, in their 1685 raid against mission Santa Catalina de Afuica, near the Ichetucknee River, the Yamasee raiders took twenty-two slaves. In 1691, the mission of San Juan de Guacara, on the Suwannee River in western Suwannee County, was similarly raided. These raids not only destroyed the mission buildings, they decimated the already epidemic-affected mission villages.[26] Raids also struck missions north and west of Apalachee, killing and enslaving villagers.

The raids into Timucua continued in the early eighteenth century. San Pedro y San Pablo de Potohiriba (in Madison County west of Suwannee County) and Santa Fé both were attacked in 1702. Apalachicola Indians who raided Santa Fé were armed and abetted by the Carolinians. Although the mission was successfully defended by the small Spanish garrison stationed there, an ill-advised counterattack resulted in the deaths of ten Christian Indians and the garrison's Spanish lieutenant.[27]

The governor of La Florida, Don Joseph de Zuñiga y Zerda, wrote to the Crown after the raid to explain what had happened.

> They [the Apalachicola] entered in the dawn watch and burned and devastated the village of Santa Fé . . . making an attack on the convent with many firearms and arrows and burning the church. . . . Finally, the fight having lasted for more than three hours, our force repulsed them, after the hasty strengthening of an indefensible stockade which served as a fence to the gate of the convent.[28]

In November 1702, Carolinian soldiers and native allies, including some Yamasee Indians, sailed from Port Royal to attack St. Augustine. The army, commanded by Gov. James Moore, was a much larger force than those of any of the previous raids. The soldiers and Indians landed

"The Enemy's Way of Burning Towns by Night" (Hulton 1977:I:149). European colonists in Florida quickly adopted the time-honored native practice of using palm thatch to roof structures, including mission churches. Using flaming arrows and spears, native raiders could easily burn a mission or a town to the ground. The text accompanying this de Bry engraving points out that such a tactic was efficient, but usually did not result in loss of life.

on the northern end of Amelia Island, where the raiders quickly dispatched the small Spanish garrison stationed at a fortified tower in what is now Fernandina Beach. The army marched down the island, attacking the missions of Santa Clara de Tupique and San Felipe, then the mission of Santa Catalina, one of the missions moved from Guale in the 1680s. The outmanned garrison stationed at Santa Catalina, along with the Franciscan priests, fled just before the raiders arrived and burned the mission to the ground.[29] The destroyed remains of the mission, located on Harrison Creek on the inland side of the island, have been found and excavated by archaeologists.[30]

The Carolinian army continued south, next reaching San Juan del Puerto on Fort George Island. In almost no time the militia and Indian warriors had taken of all the Spanish outposts and missions that lay between Amelia Island and their goal, St. Augustine. The Carolinians laid siege to that town, burning most of it, except for the fort, where the townspeople had sought refuge. The siege of the castillo continued into December before the Carolinian force withdrew.[31] Five hundred captive Indians were taken back to Charleston.

The missions in Apalachee also were under attack. In 1702 Creek allies of the Carolinians and Apalachee Indians collided on the Flint River. The next year a raid by Carolinian soldiers and natives destroyed at least one Apalachee mission. Then, in early and mid-1704, two much larger military campaigns were waged by the Carolinian militia that effectively destroyed the Apalachee mission system. The native people living at the missions were scattered or taken back to Charleston to provide labor for that colony. Three hundred men and a thousand women and children were taken and resettled as a buffer between the Carolinian settlements and the Spanish to the south. Another 325 men and perhaps as many as several thousand women and children were taken as slaves and either forced to work on Carolinian plantations or sold to plantations in the West Indies.[32]

These raids were devastating. Burned remains of the abandoned missions have been found by archaeologists all across the landscape of Leon and Jefferson counties, the realm of the Apalachee Indians.[33] The raids on the missions in Apalachee and Timucua also caused cessation of the Spanish ranching and farming operations, essentially wiping out a large part of the colony's economy.

From 1705 to 1707, additional raids into Apalachee and Timucua completed the destruction of the missions and some ineffectual

While excavating at the site of the destroyed Santa Catalina mission on Amelia Island, an archaeological team led by Kenneth Hardin of Janus Research/Piper Archaeology found a 4.5-inch-long brass seal.

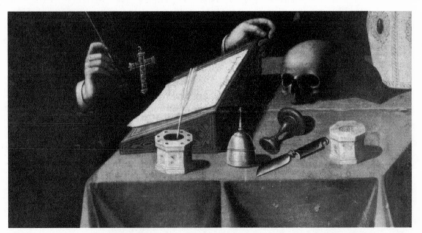

The seal is almost identical to one on the writing desk of San Augustín in this mid-seventeenth-century painting by Antonio Rodríguez.

The flat end of the seal (the doorknob-shaped end is for holding) shows, in negative, a woman with a crown holding a sword and standing beside a spiked wheel. Around her, the abbreviated text of the seal impression reads "Santa Catalina of Alexandria, Martyr," adding a dramatic exclamation to the identification of the mission as Santa Catalina. Legend has it that Catalina, a Christian living in Egypt at the end of the third century, was tortured on a spiked wheel, but miraculously was unhurt. She was then (A.D. 305) beheaded by the Roman emperor (courtesy of Janus Research/Piper Archaeology and Florida Museum of Natural History).

Spanish defenses established in the mission provinces after the raids of 1702 through 1704. The populations of Apalachee and Timucua had been killed, scattered, or enslaved. One group of Apalachee Indians had fled west. According to the governor of Spanish Florida, ten to twelve thousand American Indians had been taken as slaves as a result of the various raids by the Carolinian and native invaders.[34] The only missions remaining in Florida were recently established refugee villages near St. Augustine.

The Final Assault

With the removal of the missions and Spanish garrisons from northern Florida, the state was open to more attacks by native peoples from the north. The raiders that followed in the wake of the Carolinian militias included various Lower Creeks, Savannahs, more Yamasee, and other groups, who raided the length of the peninsula, slaving, looting, and devastating native settlements. One observer in 1709 noted that the Florida Indians, other than those living near St. Augustine, had been pushed southward to the tip of the peninsula.

The raids soon reached down into the Florida Keys, causing havoc among the native people of that region, who, like their neighbors to the north, had little defense. In 1711 the bishop of Cuba wrote:

> In the past month . . . a ship entered this port, which had come from the keys. . . . The heathen Indians of the chiefs, Carlos, Coleto, and others live in those keys. And some of the above-mentioned Indians who came in the aforesaid ship told me about very serious persecutions and hostilities, which they are experiencing and which they have experienced on other keys, which the Indians whom they call Yamasees have destroyed. That the Yamasees have killed some of the aforementioned Keys Indians; have made others flee; and that they have captured the greater part of the latter, whom, it is said, they carry off and sell, placing them into slavery at the port of [Charleston].[35]

The success of the raiders was due in part to the policies of the English colonies. After the establishment of the Virginia and Carolina colonies, colonial entrepreneurs had sought trading partners among native groups in the Southeast. Trade and exportation of deerskins were especially profitable.

One result of the deerskin trade was that natives obtained firearms. Rifles, powder, and shot gave these individuals a huge advantage in raids against people armed with bows and arrows and war clubs. Throughout the seventeenth century, native peoples with firearms— some deliberately armed by the Virginian and Carolinian colonists— caused widespread population shifts among other southeastern Native Americans.

Another factor was the slave trade, legalized in the Carolina colony in 1671. Florida Indians taken as slaves could be sold to the Carolinians by their native captors and then resold at a profit. Beginning in the

1720s, the Yamasee, who had played such a visible role in the slave trade, would themselves suffer the same fate as the Florida natives they had raided. In 1715 the Yamasee and other groups in South Carolina, including Creeks and Apalachee Indians, rebelled against the English colonists. To escape the military wrath of their former allies, many of the Yamasee fled south to St. Augustine, where they were received with open arms by the Spaniards.[36] Some settled in towns around St. Augustine, while others went to Apalachee or elsewhere in northern Florida.

Franciscan priests soon were sent to minister to the Yamasee and the remnant Florida groups. By about 1720, missionaries were serving eleven St. Augustine–region villages and at least one in Apalachee. The villages were home to Yamasee, Guale, and other refugees, as well as remnants of the native Florida Indians, including the Jororo, Pohoy, Tocobaga, and others. Efforts were made to entice natives from the north into the colony to repopulate the Spanish agricultural production areas devastated by the Carolinian raids, but they were unsuccessful. The Spaniards were unable to reestablish the ranches that had helped to sustain the colony.

The presence of these new mission towns only drew new native slave raiders. Indians from the north raided the Florida settlements, even those near St. Augustine, taking slaves. The Spaniards were unable to defend the villages. The former Yamasee slavers now suffered at the hands of the Carolinians' new allies. Many were enslaved; some Yamasee were even taken as slaves by Creek Indians, who were beginning to resettle parts of northern Florida.[37]

Missionary efforts would continue into the mid-eighteenth century in Florida, but largely only in the vicinity of St. Augustine.[38] John Hann has documented the histories of these small settlements, whose total population varied from a few hundred to less than a thousand, fluctuating as refugees came and went.[39]

As late as 1759, two doctrinas were operating in the small native town of Tolomato, then located just outside St. Augustine. Tolomato's residents included twelve Timucua speakers.[40] Nearby Nombre de Dios was home to seven Florida Indians, one of whom was Juan Alonso Cabale.[41]

The end of the mission system as an integral part of Spain's colonial efforts in La Florida effectively came with the raids of 1702 through

1704. Except for those native people living within and around St. Augustine, the labor base provided by the mission villages, which had helped to support the colony for more a century, no longer existed. Spain's hold on La Florida had been reduced to the town of St. Augustine and the small mission villages in its immediate environs.

The situation in the peninsular south of the mission provinces was no better. In 1743 two Jesuit priests, Joseph María Monaco and Joseph Xavier Alaña, established a mission named Santa María de Loreto at the mouth of the Miami River in modern Dade County to serve the refugee population living there.[42] Soldiers also were sent there to man a fort as protection against Yuchi Indians and other raiders. A report written by Father Alaña notes that the 180 people living in a village at the mission were remnants "of three nations, Keys, Carlos [Calusa], and Boca Raton."[43] Remnant populations of three other groups—Mayaimies (from Lake Okeechobee), Santaluces, and Mayacas, together totaling one hundred people or slightly more—lived inland one, two, and four days' travel, respectively. The native population of south Florida, like that in the north, was devastated.

Some native people, like those at Santa María de Loreto, as well as some of the people moving into Florida from the north, provided labor for a growing fishing industry that plied the Florida coasts. Spanish fishing boats out of St. Augustine and Cuba used Creeks and other Native Americans as crew members and to man shore operations.[44] These laborers were often taken back and forth to Cuba by boat.

Fishing ranchos were established along the coast, from Tampa Bay southward around the tip of Florida, including the Florida Keys, and up the Atlantic coast to Jupiter Inlet. Families of the native fishermen probably lived at the ranchos. Even after Spain gave up La Florida to Great Britain during the period from 1763 to 1783, the ranchos continued to operate. Archaeologists have found artifacts at several locations on the Gulf coast that probably were ranchos.[45] Some of the Spanish artifacts on the lower Atlantic coast also could be from fisheries.

By the early 1760s the indigenous population of Florida, once numbering in the hundreds of thousands, was reduced to almost nothing. Handfuls of individuals, some of whom still identified with groups by then totally decimated, were taken to Cuba when the Spanish population withdrew from Florida in 1763. The only descendants of the original inhabitants of Florida who maintained their ethnic identity past the 1760s was a group of Apalachee who had fled west, ending up in Louisiana on the Red River. They numbered forty-five individuals in 1825.[46] For the Florida Indians it was the end of time.

Epilogue

Even while the final demise of the indigenous groups of Florida was taking place, new native groups were beginning to colonize the state. Some originally may have come as raiders or as hunters. Others came to avoid the military uncertainty in the regions in which they had been living.

Many of these native colonizers were descendants of earlier native groups, who, in the aftermath of two centuries of disruption and change, had coalesced into the Creek Indians by 1700. As the colonial-period native societies of Georgia and eastern Alabama were reduced in population and as the remnants of those groups amalgamated and exercised other adaptive strategies, the political unit known as the Creek Confederacy had emerged.

Documents indicate the first Creek towns in Florida date to the 1750s. At that time the Creeks may have encountered handfuls of Florida Indians who remained in isolated pockets in remote areas. If so, those remnant populations were thoroughly incorporated into the newcomers, for the material assemblages found at the early Creek archaeological sites in Florida are most similar to contemporary Creek sites to the north, rather than to the assemblages of any of the indigenous Florida Indians.

The earliest Creek-Seminole towns in Florida were in the old mission provinces of Apalachee and Timucua, especially around what today are the Tallahassee–Lake Miccosukee and Gainesville–Paynes Prairie localities. Some were at abandoned mission sites, while others were established in new locations. Other early Creek towns in Florida were on the Apalachicola River and west of Gainesville over to the lower Suwannee River. At the time, the mid-eighteenth century, these settlements were far away from the native villages that surrounded St. Augustine.

More Creek Indians migrated to Florida during the first quarter of the nineteenth century, raising their number to about five thousand. New towns were established from the Gainesville area south to Tampa Bay. The name Seminole had begun to be used sparingly in the later eighteenth century, and in the nineteenth century it came to refer to the descendants of the Creek people who had moved into Florida. Scholars agree the name *Seminole* was originally derived from the Spanish word *cimarrone*, a word long in use by the Spaniards to refer to Indians living apart from missions or other Spanish-Indian settlements.

Florida was made a territory of the United States of America in 1819, and soon afterward American settlers from Georgia and the Carolinas began to move into the northern part of the state, causing conflict with the Seminole people already living there. The Treaty of Moultrie Creek, signed in 1823, was an attempt to resolve the situation by moving the Seminole Indians southward beyond the moving American frontier to land in central Florida south of Ocala. But conflict continued, ultimately resulting in warfare.

The final result of the guerrilla-like Second Seminole War (1835–42) was the forced removal of most Seminoles to Indian Territory in modern Oklahoma. A very few people, estimated at two to three hundred, sought refuge in the isolated Everglades and swamps of southern Florida.

But the southward push of the frontier associated with the American settlement of Florida, which had become a state in 1845, led to still more conflict with the bands of Seminoles who remained. The Third Seminole War, sometimes called the Billy Bowlegs War, ensued. Between 1855 and 1858, a series of limited engagements were fought in southern Florida. Federal troops penetrated deep into the interior of south Florida to hunt down the Seminoles. About two hundred people were removed to Indian Territory, again leaving only very small refugee populations living in the Everglades, the Big Cypress Swamp, and the Ten Thousand Islands, locations very difficult for the federal troops to reach. It is the descendants of those Seminoles who live in Florida today.

Although it is common to refer to all of these people as Seminole Indians, in reality they speak two different Creek languages. One is Muskogee, sometimes called Creek, and the other is Mikasuki, sometimes called Hitchiti. Both are Muskogean languages, the same family of languages present in much of the Southeast, from the Apalachee region north, in the colonial period.

Since the end of the nineteenth century, the number of American Indians in Florida has continued to increase yearly. The 1990 U.S. census recorded 36,000 people in Florida claiming Native American descent, including people from forty-eight different groups. That figure is one hundred times the 358 native people counted in the 1900 census.

Federally recognized native groups in Florida today are the Miccosukees, the Seminoles, and the Poarch Creeks. The latter reside mainly in Escambia County in the westernmost panhandle. Their tribal headquarters are just to the north, near Atmore, Alabama.

Also living in Florida are native people affiliated with a number of other groups, including Lumbee, Choctaw, Chippewa, and other Creeks. Indeed, there are more Cherokee people in Florida than any other native group. Many of these modern native Florida Indians are recent residents, who, like other Americans, have moved to Florida to take advantage of its climate and opportunities.

The invasion of Florida by colonial powers annihilated the native people whose ancestors had lived here for thousands of years. Yet once again Florida is home to a growing number of Native American Indians. As we enter the twenty-first century, those people promise to play a significant role in Florida's future and in helping all of us to understand the past.

 **NOTES**

Chapter 1: Searching for the Past

1. The process of making population estimates is as controversial as the figures themselves. For some of the flavor of the debate, see Dobyns (1983, 1993a), Milanich (1987), and Hann (1990a).

2. Many of these colonial-period archaeological sites are mentioned in Smith (1956), Goggin (1960, 1968), Deagan (1987a), and Mitchem (1989b).

3. For an account of that expedition see Connolly and Anderson (1987).

4. Archaeological studies of various European artifacts found in Spanish Florida include Goggin (1954, 1960, 1968), Fairbanks (1968a, 1968b), Deagan (1978b, 1987a), Smith and Good (1982), Leader (1985), South, Skowronek, and Johnson (1988), Mitchem and Leader (1988), Mitchem and McEwan (1988), and Marken (1994).

5. Historical studies include Griffin and Manucy (1962), Manucy (1962, 1985), Lyon (1977, 1992), and Hann (1986a).

6. Shapiro (1987), McEwan (1991, 1993).

7. The contributions by John Hann, a historian with the Florida Bureau of Archaeological Research's San Luís mission project, are enormous (see Hann 1986a, 1986b, 1986c, 1986d, 1987, 1988a, 1988b, 1988c, 1988d, 1989a, 1989b, 1990b, 1991, 1992a, 1992b, 1993a, 1993b, 1993c, 1994a).

8. For information on the archaeology of colonial St. Augustine and its role in colonial Florida, see Deagan (1977, 1981, 1983, 1985, 1993).

9. John Griffin (1949) was one of the first people to recognize the potential of historical archaeology in Florida.

10. I would be remiss if I did not also note the contributions of Lyle N. McAlister, a historian specializing in Spanish colonial history. For many years he taught courses and trained graduate students at the University of

Florida. He had a profound influence on historians Bushnell, Hoffman, and Lyon. Many graduate students in archaeology also have benefited from his courses and supervision. A history of research on the missions is Marrinan (1985).

Chapter 3: Native People in Southern Florida

1. Castañeda, Cuesta, and Hernández (1983:366). Caracoles most likely referred specifically to *Busycon* shells; today the term more commonly refers to snails.
2. Recent archaeological investigations of the Caloosahatchee culture have been published in a volume edited by William Marquardt (1992). Also see Randolph Widmer's (1988) pioneering synthesis, George Luer's (1989a, 1991) work on canoe canals, and Milanich (1994:311–323). Basic references on the Calusa Indians of the colonial period are Goggin and Sturtevant (1964), Lewis (1978), Marquardt (1984, 1986, 1987, 1988), and Hann (1991). Primary documents regarding the Calusa and the Spaniards in the 1560s are published in Zubillaga (1946). Translations of some of those documents and others, as well as accounts of Pedro Menéndez de Avilés's visits to the Calusa, are found in Solís de Merás (1964) and Barrientos (1965).
3. True (1945:26–27).
4. True (1945:51; see also 30–31).
5. Lewis (1978:37), Hann (1991:310–311).
6. Hann (1991:312).
7. For more on the Key Marco site, see Cushing (1897) and Gilliland (1975, 1989).
8. Hann (1991:177).
9. Sturtevant (1978:143).
10. For instance, Cushing (1897), Stirling (1935), Goggin (1949), Sears (1967:100; 1982), and Fairbanks (1968b).
11. True (1945:34).
12. Lawson (1992:88–89).
13. "May" or "Mai" may mean "freshwater" in one or more of the native languages of Florida. John Hann provided me with information suggesting it might specifically refer to a canoe landing rather than just freshwater.
14. Goggin and Sturtevant (1964) and Lewis (1978).
15. Luer (1989a, 1991).
16. Lewis (1978:40–41); Hann (1991:305–308). A fanega is approximately 1.5 bushels, an arroba is 25 pounds, and a quintal is a hundredweight, or 100 pounds.
17. Hann (1991:255).
18. Juan López de Velasco (in Hann 1991:312).
19. That collection has in the past erroneously been thought to have come from Punta Rassa, a location on the south side of the mouth of the Caloosa-

hatchee River (Goggin n.d.:272–278). George Luer, an archaeologist who has published extensively on Florida Gulf coastal archaeology, has ascertained that the artifacts in the University Museum came from Mound Key and were acquired for that museum by Joseph Wilcox. Wilcox purchased them from the individuals who had dug them up. The artifacts were mailed to the museum from the post office at Punta Rassa, hence the confusion. A portion of the collection was later sent to the National Museum of the American Indian (Luer 1985, 1994).

20. Goggin (n.d.:277).
21. Allerton, Luer, and Carr (1984), Luer (1985).
22. Griffin (1946).
23. Hudson (1976:135–136).
24. McGoun (1981).
25. Sears (1982), Branstetter (1989).
26. Hann (1991:237). For more information on Calusa chiefs, including succession, and other Calusa officials, see Goggin and Sturtevant (1964:188–194).
27. Solís de Merás (1964:148).
28. Hann (1991:239, 257, 266).
29. Hann (1991:198).
30. Milanich (1994:298–311).
31. Hann (1991:314).
32. The excavations are reported in Griffin et al. (1985).
33. Several ethnohistoric studies of the Tequesta are available (Goggin 1940; McNicoll 1941; Parks 1985). All of these rely heavily on the same Spanish documents, especially the sixteenth-century materials published in Zubillaga (1946). Documents containing pertinent information are translated in Hann (1991); others from the 1560s and early 1570s are in Solís de Merás (1964) and Barrientos (1965).
34. Solís de Merás (1964:210, 222, 224).
35. In Hann (1991:319).
36. For instance, Milanich (1994:140, 149, 169, 178–179, 260–262, 269, 292–297, 351, 398, 401–407).
37. Stirling (1935), Williams (1983).
38. Jaffee (1976).
39. Zubillaga (in Hann 1991:115, 283).
40. Interpretations of those documents are found in Sturtevant (1978) and Parks (1985).
41. Wheeler (1992).
42. Jaffee (1976).
43. The Belle Glade culture can be traced back to at least 500 B.C. (Sears 1982; Milanich 1994:279–298).
44. For instance, Mowers and Williams (1972).
45. Calderón (in Hann 1991:314).

46. Dickinson's extraordinary and informative account of what befell the survivors is found in Andrews and Andrews (1945).
47. Andrews and Andrews (1945:28).
48. Andrews and Andrews (1945:58).
49. Andrews and Andrews (1945:35).
50. Some of that evidence is reviewed in Milanich (1994:117, 137, 140, 149–150, 179, 192–194, 272, 407). A thorough study of black drink and its history and use among southeastern native people is *The Black Drink—A Native American Tea* (Hudson 1979).
51. Andrews and Andrews (1945:46–47).
52. An overview of the archaeology and ethnography of the native people of the Florida Keys can be found in Goggin and Sommer (1949) and Goggin (1950).
53. López de Velasco (in Hann 1991:312–313).
54. Fontaneda (in True 1945:25, 26, 31), Hann (1991:22, 200, 316).
55. Hann (1991:22, 177, 186, 191, 201).
56. Sturtevant (1978:143–144), Hann (1991:335).
57. Parks (1985:69).

Chapter 4: Native People in Central Florida

1. Hann (1989a:185).
2. Hann (1991:7; the words in brackets are Hann's).
3. Hann (1991:314).
4. Hann (1991:86–87).
5. Andrews and Andrews (1945:45).
6. The Indian River culture was defined by Irving Rouse (1951), who equated it with the Ais Indians; also see Milanich (1994:249–254).
7. Willey (1954).
8. Smith (1956:50–51). Nineteenth-century archaeologists also reported European artifacts from this locality.
9. Hann (1991:82–83).
10. Hann (1991:151).
11. Hann (1991:30, 214).
12. Hann (1991:142–156).
13. Hann (1991:147).
14. Hann (1991:144).
15. Hann (1993a:130).
16. John Hann provided this information, which is based on Spanish documents.
17. Benson (1967), Karklins (1974), and Griffin and Smith (1948).
18. Hann (1991:111).
19. Hann (1993a:111, 118).
20. Hann (1991:115).
21. Solís de Merás (1964:205).
22. Solís de Merás (1964:205).

23. See Goggin (1952), Miller (1991), and Milanich (1994:243–274).

24. Aten (1961), Purdy (1987:34).

25. Hann (1990b:487, 506–507, 1991:143).

26. Luer and Almy (1981), Luer et al. (1987), Mitchem (1989b), Milanich (1994:389–412); also see Milanich and Hudson (1993:61–70). An overview of the Tocobaga and other Tampa Bay groups is found in Bullen (1978).

27. Fontaneda (in True 1945:30, 31, 38) and French accounts from the 1560s mention a group called Mogoso, but this is not the Mocoso of the de Soto narratives. Certainly the latter do not appear in any accounts associated with the Menéndez Gulf coast initiatives of the 1560s.

28. Documents regarding the incident are in Quinn (1979) and Hann (1991:9–12).

29. Hann (1991:21, 23–26).

30. The documents are translated in Hann (1991:327, 332, 358, 361, 370).

31. Hann (1989b:193, 198).

32. Zubillaga (1946:272–277, 291–297, 303–304), Solís de Merás (1964:223–230, 242), Hann (1991).

33. Griffin and Bullen (1950), Bushnell (1966), Neill (1968), and Mitchem (1989b).

34. Hann (1991:310; the words in brackets are Hann's).

35. The account of Menéndez's visit to Tocobaga is found in Solís de Merás (1964:224–228).

36. Solís de Merás (1964:228–229, 233).

37. Cabeza de Vaca (1922).

38. Elvas (1922:23).

39. Elvas (1922:28–29).

40. Garcilaso (in Varner and Varner 1951:65).

41. Hann (1991:318); and see Worth (1995).

42. Neill (1978:224–225), Mitchem and Weisman (1987:156–158), Mitchem (1989b:48–49).

Chapter 5: Native People in Northern Florida

1. For information on Father Pareja's writings and the Timucua language, see Gatschet (1877–80), Adam and Vinson (1886), Swanton (1929), Granberry (1956, 1993), and Milanich and Sturtevant (1972).

2. Worth (1992:156–157). The Timucua-speaking Oconi should not be confused with the Muskogean-speaking Ocone, who were living on the Chattahoochee River in 1685 and moved into central Georgia to the Oconee River by 1695 (Swanton 1922:180). The Timucuan and Muskogean languages are very different.

3. Swanton (1946:193), Hann (1994b).

4. The Timucua have been the subject of numerous ethnohistorical and archaeological studies; see Swanton (1922, 1946), Ehrmann (1940), Spellman (1948), Goggin (1953), Seaberg (1955), Milanich (1972, 1978),

Deagan (1978a), Johnson and Nelson (1990), Johnson (1991), Hann (1992b), and Milanich and Hudson (1993:169–185).

   After I completed a draft of this chapter in early 1994, John Hann provided me with a draft of his new book on the Timucua. Hann's book is an excellent and thorough scholarly overview that incorporates archival materials that have been little used or not seen at all by previous scholars. In several places, Hann's new study provided information that I used to correct errors of fact or interpretation in my manuscript. Where I used his manuscript I have cited it as "Hann 1994b." When published, Hann's book will be the basic reference on the Timucua speakers, just as his books on the Calusa and the Apalachee are document-based references for those groups.

 5. Bennett (1964:66), Lawson (1992:56, 62, 65, 67, 70, 72).
 6. Mexia (n.d.), Moore (1894a, 1894b, 1896a, 1896b), Griffin and Smith (1949), Bullen and Griffin (1952), Deagan (1983), and Piatek (1992).
 7. Barrientos (in Solís de Merás 1964:159).
 8. Lawson (1992:64).
 9. True (1945:35), Lawson (1992:129).
10. Hann (1994b).
11. This is a part of a subregion that archaeologists have named the St. Marys region (see Milanich 1994:248–249).
12. Milanich (1971b).
13. Goggin (1952).
14. Johnson (1991).
15. Hann (1994b:353).
16. Lawson (1992:94).
17. Goggin (1952:55, 125).
18. Fontaneda (in True 1945:46).
19. Sleight (1949).
20. Names of other mission-period eastern groups and their villages can be found in Hann (1994b), which contains similar information for the western Timucua speakers; also see Faupel (1992b) and Milanich and Hudson (1993:196, 198–199).
21. Milanich (1971a, 1972, 1994:333–348).
22. See Johnson (1991) for a discussion of trails in north Florida.
23. The term "northern Utina" is a misnomer. Early scholars thought north Florida was the home of the eastern Timucua Utina, and the name Utina, referring to the native people of north Florida, entered the literature. To differentiate between the two I will refer to the western Timucua Utina as the northern Utina. For more on who the northern Utina were and were not, see Johnson (1991).
24. Johnson and Nelson (1990), Johnson (1991), Worth (in Weisman 1992), and Milanich (1994:348–353).
25. Mitchem et al. (1985), Mitchem (1989b), Mitchem and Hutchinson (1989).

26. The Fort Walton culture and the Leon-Jefferson assemblage are well known (Tesar 1980, 1981; Scarry 1984, 1990b, 1994; Milanich 1994:356–380). Some archaeologists have opted to call the Leon-Jefferson ceramic complex the Lamar complex, thereby associating it with the Lamar culture which is widespread in Georgia. I prefer to retain the original nomenclature (Smith 1948a; Boyd, Griffin, and Smith 1951) in order to emphasize the unique history and nature of the colonial, especially mission, period Apalachee Indians. The definitive historical study of the Apalachee Indians is John Hann's *Apalachee: The Land between the Rivers* (1988a). Recently he has published a shorter overview (Hann 1994a).

27. Lawson (1992).

28. See Hann (1988a:24–69, 353–361).

29. Hann (1988a:58, 365–370).

30. The Apalachee language is discussed in Hann (1988a:118–125).

31. Griffin (1947), Mitchem (1989a), Scarry (1990a); the Pensacola culture is described in Fuller (1985) and Milanich (1994:380–387).

32. For more information on panhandle native groups, see Swanton (1922:141–146), Boyd (1958), Gardner (1966, 1969), and Hann (1988c, 1993c).

33. John Hann and Nancy White have both suggested the Chatot as the source of Choctawhatchee Bay's name.

34. Swanton (1922:135).

35. Hann (1993c:72–73).

Part II: The Invasion

1. Chamberlain (1948:24–25).

2. Garcilaso (in Varner and Varner 1951:118).

Chapter 6: The Invasion Begins

1. For a clever and informative twist on just who discovered whom, see William Sturtevant's article "The First American Discoverers of Europe" (1993).

2. Archaeologist Kathleen Deagan has excavated in what is believed to be Guacanacaric's village on the northern coast of Haiti (Deagan 1987b, 1988, 1989).

3. Deagan and Venezuelan archaeologist José Cruxent continue to investigate the site of La Isabela (Deagan 1992; Deagan and Cruxent 1993).

4. Davis (1935), Morison (1974:499–516), and Weddle (1985:38–53).

5. Harrisse (1968:135–141).

6. In the account of Juan Ponce's landing, the latitude is given as 30°8' north. But this measurement, apparently like others recorded on the voyage, is in error. For more on faulty latitudes recorded by the expedition, see Weddle (1985:41–42), Milanich and Hudson (1993:43–45), and Hoffman (1994b:54, 56); also see below in this chapter.

7. Harrisse (1961) is a classic study of early map interpretation; also see Castañeda, Cuesta, and Hernández (1983:366).

8. Weddle (1985:95–108).

9. Davis (1935:17–18).

10. Davis (1935:18).

11. See Davis (1935:52–64) for these and other pertinent documents.

12. Oviedo (in Davis 1935:59).

13. The 1516 voyage of Miruelo was not to Apalachee Bay, as previously supposed. The preponderance of evidence at hand suggests the Bay of Miruelo is Tampa Bay. The Chaves Espejo describes the Bay of Miruelo, but the description fits Tampa Bay, not Apalachee Bay. The same rutter places the Bay of Miruelo far north of Tampa Bay at 30°40′ latitude (Castañeda, Cuesta, and Hernández 1983:366). If Miruelo sailed to Tampa Bay, naming it Bay of Miruelo, he apparently gave it a latitude much too far north of the correct location. As we have seen, this also seems to have been the case with some of the latitudes recorded by the Juan Ponce de León expedition.

   The indentification of Bahía Honda as Tampa Bay has been established by Milanich and Hudson (1993:39–48), based on the de Soto narratives and other evidence. De Soto subsequently renamed the bay Bahía de Espiritu Santo. Although Hudson and I noted that the description of the Bay of Miruelo fit Tampa Bay, we missed the equivalence of Espiritu Santo with the Bay of Miruelo spelled out by López de Velasco in the 1570s (in Hann 1991:310). In other words, Bahía de Miruelo = Espiritu Santo = Bahía Honda = Tampa Bay. Exactly which Spanish expedition awarded Tampa Bay the name Bahía Honda is uncertain. Perhaps it was done by the 1519 Pineda voyage.

14. Hoffman (1980).

15. The two Spaniards had set out independently, but joined forces after meeting in the Bahamas. The definitive studies of this and the 1525 ·xpedition are by Hoffman (1984, 1990).

16. Hoffman (1990:4, 10).

17. Hoffman (1984:419).

18. A translation of Peter Martyr's account is found in MacNutt (1912).

19. Pearson (1977), Wallace (1975).

20. Studies of the expedition and its contract include: Lyon (1976:220–223), Hoffman (1990:34–50, 60–83; 1994a), and Harrisse (1961:198–213). Hoffman's 1990 book, *A New Andalucia and a Way to the Orient,* is a masterful historical account of not only the expeditions sponsored and led by Ayllón, but other Spanish activities in the southeastern United States in the sixteenth century as well. I have relied heavily on it in my writing about the 1526 expedition.

21. Hoffman (1990:71–73).

22. Hoffman (1990:75–80).

23. I completed a draft of this section in early 1993. Late that year I learned that Paul Hoffman had written an article on the Narváez expedition that was to be published in 1994 in a book edited by Charles Hudson and Carmen Chaves Tesser. They kindly provided me with a copy of Hoffman's article, now published, (Hoffman 1994b), which I have cited here. Hoffman and I agree on the general route of the expedition in Florida, including the error in latitude found in the Chaves rutter. Our interpretations differ only in some minor aspects. His study represents the best modern historical research on the expedition and contains information previously unknown. I also am grateful to Hoffman for making me aware of the Chaves rutter (Castañeda, Cuesta, and Hernández 1983) several years ago. In my research on the Narváez expedition I used unpublished translations of two versions of Cabeza de Vaca's account provided by John Hann (1988d).

24. Cabeza de Vaca (1922:1), Lyon (1976:220–221), Weddle (1985:163, 185–207), and Hoffman (1990:58–59; 1994b).

25. Hoffman (1994b:53).

26. Cabeza de Vaca (1922).

27. Cabeza de Vaca (1922:10–11).

28. Cabeza de Vaca (1922:11–13).

29. Cabeza de Vaca (1922:191–192).

30. Castañeda, Cuesta, and Hernández (1983).

31. Cabeza de Vaca (1922:16).

32. Cabeza de Vaca (1922:18).

33. Cabeza de Vaca (1922:19).

34. Cabeza de Vaca (1922:24).

35. Garcilaso (in Varner and Varner 1951:186).

36. Cabeza de Vaca (1922:29).

37. Weddle (1985:191).

38. Cabeza de Vaca (1922:35).

39. Cabeza de Vaca (1922:40).

40. Cabeza de Vaca (1922:51).

41. Mitchem (1989a), Marrinan, Scarry, and Majors (1990), and Scarry (1990a).

42. Mitchem (1989a).

43. Griffin (1947), Marrinan, Scarry, and Majors (1990), and Scarry (1990a).

44. Weddle (1985:202).

45. Marco de Niça in Cabeza de Vaca (1922:203–231).

Chapter 7: A Tide Unchecked

1. Elvas (1922:6).

2. Elvas (1922:6–9).

3. Smith (1866).

4. Ranjel (1922:50–51).

5. See Milanich and Hudson (1993) for a recent study of the expedition in Florida. Three extant firsthand accounts of the expedition (Biedma 1922, Elvas 1922, Ranjel 1922) are available in various editions and translations (e.g., Milanich 1991, Clayton, Knight, and Moore 1993; also see Swanton 1985, Hudson 1994).

6. Ewen (1988, 1989a, 1989b, 1990), Tesar and Jones (1989), Milanich and Hudson (1993:222–226).

7. Mitchem and Weisman (1984), Mitchem (1989a).

8. Mitchem (1989b), Hutchinson (1991).

9. Hoffman (1990:69).

10. Hoffman (1990:144–150).

11. Hoffman (1990:147).

12. Hoffman (1983).

13. The Luna expedition has been the subject of a number of studies, including Priestley (1928), Weddle (1985:251–284), Curren, Little, and Holstein (1989), Hudson et al. (1989a, 1989b), and Hoffman (1990:144–202).

14. Hudson et al. (1989a:128).

15. Hoffman (1990:173–179).

Chapter 8: Colonization and First Settlement

1. Hoffman (1990:192).

2. Hoffman (1990:187–202).

3. Ribault (1964:53).

4. For information on Ribault's expedition, see Ribault (1964), Hoffman (1990:209–212), and Lawson (1992:16–45).

5. Hoffman (1990:214–215).

6. Lorant (1946), Hulton (1977).

7. McPhail (1975), Sturtevant (1977), Faupel (1992a, 1992b); also see Skelton (1977). For more information on the Le Moyne–de Bry engravings and other early images of native people in Florida and elsewhere in the Americas, see Sturtevant (1976, 1992), Feest (1988), and Milbrath (1989).

8. Hoffman (1990:215–230), Lawson (1992).

9. Lawson (1992:119).

10. Lawson (1992:60–62).

11. Lawson (1992:7, 105).

12. Lawson (1992:127–128).

13. Lawson (1992:129).

14. Lyon (1976:120, 130).

15. Lyon (1976:125).

16. Lyon (1976:128–129).

17. From the East Coast Florida Memoirs, 1837–1886 (in Long 1967:46).

18. Dau (1934:85–86).

19. Long (1967).

20. Horvath (1992), Rogers (1992).

21. Lawson (1992:17).
22. Lawson (1992:17–18).
23. At times, because they did not understand this exchange fully, the Europeans reciprocated inappropriately; see Lankford (1984).
24. Lawson (1992:88–92).
25. Lawson (1992:74–76).
26. Berdaches (a French term) were found in other American Indian societies as well. They were males who were viewed socially as being neither male or female. Consequently, such individuals could fill roles and do tasks not traditionally associated with either gender.
27. Lawson (1992:96–102).
28. Lawson (1992:105).
29. Bennett (1964:90).
30. Lawson (1992:94).
31. For information on Menéndez, see Lyon (1976, 1987, 1988).
32. Lyon (1976:213–219).
33. Lyon (1976:147–150).
34. Hann (1991:301).
35. Solís de Merás (1964:151).
36. Hann (1991:235–236).
37. For more on Santa Elena, see Lyon (1984) and South, Skowronek, and Johnson (1988).
38. Parks (1985:21–25).
39. Lyon (1988:6–7).
40. Lyon (1988:7–8).
41. Lyon (1988:9–10).
42. Hudson (1990).
43. The story of the Jesuits in sixteenth-century La Florida has been written by Jesuit scholars, who also have published important correspondence penned by priests serving in the colony (Alegre 1956, Zubillaga 1941, 1946; both of these books are in Spanish with Latin notes; also see, Vargas Ugarte 1935; Lewis and Loomie 1953).

Part III: The Aftermath

1. Lyon (1976:50, 222).

Chapter 9: The Franciscan Frontier

1. The section on the early history of the Franciscans draws on Geiger (1937).
2. Worth (in press).
3. Worth (1992:chapter 3).
4. Worth (1992:212, 283, 306).
5. Hann (1993a).
6. Geiger (1940:120); also see Larson (1978).
7. Worth (in press:appendix B); also see Hann (1994:348–352).

8. For more on this conflict, see Matter (1990).

9. Geiger (1937:255).

10. Geiger (1937:88–115), Hann (1994:296–306).

11. Milanich (1971b); also see McMurray (1973) and Dickinson (1989). John Hann, citing inferential documentary evidence, alternatively has suggested that the native pottery similar to that from Cumberland Island found at San Juan del Puerto could be from Tacatacuru Indians, who may have been the mission's original inhabitants.

12. Information on the Guale mission system can be found in a forthcoming book by John Worth (in press).

13. Goggin (1953), Deagan (1972), Johnson (1987, 1990), Weisman (1992, 1993), Hoshower (1992), Hoshower and Milanich (1993).

14. Geiger (1937:87, 147, 149–150).

15. Weisman (1992:34, 54–64, 66).

16. Geiger (1937:227–228). John Hann's forthcoming book provides a detailed history of the Spanish mission system among the eastern and western Timucua speakers (Hann 1994b:chapters 9–14).

17. Symes and Stephens (1965).

18. Milanich and Johnson (1989), Johnson (1993).

19. Worth (1992:59–60).

20. Hann (1994b:357).

21. Excavations at the Baptizing Spring site are reported in Loucks (1978, 1993). Test excavations at Indian Pond were carried out by Kenneth Johnson (1987, 1991), who recently has located the mission buildings. Identifications of the sites as the missions of San Juan and Santa Cruz were made by John Worth (1992:59).

22. Hann (1990b:473–476), Worth (1992:70–71; for a complete listing of place names in western Timucua in the first half of the seventeenth century see appendices A and B in Worth).

23. Hann (1990b:460, 469–470, 487).

24. Hann (1994a:353).

25. See Hann (1990b) for a listing of Florida missions.

26. Hann (1988a:27–30).

27. See Hann (1988a:354–355, 1990b).

28. Hann (1988a:356).

29. Hann (1991).

30. Hann (1993b:86).

31. McEwan (1992:35–36).

32. Hita Salazar (1675), Wenhold (1936), Geiger (1940:125–131).

33. For instance, Boyd (1948), Goggin (1953), Milanich (1978), Hann (1990b).

34. Boyd (1938).

35. Examples are Hann (1988d, 1994), Johnson (1991), and Worth (1992).

36. Loucks (1978, 1993).

37. Loucks (1993:213).

38. Investigations include Johnson (1986, 1991) and Johnson, Nelson, and Terry (1988).
39. Worth (1992).
40. For more on the rebellion, see Pearson (1968), Hann (1986d), and Worth (1992). The southern trail, referred to here as the mission road, must have been in operation soon after the rebellion, though John Hann has pointed out that documentary evidence for its existence before 1675 has not yet been found.
41. Worth (1992:298).
42. A detailed discussion of the restructuring of Timucua province after the rebellion can be found in Worth (1992:288–315).

Chapter 10: Life in the Mission Provinces

1. Dobyns (1983:10).
2. Geiger (1937:82–86).
3. John Worth (1994) recently has published important new information on the location of Tama.
4. Milanich and Hudson (1993:170–186).
5. Geiger (1937:227–228).
6. Hann (1986d:90–91).
7. Geiger (1940:121).
8. Hann (1986a:104–105; 1988a:29–30, 354–355).
9. Though, as previously noted, this might have been because non-Apalachee Indians were moved to new missions in the province. See Hann (1988a:160–174) for an overview of Apalachee Indian demography during the period of the missions.
10. I am grateful to Bruce Chapell, archivist at the University of Florida's P.K. Yonge Library of Florida History, for providing this translation; also see Milanich and Saunders (1986:2–4)
11. Bushnell (1986:10–11), Saunders (1993).
12. Thomas (1987, 1993).
13. Saunders (1990).
14. Weisman (1992, 1993), Hoshower and Milanich (1993).
15. See Arnade (1959:14–15) regarding the destruction of Santa Catalina on Amelia Island by raiders who burned it with flaming arrows.
16. Boyd, Smith, and Griffin (1951:125), Shapiro, Vernon, and Poe (in Shapiro 1987:176).
17. Hann (1993b).
18. Hann (1991:113). John Hann has suggested that the request for augers may reflect a change in carpentry techniques, from the use of spikes and nails to the use of pin and tenon construction.
19. Saunders (1993).
20. Hann (1993b, 1994b).
21. Weisman (1992).
22. Weisman (1992:figures 24–25).

23. Hann (1986a).
24. Hann (1986a:153–154).
25. Geiger (1937:255).
26. Arnade (1959:14–15).
27. Hann (1986a:156).
28. For instance, Jones (1970, 1971, 1972b), Milanich and Saunders (1986), Jones, Hann, and Scarry (1991), Weisman (1992:73), and Hoshower and Milanich (1993). See Larsen (1993) for an overview of the bioarchaeology of mission populations.
29. Saunders (1993).
30. The mission of San Martín at Fig Springs is an exception. Excavations have shown that its Spanish buildings and associated burials are only three degrees east of true north (Weisman 1992; Hoshower and Milanich 1993).
31. Geiger (1937:254).
32. Hann (1994b:293–95).
33. Geiger (1937:78–79, 82–83).
34. Hann (1988a:134; 1989b:19).
35. Bushnell (1989).
36. Pearson (1968), Hann (1986d, 1993c).
37. Hann (1988a:99).
38. Geiger (1937:80–81, 187).
39. Hann (1994b:290).
40. Hann (1994b:368–369).
41. Geiger (1937:29, 148, 254, 259).
42. Oré (1936:104–105), Geiger (1937:29, 254).
43. Hann (1994b:321).
44. Hann (1986a:154).
45. Reports on botanical remains found in archaeological excavations at mission sites include Ruhl (1990, 1993), Newsom and Quitmyer (in Weisman 1992), and Scarry (1993).
46. Hann (1994b).
47. Vernon and Cordell (1993).
48. Lyon (1992:14).
49. During the colonial period, hybridization of the native, precolumbian corn species took place, resulting in a steady increase in the size of cobs and number of kernels (Kohler 1979). Most likely the hybridization occurred when new types of corn were brought to Florida by the Spanish.
50. Hann (1991:111).
51. For instance, Weisman (1992:143, 145).
52. Reitz (1990, 1993).
53. Hann (1988b).
54. Loucks (1978), Weisman (1992).
55. Geiger (1937:29–30).
56. Geiger (1937:30).
57. Milanich and Sturtevant (1972:25).

58. Oré (1936:114–115).
59. Bushnell (1978a), Hann (1988a:73–95, 328–353; 1993c).
60. Geiger (1937:90).
61. Bushnell (1989), Hann (1988a:126–159), Worth (1992).
62. Hann (1988a:89; 1993c).
63. Bushnell (1981:23).
64. Hann (1993c:89).
65. Hann (1988a:59); excavations in the fort are reported in McEwan and Poe (1994).
66. Worth (1992:140–146).
67. For instance, Hann (1986d:89; 1988a:136).
68. Hann (1993c).
69. Hann (1993c). For more on trade between Florida native people and the Spaniards, see Covington (1959), who notes that items traded by Florida Indians to Cuba included cardinal birds.
70. Hann (1993c).
71. Boniface (1971), Hann (1988a), Worth (1992:99–115).
72. Bushnell (1978b), Worth (1992:100–106).
73. Baker (1993).
74. Worth (1992:105).
75. Bushnell (1981:132–133).
76. Worth (1992:103).
77. Bushnell (1978b:424).
78. Bushnell (1978b:428–429).
79. Worth (1992:106–113).
80. Goggin (1953).
81. Bushnell (1981:81).
82. Bushnell (1978b:427). John Worth pointed out that in Spanish *chicharro* means "beans," an apt name for a ranch.
83. Hann (1994b:377).
84. More about the ranches is found in Hann (1994b:375–391).
85. Arnade (1965), Boniface (1971).
86. Arnade (1965:9), McEwan (1991:38), Hann (1988a:53–54, 133).
87. Bushnell (1981:14).
88. Hann (1988a:53, 59).
89. Boniface (1971:200–201).
90. McEwan (1991:55).

Chapter 11: The End of Time

1. Hutchinson (1991).
2. Weisman (1992:124–140), Worth (in Weisman 1992:171–178).
3. Seaberg (1955).
4. Hann (1988a:22–23).
5. Hann (1986d:111).
6. Hann (1988a:23).

7. Hann (1988a:175–180; 1994:288, 347, 398–399); also see Worth (1992:163–170).
8. Hann (1988a:175).
9. Pareja (in Hann 1994b:347).
10. Hann (1994b:398–399).
11. Worth (1992:163–170, 179).
12. Hann (1994b:347–348).
13. Hann (1994b:485–486).
14. A growing literature on this subject exists. For instance, see the articles in Bray (1993). A major figure in the debate is anthropologist Henry Dobyns (1983, 1993a, 1993b), whose publications have stimulated research by archaeologists (e.g., Ramenofsky 1987), as well as historians and historical demographers.
15. Dobyns (1983, 1993b).
16. Worth (1992:179).
17. Hann (1994b:313).
18. Hann (1990b:460). In a few instances native people from Mexico also were brought to Florida to work on Spanish ranches. John Worth (1992) presents examples of the latter as well as a discussion of the likelihood of intra-Timucua migration and possible relationships to ceramic change. Worth notes that Santa María de Arapaha was most likely just north of the present-day Florida-Georgia border.
19. Hann (1988a).
20. The size and number of archaeological sites in the Apalachee region supports the contention that the population of the Apalachee Indians declined between ca. 1500 and the time of the Spanish missions (Smith and Scarry 1988).
21. See Bolton and Ross (1925), Boyd, Smith, and Griffin (1951), and Arnade (1959).
22. Hann (1994b:506–509), Worth (in press).
23. The castillo's construction is the focus of a monograph by Arana and Manucy (1977).
24. Arnade (1959:1).
25. The presence of Yamasee Indians at the missions has been documented by Hann (1987), Thomas (1987:56–57), Gannon (1965:71–72), and Worth (in press); archaeological evidence from Cumberland and Amelia islands is presented in Milanich (1971b) and Saunders (1987, 1993).
26. Boyd, Smith, and Griffin (1951:8, 11), Gannon (1965:72), Covington (1967), Hann (1994b).
27. Boyd, Smith, and Griffin (1951:11–12, 36–37).
28. Boyd, Smith, and Griffin (1951:37).
29. Arnade (1959), Bushnell (1986).
30. Archaeological investigations of that mission have been reported by Hardin (1986), Milanich and Saunders (1986), and Saunders (1987, 1993). Several sites corresponding to contemporary villages and missions

also have been identified (Bullen and Griffin 1952; Hemmings and Deagan 1973).

31. Arnade (1959) has detailed the attack.
32. The raids on Apalachee have been the focus of a number of studies, including Boyd, Smith, and Griffin (1951), Jones (1972a), and Hann (1988a).
33. In an ironic twist, the destruction of the Apalachee missions by burning preserved much of the evidence of their existence. From their charred remains archaeologists, acting like arson investigators, have reconstructed a great deal of information about mission architecture and life. See Smith (1948b), Jones (1970, 1971, 1972b), Morrell and Jones (1970), Jones and Shapiro (1990), Jones, Hann, and Scarry (1991), Marrinan (1993), and McEwan (1991, 1993).
34. Covington (1967:13).
35. Hann (1991:46).
36. Covington (1968, 1970), Hann (1989a).
37. Covington (1970).
38. Hann (1989a).
39. Hann (1994b:569–592).
40. Kapitzke (1993:4).
41. Hann (1994b:592).
42. The story of that mission is told in Sturtevant (1978), Parks (1985), and Hann (1991)
43. Parks (1985:56).
44. Covington (1959), Hammond (1973); also see Sturtevant (1978).
45. Neill (1968), Luer (1989b, 1991).
46. Covington (1964), Hunter (1994).

 **REFERENCES**

The following abbreviations are used in the references:

AHRM   Division of Archives, History and Records Management, Florida Department of State, Tallahassee

BAE   Bureau of American Ethnology, Smithsonian Institution, Washington, D.C.

BAR   Bureau of Archaeological Research, Division of Historical Resources, Florida Department of State, Tallahassee

BHSP   Bureau of Historic Sites and Properties, Division of Archives, History and Records Management, Florida Department of State, Tallahassee

DA   Department of Anthropology, Florida Museum of Natural History, Gainesville (formerly Florida State Museum)

FMNH   Florida Museum of Natural History, Gainesville

FSU   Department of Anthropology, Florida State University, Tallahassee

SEAC   Southeast Archaeological Center, National Park Service, Tallahassee

UWFIA   Institute of Archaeology, University of West Florida, Pensacola (formerly Office of Cultural and Archaeological Research)

Adam, Lucien, and Julien Vinson, eds.
   1886   *Arte de la Lengua Timuquana, Compuesto por El P. Francisco Pareja.* Bibliotheque Linguistique Américaine 11. Paris.

Alegre, Francisco Javier
   1956   *Historia de la Compañia de Jesus en Nueva España.* Vol. 1. Bibliotheca Instituti Historici S.J., vol. 9. Rome: Institutum Historicum S.J. (Original edition 1842).

Allerton, David, George M. Luer, and Robert S. Carr
  1984   Ceremonial Tablets and Related Objects from Florida. *Florida Anthropologist* 37:5–54.
Andrews, E., and C. Andrews, eds.
  1945   *Jonathan Dickinson's Journal; or God's Protecting Providence.* New Haven, Conn.: Yale University Press.
Arana, Luis, and Albert Manucy
  1977   *The Building of the Castillo de San Marcos.* Eastern National Park and Monument Association.
Arnade, Charles
  1959   *The Siege of St. Augustine in 1702.* Gainesville: University of Florida Press.
  1965   Cattle Raising in Spanish Florida: 1513–1763. *St. Augustine Historical Society Publication* 21:1–11.
Aten, Lawrence E.
  1961   Excavation and Salvage at Starks Hammock, Volusia County, Florida. *Florida Anthropologist* 14:37–45.
Axtell, James
  1985   *The Invasion Within: The Conquest of Cultures in Colonial North America.* New York: Oxford University Press.
Baker, Henry A.
  1993   Spanish Ranching and the Alachua Sink Site: A Preliminary Report. *Florida Anthropologist* 46:82–100.
Barrientos, Bartolomé
  1965   *Pedro Menéndez de Avilés, Founder of Florida.* Translated by Anthony Kerrigan. Gainesville: University of Florida Press.
Bennett, Charles
  1964   *Laudonnière and Fort Caroline.* Gainesville: University of Florida Press.
Benson, Carl A.
  1967   The Philip Mound: A Historic Site. *Florida Anthropologist* 20:118–132.
Biedma, Luys Hernández de
  1922   Relation of the Conquest of Florida. In *Narratives of the Career of Hernando de Soto in the Conquest of Florida,* vol. 2, edited by Edward G. Bourne, pp. 1–40. New York: Allerton.
Bolton, Herbert E., and Mary Ross
  1925   *The Debatable Land.* Berkeley: University of California Press.
Boniface, Brian
  1971   A Historical Geography of Spanish Florida, circa 1700. Master's thesis, University of Georgia, Athens.
Boyd, Mark F.
  1938   Map of the Road from Pensacola to St. Augustine, 1778. *Florida Historical Quarterly* 17:1–23.

1948   Enumeration of Florida Spanish Missions in 1675. *Florida Historical Quarterly* 24:181–188.

1958   *Historic Sites in and around the Jim Woodruff Reservoir Area, Florida-Georgia.* Bulletin 169, River Basin Survey Papers 14. BAE.

Boyd, Mark F., Hale G. Smith, and John W. Griffin

1951   *Here They Once Stood: The Tragic End of the Apalachee Missions.* Gainesville: University of Florida Press.

Branstetter, Laura

1989   Research on the Tallant Collection: Final Report. Undergraduate honors thesis, University of South Florida, New College, Sarasota.

Bray, Warwick, ed.

1993   *The Meeting of Two Worlds: Europe and the Americas, 1492–1650.* Proceedings of the British Academy, no. 81. Oxford: Oxford University Press.

Bullen, Ripley P.

1978   Tocobaga Indians and the Safety Harbor Culture. In *Tacachale, Essays on the Indians of Florida and Southeast Georgia during the Historic Period,* edited by Jerald T. Milanich and Samuel Proctor, pp. 50–58. Gainesville: University Presses of Florida.

Bullen, Ripley P., and John W. Griffin

1952   An Archaeological Survey of Amelia Island, Florida. *Florida Anthropologist* 5:37–64.

Bushnell, Amy Turner

1978a   That Demonic Game: The Campaign to Stop Indian Pelota Playing in Spanish Florida, 1675–1684. *The Americas* 35:1–19.

1978b   The Menéndez-Marquez Cattle Barony at La Chua and the Determinants of Economic Expansion in 17th Century Florida. *Florida Historical Quarterly* 56:407–431.

1981   *The King's Coffer: Proprietors of the Royal Treasury, 1565–1702.* Gainesville: University Presses of Florida.

1986   *Santa María in the Written Record.* Miscellaneous Project Report 21. DA.

1989   Ruling "The Republic of Indians" in Seventeenth-Century Florida. In *Powhatan's Mantle, Indians in the Colonial Southeast,* edited by Peter H. Wood, Gregory A. Waselkov, and M. Thomas Hatley, pp. 134–150. Lincoln: University of Nebraska Press.

Bushnell, Frank

1966   A Preliminary Excavation of the Narváez Midden, St. Petersburg, Florida. *Florida Anthropologist* 19:115–124.

Cabeza de Vaca, Alvar Núñez

1922   *The Journey of Alvar Núñez Cabeza de Vaca and His Companions from Florida to the Pacific, 1528–1536.* Edited by Adolph F. Bandelier, translated by Fanny Bandelier. New York: Allerton.

Castañeda, Paulino, Mariano Cuesta, and Pilar Hernández
   1983   *Transcripción, Estudio y Notas del "Espejo de Navegantes" de Alonso
            Chaves*. Madrid: Instituto de Historia y Cultura Naval.
Chamberlain, Robert S.
   1948   *The Conquest and Colonization of Yucatan, 1517–1550*. Carnegie Institu-
            tion of Washington Publication no. 582. Washington, D.C. Carnegie
            Institution.
Clayton, Lawrence A., Vernon James Knight Jr., and Edward C.
Moore, eds.
   1993   *The De Soto Chronicles: The Expedition of Hernando de Soto to North
            America in 1539–1543*. 2 vols. Tuscaloosa: University of Alabama
            Press.
Connolly, Bob, and Robin Anderson
   1987   *First Contact: New Guinea's Highlanders Encounter the Outside World*.
            New York: Penguin Books.
Covington, James W.
   1959   Trade Relations between Southwestern Florida and Cuba—
            1600–1840. *Florida Historical Quarterly* 38:114–128.
   1964   The Apalachee Indians Move West. *Florida Anthropologist*
            17:221–225.
   1967   Some Observations Concerning the Florida-Carolina Indian Slave
            Trade. *Florida Anthropologist* 20:10–18.
   1968   Stuart's Town, the Yamasee Indians and Spanish Florida. *Florida
            Anthropologist* 21:8–13.
   1970   The Yamasee Indians in Florida: 1715–1763. *Florida Anthropologist*
            23:119–128.
Curren, Caleb, Keith J. Little, and Harry O. Holstein
   1989   Aboriginal Societies Encountered by the Tristán de Luna Expedi-
            tion. *Florida Anthropologist* 42:381–395.
Cushing, Frank H.
   1897   Exploration of Ancient Key-dweller Remains on the Gulf Coast of
            Florida. *Proceedings of the American Philosophical Society*
            25(153):329–448.
Dau, Frederick
   1934   *Florida Old and New*. New York: G.P. Putnam's Sons.
Davis, T. Frederick
   1935   Juan Ponce de Leon's Voyages to Florida. *Florida Historical Quarterly*
            14:5–70.
Deagan, Kathleen A.
   1972   Fig Springs: The Mid-Seventeenth Century in North-Central
            Florida. *Historical Archaeology* 6:23–46.
   1977   The Search for Sixteenth Century St. Augustine. *Conference on His-
            toric Sites Archaeology Papers* 12:266–285.
   1978a   Cultures in Transition: Fusion and Assimilation among the Eastern
            Timucua. In *Tacachale, Essays on the Indians of Florida and Southeastern*

Georgia during the Historic Period, edited by Jerald T. Milanich and Samuel Proctor, pp. 88–119. Gainesville: University Presses of Florida.

1978b   The Material Assemblage of Sixteenth Century Spanish Florida. *Historical Archaeology* 12:25–50.

1981   Downtown Survey: The Discovery of 16th Century St. Augustine in an Urban Area. *American Antiquity* 46(3):626–633.

1983   *Spanish St. Augustine: The Archaeology of a Colonial Creole Community.* New York: Academic Press.

1985   The Archaeology of Sixteenth Century St. Augustine. *Florida Anthropologist* 38:6–34.

1987a   *Artifacts of the Spanish Colonies of Florida and the Caribbean, 1500–1800.* Vol. 1, *Ceramics, Glassware, and Beads.* Washington, D.C.: Smithsonian Institution Press.

1987b   Searching for Columbus's Lost Colony. *National Geographic* 172(5):672–675.

1988   The Archaeology of the Spanish Contact Period in the Circum-Caribbean Region. *Journal of World Prehistory* 2:187–233.

1989   The Search for La Navidad, Columbus's 1492 Settlement. In *First Encounters, Spanish Explorations in the Caribbean and the United States, 1492–1570,* edited by Jerald T. Milanich and Susan Milbrath, pp. 41–54. Gainesville: University of Florida Press/FMNH.

1992   La Isabela, Foothold in the New World. *National Geographic* 181(1):40–53.

1993   St. Augustine and the Mission Frontier. In *Spanish Missions of La Florida,* edited by Bonnie G. McEwan, pp. 87–110. Gainesville: University Press of Florida.

Deagan, Kathleen, and José M. Cruxent

1993   From Contact to *Criollos:* The Archaeology of Spanish Colonization in Hispaniola. In *The Meeting of Two Worlds, Europe and the Americas, 1492–1650,* edited by Warwick Bray, pp. 67–104. Proceedings of the British Academy, no. 81. Oxford: Oxford University Press.

DeBry, Theodor

1591   *Brevis narratio eorum quae in Florida Americae Provincia.* Frankfurt.

Dickinson, Martin F.

1989   Delineating a Site through Limited Research: The Mission of San Juan del Puerto (8Du53), Fort George Island, Florida. *Florida Anthropologist* 42:396–409.

Dobyns, Henry F.

1983   *Their Number Become Thinned: Native Population Dynamics in Eastern North America.* Knoxville: University of Tennessee Press.

1993a   Debate: Building Stones and Paper from Native American Historical Numbers. *Latin American Population History Bulletin* 24:11–19.

1993b   Disease Transfer at Contact. *Annual Review of Anthropology* 22:273–291.

Ehrmann, W. W.
    1940   The Timucuan Indians of 16th Century Florida. *Florida Historical Quarterly* 18:168–191.

Elvas (Gentleman of Elvas)
    1922   True Relation. In *Narratives of the Career of Hernando de Soto in the Conquest of Florida,* vol. 1, edited by Edward G. Bourne, pp. 1–222. New York: Allerton.

Ewen, Charles R.
    1988   *The Discovery of de Soto's First Winter Encampment in Florida.* De Soto Working Paper 7. Alabama De Soto Commission, University of Alabama, State Museum of Natural History. Tuscaloosa.

    1989a   Anhaica: Discovery of Hernando de Soto's 1539–1540 Winter Camp. In *First Encounters, Spanish Explorations in the Caribbean and the United States, 1492–1570,* edited by Jerald T. Milanich and Susan Milbrath, pp. 110–118. Gainesville: University of Florida Press/FMNH.

    1989b   The De Soto Apalachee Project: The Martin Site and Beyond. *Florida Anthropologist* 42:361–368.

    1990   Soldier of Fortune: Hernando de Soto in the Territory of the Apalachee, 1539–1540. In *Columbian Consequences.* Vol. 2, *Archaeological and Historical Perspectives on the Spanish Borderlands East,* edited by David Hurst Thomas, pp. 83–92. Washington D.C.: Smithsonian Institution Press.

Fairbanks, Charles H.
    1968a   Early Spanish Colonial Beads. *Conference on Historic Site Archaeology Papers* 2:3–21.

    1968b   Florida Coin Beads. *Florida Anthropologist* 21:102–105.

Faupel, W. John
    1992a   An Appraisal of the Illustrations. In *A Foothold in Florida: The Eye-Witness Account of Four Voyages made by the French to that Region,* by Sarah Lawson and W. John Faupel, pp. 150–178. East Grinstead, West Sussex, England: Antique Atlas Publications.

    1992b   An Appraisal of the Map *Floridae Americae Provincia.* In *A Foothold in Florida: The Eye-Witness Account of Four Voyages made by the French to that Region,* by Sarah Lawson and W. John Faupel, pp. 193–206. East Grinstead, West Sussex, England: Antique Atlas Publications.

Feest, Christian F.
    1988   Jacques Le Moyne Minus Four. *European Review of Native American Studies* 1(1):33–38.

Fuller, Richard S.
    1985   The Bear Point Phase of the Pensacola Variant: The Protohistoric Period in Southwest Alabama. *Florida Anthropologist* 38:150–155.

Gannon, Michael V.
    1965   *The Cross in the Sand: The Early Catholic Church in Florida, 1513–1870.* Gainesville: University of Florida Press.

Gardner, William M.

1966   The Waddells Mill Pond Site. *Florida Anthropologist* 19:43–64.

1969   An Example of the Association of Archaeological Complexes with Tribal and Linguistic Grouping: The Fort Walton Complex of Northwest Florida. *Florida Anthropologist* 22:1–11.

Gatschet, Albert S.

1877–80   The Timucuan Language. *Proceedings of the American Philosophical Society* 16:625–642, 17:490–504, 18:465–502.

Geiger, Maynard

1937   *The Franciscan Conquest of Florida, 1573–1618.* Washington, D.C.: Catholic University of America Press.

1940   *Biographical Dictionary of the Franciscans in Spanish Florida and Cuba (1528–1841).* Franciscan Studies 21. Paterson, N.J.: St. Anthony's Guild Press.

Gilliland, Marion S.

1975   *The Material Culture of Key Marco, Florida.* Gainesville: University Press of Florida.

1989   *Key Marco's Buried Treasure: Archaeology and Adventure in the Nineteenth Century.* Gainesville: University Presses of Florida.

Goggin, John M.

n.d.   The Archaeology of the Glades Area, Southern Florida. [Written about 1949, with additions in subsequent years into the 1950s.] Manuscript. On file, DA.

1940   The Tekesta Indians of Southern Florida. *Florida Historical Quarterly* 18:274–284.

1949   Cultural Occupation at Goodland Point, Florida. *Florida Anthropologist* 2(3–4):65–90.

1950   The Indians and History of the Matecumbe Region. *Tequesta* 10:13–24.

1952   *Space and Time Perspectives in Northern St. Johns Archaeology, Florida.* Yale University Publications in Anthropology, no. 47. New Haven: Yale University Press.

1953   An Introductory Outline of Timucuan Archaeology. *Southeastern Archaeological Conference Newsletter* 3(3):4–17.

1954   Historic Metal Plummet Pendants. *Florida Anthropologist* 7:27.

1960   The *Spanish Olive Jar: An Introductory Study.* Yale University Publications in Anthropology, no. 62. New Haven: Yale University Press.

1968   *Spanish Majolica in the New World.* Yale University Publications in Anthropology, no. 72. New Haven: Yale University Press.

Goggin, John M., and Frank H. Sommer III

1949   *Excavations on Upper Matecumbe Key, Florida.* Yale University Publications in Anthropology, no. 41. New Haven: Yale University Press.

Goggin, John M., and William C. Sturtevant

1964   The Calusa: A Stratified Nonagricultural Society (with Notes on Sibling Marriage). In *Explorations in Cultural Anthropology: Essays in*

Honor of George Peter Murdock, edited by Ward H. Goodenough, pp. 179–219. New York: McGraw-Hill.

Granberry, Julian

    1956   Timucua I: Prosodics and Phonemics of the Mocama Dialect. *International Journal of American Linguistics* 22:97–105.

    1993   *A Grammar and Dictionary of the Timucua Language.* Tuscaloosa: University of Alabama Press.

Griffin, John W.

    1946   Historic Artifacts and the "Buzzard Cult" in Florida. *Florida Historical Quarterly* 24:295–301.

    1947   Comments on a Site in the St. Marks National Wildlife Refuge, Wakulla County, Florida. *American Antiquity* 13:182–183.

    1949   The Historic Archaeology of Florida. In *The Florida Indian and His Neighbors,* edited by John W. Griffin, pp. 45–54. Winter Park, Florida: Rollins College Inter-American Center.

Griffin, John W., and Ripley P. Bullen

    1950   *The Safety Harbor Site, Pinellas County, Florida.* Florida Anthropological Society Publications no. 2. Gainesville: Florida Anthropological Society.

Griffin, John W., and Albert Manucy

    1962   The Development of Housing in Saint Augustine to 1783. In *Evolution of the Oldest House.* Notes in Anthropology 7, pp. 3–19. FSU.

Griffin, John W., Sue B. Richardson, Mary Pohl, Carl D. McMurray, C. Margaret Scarry, Suzanne K. Fish, Elizabeth S. Wing, L. Jill Loucks, and Marcia K. Welch

    1985   *Excavations at the Granada Site. Archaeology and History of the Granada Site.* Vol 1. AHRM.

Griffin, John W., and Hale G. Smith

    1948   *The Goodnow Mound, Highlands County, Florida.* Contributions to the Archaeology of Florida, no. 1. Tallahassee: Florida Board of Forestry and Parks, Florida Park Service.

    1949   Nocoroco, a Timucuan Village of 1605 Now in Tomoka State Park. *Florida Historical Quarterly* 27:340–361.

Hammond, E. A.

    1973   Spanish Fisheries of Charlotte Harbor. *Florida Historical Quarterly* 51:355–380.

Hann, John H.

    1986a   Church Furnishings, Sacred Vessels and Vestments Held by the Missions of Florida: Translation of Two Inventories. *Florida Archaeology* 2:147–164. BAR.

    1986b   Demographic Patterns and Changes in Mid-Seventeenth Century Timucua and Apalachee. *Florida Historical Quarterly* 64:371–392.

    1986c   Translation of Alonso de Leturiondo's Memorial to the King of Spain. *Florida Archaeology* 2:165–225. BAR.

1986d   Translation of Governor Rebolledo's 1657 Visitation of Three Florida Provinces and Related Documents. *Florida Archaeology* 2:81–145. BAR.

1987   Twilight of the Mocamo and Guale Aborigines as Portrayed in the 1695 Spanish Visitation. *Florida Historical Quarterly* 66:1–24.

1988a   *Apalachee: The Land between the Rivers.* Gainesville: University of Florida Press/FMNH.

1988b   Apalachee Counterfeiters in St. Augustine. *Florida Historical Quarterly* 67:53–88.

1988c   Florida's Terra Incognita: West Florida's Natives in the Sixteenth and Seventeenth Century. *Florida Anthropologist* 41:61–107.

1988d   Translation of the Florida Section of the Alvar Núñez Cabeza de Vaca Accounts of the 1528 Trek from South Florida to Apalachee Led by Pánfilo de Narváez. Manuscript. On file, BAR.

1989a   St. Augustine's Fallout from the Yamassee War. *Florida Historical Quarterly* 68:180–200.

1989b   Western Timucua and Its Missions. Manuscript. On file, BAR.

1990a   De Soto, Dobyns, and Demography in Western Timucua. *Florida Anthropologist* 43:3–12.

1990b   Summary Guide to Spanish Florida Missions and Visitas with Churches in the Sixteenth and Seventeenth Centuries. *The Americas* 46:417–513.

1991   *Missions to the Calusa.* Gainesville: University of Florida Press/FMNH.

1992a   Heathen Acuera, Murder, and a Potano *Cimarrona:* The St. Johns River and the Alachua Prairie in the 1670s. *Florida Historical Quarterly* 70:451–474.

1992b   Political Leadership among the Natives of Spanish Florida. *Florida Historical Quarterly* 71:188–208.

1993a   The Mayaca and Jororo and Missions to Them. In *Spanish Missions of La Florida,* edited by Bonnie G. McEwan, pp. 111–140. Gainesville: University Press of Florida.

1993b   1630 Memorial of Fray Francisco Alonso de Jesus on Spanish Florida's Missions and Natives. *The Americas* 50:85–105.

1993c   Visitations and Revolts in Florida, 1656–1695. *Florida Archaeology* 7:1–296. BAR.

1994a   The Apalachee of the Historic Era. In *The Forgotten Centuries, Indians and Europeans in the American South, 1521–1704,* pp. 327–354. Athens: University of Georgia Press.

1994b   Land of the Timucua Speakers [tentative title]. Gainesville: University Press of Florida. In press.

Hardin, Kenneth W.

1986   The Santa María Mission Project. *Florida Anthropologist* 39:75–83.

Harrisse, Henry

  1961   *The Discovery of North America: A Critical, Documentary, and Historical Investigation*. Amsterdam: N. Israel (Publishing Department). [Originally published 1892, London.]

  1968   *John Cabot, Discoverer of North America, and his Son*. New York: Argosy-Antiquarian Ltd. [Originally published in English 1896, London.]

Hemmings, E. Thomas, and Kathleen A. Deagan

  1973   *Excavations on Amelia Island in Northeast Florida*. Contributions of the Florida State Museum, Anthropology and History, no. 18. Gainesville.

Herrera y Tortesilla, Antonio de

  1601   *Historia General de los Hechos de los Castellanos en las Islas y Tierra Firme del Mar Oceano*. Madrid.

Hita Salazar, Pablo de

  1675   [Letter to the Spanish Crown. St. Augustine, August 24, 1675.] Archivo General de Indias, Santo Domingo 839. Photostat in the Stetson Collection, P. K. Yonge Library of Florida History, University of Florida, Gainesville.

Hoffman, Paul E.

  1980   A New Voyage of North American Discovery: The Voyage of Pedro de Salazar to the Island of Giants. *Florida Historical Quarterly* 58:415–426.

  1983   Legend, Religious Idealism, and Colonies: The Point of Santa Elena in History, 1552–1566. *South Carolina Magazine of History* 84:59–71.

  1984   The Chicora Legend and Franco-Spanish Rivalry. *Florida Historical Quarterly* 62:419–438.

  1990   *A New Andalucia and a Way to the Orient: The American Southeast during the Sixteenth Century*. Baton Rouge: Louisiana State University Press.

  1994a   Lucas Vázquez de Ayllón's Discovery and Colony. In *The Forgotten Centuries: Indians and Europeans in the American South, 1521–1704*, edited by Charles Hudson and Carmen Chaves Tesser, pp. 36–49. Athens: University of Georgia Press.

  1994b   Narváez and Cabeza de Vaca in Florida. In *The Forgotten Centuries: Indians and Europeans in the American South, 1521–1704*, edited by Charles Hudson and Carmen Chaves Tesser, pp. 50–73. Athens: University of Georgia Press.

Horvath, Elizabeth A.

  1992   Archeological Investigations at the Armstrong Site: A Preliminary Report on a Possible Ribault Fleet Survivor's Camp. Paper presented at the Society for Historical Archaeology Conference on Historical and Underwater Archaeology, Kingston, Jamaica.

Hoshower, Lisa M.

  1992   Bioanthropological Analysis of a Seventeenth Century Native American–Spanish Mission Population: Biocultural Impacts on the Northern Utina. Ph.D. diss., University of Florida, Gainesville.

Hoshower, Lisa M., and Jerald T. Milanich

1993 Excavations in the Fig Springs Mission Burial Area. In *Spanish Missions of La Florida,* edited by Bonnie G. McEwan, pp. 217–243. Gainesville: University Press of Florida.

Hudson, Charles

1976 *The Southeastern Indians.* Knoxville: University of Tennessee Press.

1990 *The Juan Pardo Expeditions: Spanish Explorers and the Indians of the Carolinas and Tennessee, 1566–1568.* Washington, D.C.: Smithsonian Institution Press.

1994 The Hernando de Soto Expedition, 1539–1543. In *The Forgotten Centuries: Indians and Europeans in the American South, 1521–1704,* edited by Charles Hudson and Carmen Chaves Tesser, pp. 74–103. Athens: University of Georgia Press.

Hudson, Charles, ed.

1979 *The Black Drink—A Native American Tea.* Athens: University of Georgia Press.

Hudson, Charles, Marvin T. Smith, Chester B. DePratter, and
Emilia Kelley

1989a The Tristán de Luna Expedition, 1559–1561. In *First Encounters, Spanish Explorations in the Caribbean and the United States, 1492–1570,* edited by Jerald T. Milanich and Susan Milbrath, pp. 119–134, Gainesville: University of Florida Press/FMNH.

1989b The Tristán de Luna Expedition, 1559–1561. *Southeastern Archaeology* 8:31–45.

Hulton, Paul

1977 *The Work of Jacques Le Moyne de Morgues, a Huguenot Artist in France, Florida and England.* 2 vols. London: British Museum Publications Ltd.

Hunter, Donald G.

1994 Their Final Years: The Apalachee and other Immigrant Tribes on the Red River, 1763–1834. *Florida Anthropologist* 47:3–46.

Hutchinson, Dale L.

1991 Post-contact Native American Health and Adaptation: Assessing the Impact of Introduced Disease in Sixteenth-Century Gulf Coast Florida. Ph.D. diss., University of Illinois, Urbana.

Jaffee, Howard

1976 Preliminary Report on a Midden Mound and Burial Mound of the Boynton Mound Complex (8PB56). *Florida Anthropologist* 29:145–152.

Jennings, Francis

1975 *The Invasion of America: Indians, Colonialism, and the Cant of Conquest.* Chapel Hill: University of North Carolina Press.

Johnson, Kenneth W.

1986 *Archaeological Survey of Contact and Mission Period Sites in Northern Peninsular Florida.* Miscellaneous Project Report 37. DA.

1987   *The Search for Aguacaleyquen and Cali.* Miscellaneous Project Report 33. DA.

1990   The Discovery of a Seventeenth Century Spanish Mission in Ichetucknee State Park, 1986. *Florida Journal of Anthropology* 15:39–46.

1991   The Utina and the Potano Peoples of Northern Florida: Changing Settlement Systems in the Spanish Colonial Period. Ph.D. diss., University of Florida, Gainesville.

1993   Mission Santa Fé de Toloca. In *Spanish Missions of La Florida,* edited by Bonnie G. McEwan, pp. 141–164. Gainesville: University Press of Florida.

Johnson, Kenneth W., and Bruce C. Nelson

1990   The Utina: Seriations and Chronology. *Florida Anthropologist* 43:48–62.

Johnson, Kenneth W., Bruce C. Nelson, and Keith A. Terry

1988   *The Search for Aguacaleyquen and Cali, Season 2.* Miscellaneous Project Report 38. DA.

Jones, B. Calvin

1970   Missions Reveal State's Spanish-Indian Heritage. *Archives and History News* 1(2):1–3. AHRM.

1971   State Archaeologists Unearth Spanish Mission Ruins. *Archives and History News* 2(4):2. AHRM.

1972a   Colonel James Moore and the Destruction of the Apalachee Missions in 1704. *Florida Bureau of Historic Sites and Properties Bulletin* 2:25–33.

1972b   Spanish Mission Sites Located and Test Excavated. *Archives and History News* 3(6):1–2. AHRM.

Jones, B. Calvin, John Hann, and John F. Scarry

1991   San Pedro y San Pablo de Patale: A Seventeenth-Century Spanish Mission in Lean County, Florida. *Florida Archaeology* 5:1–201. BAR.

Jones, B. Calvin, and Gary N. Shapiro

1990   Nine Mission Sites in Apalachee. In *Columbian Consequences.* Vol. 2, *Archaeological and Historical Perspectives on the Spanish Borderlands East,* edited by David Hurst Thomas, pp. 491–509. Washington, D.C.: Smithsonian Institution Press.

Kapitzke, Robert

1993   The "Calamities of Florida": Father Solana, Governor Palacio y Valenzuela, and the Desertions of 1758. *Florida Historical Quarterly* 72:1–18.

Karklins, Karlis

1974   Additional Notes on the Philip Mound, Polk County, Florida. *Florida Anthropologist* 27:1–8.

Kohler, Tim A.

1979   Corn, Indians, and Spaniards in North-central Florida: A Technique for Measuring Evolutionary Changes in Corn. *Florida Anthropologist* 32:1–17.

Lankford, George E., III

1984   Saying Hello to the Timucua. *Mid-America Folklore* 12:7–23.

Larsen, Clark Spencer

1993   On the Frontier of Contact: Mission Bioarchaeology in La Florida. In *Spanish Missions of La Florida,* edited by Bonnie G. McEwan, pp. 322–356. Gainesville: University Press of Florida.

Larson, Lewis H., Jr.

1978   Historic Guale Indians of the Georgia Coast and the Impact of the Spanish Mission Effort. In *Tacachale, Essays on the Indians of Florida and Southeastern Georgia during the Historic Period,* edited by Jerald T. Milanich and Samuel Proctor, pp. 120–140. Gainesville: University Presses of Florida.

Lawson, Sarah, trans.

1992   The Notable History of Florida. In *A Foothold in Florida: The Eye-Witness Account of Four Voyages made by the French to that Region,* by Sarah Lawson and W. John Faupel, pp. 1–148. East Grinstead, West Sussex, England: Antique Atlas Publications.

Leader, Jonathan

1985   Metal Artifacts from Fort Center: Aboriginal Metalworking in the Southeastern United States. Master's thesis, University of Florida, Gainesville.

Lewis, Clifford M.

1978   The Calusa. In *Tacachale: Essays on the Indians of Florida and Southeast Georgia during the Historic Period,* edited by Jerald T. Milanich and Samuel Proctor, pp. 19–49. Gainesville: University of Florida Press/ FMNH.

Lewis, Clifford M., and Albert J. Loomie

1953   *The Spanish Jesuit Missions in Virginia: 1570–1572.* Chapel Hill: University of North Carolina Press.

Long, George A.

1967   Indian and Historic Sites Report, John F. Kennedy Space Center, NASA. On file. Fairbanks Collection, DA.

Lorant, Stefan

1946   *The New World: The First Pictures of America.* New York: Duell, Sloan & Pearce.

Loucks, L. Jill

1978   Political and Economic Interactions between the Spaniards and Indians: Archeological and Ethnohistorical Perspectives of the Mission System in Florida. Ph.D. diss., University of Florida, Gainesville.

1993   Spanish-Indian Interaction on the Florida Missions: The Archaeology of Baptizing Spring. In *Spanish Missions of La Florida,* edited by Bonnie G. McEwan, pp. 193–216. Gainesville: University Press of Florida.

Luer, George M.

1985   An Update on Some Ceremonial Tablets. *Florida Anthropologist* 38: 273–274, 281.

1989a   Calusa Canals in Southwestern Florida: Routes of Tribute and Exchange. *Florida Anthropologist* 42:89–130.

1989b   A Seminole Burial on Indian Field (8LL39), Lee County, Southwestern Florida. *Florida Anthropologist* 42:237–240.

1991   Historic Resources at the Pineland Site, Lee County, Florida. *Florida Anthropologist* 44:59–75.

1994   A Third Ceremonial Tablet from the Goodnow Mound, Highlands County, Florida: With Notes on Some Peninsular Tribes and other Tablets. *Florida Anthropologist* 47:180–188.

Luer, George M., and Marion M. Almy

1981   Temple Mounds in the Tampa Bay Area. *Florida Anthropologist* 34: 127–155.

Luer, George M., Marion M. Almy, Dana Ste. Claire, and Robert Austin

1987   The Myakkahatchee Site (8So397), A Large Multi-Period Inland from the Shore Site in Sarasota County, Florida. *Florida Anthropologist* 40:137–153.

Lyon, Eugene

1976   *The Enterprise of Florida.* Gainesville: University of Florida Press.

1977   St. Augustine 1580: The Living Community. *El Escribano* 14:20–33.

1984   *Santa Elena: A Brief History of the Colony, 1566–1587.* Institute of Archaeology and Anthropology, Research Manuscript Series, no. 192. Columbia, S.C.

1987   Aspects of Pedro Menéndez de Avilés the Man. *El Escribano* 24:39–52.

1988   Pedro Menéndez's Strategic Plan for the Florida Peninsula. *Florida Historical Quarterly* 67:1–14.

1992   Richer Than We Thought—The Material Culture of Sixteenth Century St. Augustine. *El Escribano* 29:1–117.

MacNutt, Francis M., trans.

1912   *The Eight Decades of Peter Martyr d'Anghera.* 2 vols. New York: G.P. Putnam.

Manucy, Albert C.

1962   *The Houses of St. Augustine: Notes on the Architecture from 1565–1821.* St. Augustine: St. Augustine Historical Society.

1985   The Physical Setting of Sixteenth Century St. Augustine. *Florida Anthropologist* 38:34–53.

Marken, Mitchell W.

1994   *Pottery from Spanish Shipwrecks, 1500–1800.* Gainesville: University Press of Florida.

Marquardt, William H.

1984   *The Josslyn Island Mound and Its Role in the Investigation of Southwest Florida's Past.* Miscellaneous Project Report 22. DA.

1986   The Development of Cultural Complexity in Southwest Florida: Elements of a Critique. *Southeastern Archaeology* 5:63–70.

1987   The Calusa Social Formation in Protohistoric South Florida. In *Power Relations and State Formations,* edited by Thomas C. Patterson and Christine W. Gailey, pp. 98–116. Washington, D.C.: Archaeology Section, American Anthropological Association.

1988   Politics and Production among the Calusa of South Florida. In *Hunters and Gatherers.* Vol. 1, *History, Environment, and Social Change among Hunting and Gathering Societies,* edited by David Richies, Tim Ingold, and James Woodburn, pp. 161–188. London: Berg Publishers.

Marquardt, William H., ed.

1992   *Culture and Environment in the Domain of the Calusa.* Institute of Archaeology and Paleoenvironmental Studies, Monograph 1, DA.

Marrinan, Rochelle A.

1985   The Archaeology of the Spanish Missions of Florida: 1566–1704. In *Indians, Colonists, and Slaves, Essays in Memory of Charles H. Fairbanks,* edited by Kenneth W. Johnson, Jonathan M. Leader, and Robert C. Wilson, pp. 241–252. Florida Journal of Anthropology Special Publication, no. 4. Gainesville.

1993   Archaeological Investigations at Mission Patale, 1984–1992. In *Spanish Missions of La Florida,* edited by Bonnie G. McEwan, pp. 244–294. Gainesville: University Press of Florida.

Marrinan, Rochelle A., John F. Scarry, and Rhonda L. Majors

1990   Prelude to de Soto: The Expedition of Pánfilo de Narváez. In *Columbian Consequences.* Vol. 2, *Archaeological and Historical Perspectives on the Spanish Borderlands East,* edited by David Hurst Thomas, pp. 71–82. Washington D.C.: Smithsonian Institution Press.

Matter, Robert Allen

1990   *Pre-Seminole Florida, Spanish Soldiers, Friars, and Indian Missions, 1513–1763.* New York: Garland Publishing.

McEwan, Bonnie G.

1991   San Luis de Talimali: The Archaeology of Spanish-Indian Relations at a Florida Mission. *Historical Archaeology* 25:36–60.

1992   *Archaeology of the Apalachee Village at San Luis de Talamali.* Florida Archaeological Reports, no. 28. BAR.

1993   Hispanic Life on the Seventeenth-Century Florida Frontier. In *Spanish Missions of La Florida,* edited by Bonnie G. McEwan, pp. 295–321. Gainesville: University Press of Florida.

McEwan, Bonnie G., and Charles B. Poe

1994   Excavations at Fort San Luis. *Florida Anthropologist* 47:90–106.

McGoun, William E.

1981   Medals of Conquest in Calusa Florida. Master's thesis, Florida Atlantic University, Boca Raton.

McMurray, Judith A.

1973   The Definition of the Ceramic Complex at San Juan del Puerto. Master's thesis, University of Florida, Gainesville.

McNicoll, Robert E.

1941   The Caloosa Village Tequesta, a Miami of the Sixteenth Century. *Tequesta* 1:11–20.

McPhail, J. R.

1975   An Investigation into the Engravings by Theodor DeBry of Jacques Le Moyne's Original Paintings of Florida. Undergraduate honors thesis, Department of Anthropology, University of Florida, Gainesville.

Mexia, Alvaro

n.d.   Useful and Convenient Directions, Giving Faithfully the Rivers, Channels, Lagoons, Woodlands, Settlements, Embarcation and Landing-Places, and Hamlets Encountered from the City of St. Augustine to the Bar of Ais [ca. 1605], translated by Charles Higgs. Manuscript. Fairbanks Collection, DA.

Milanich, Jerald T.

1971a   *The Alachua Tradition of North-central Florida.* Contributions of the Florida State Museum, Anthropology and History, no. 17. Gainesville.

1971b   Surface Information from the Presumed Site of the San Pedro de Mocamo Mission. *Conference on Historic Site Archaeology Papers* 5:114–121.

1972   Excavations at the Richardson Site, Alachua County, Florida: An Early 17th Century Potano Indian Village (with Notes on Potano Culture Change). *Florida Bureau of Historic Sites and Properties B. lletin* 2:35–61.

1978   The Western Timucua: Patterns of Acculturation and Change. In *Tacachale, Essays on the Indians of Florida and Southeastern Georgia during the Historic Period,* edited by J. T. Milanich and S. Proctor, pp. 59–88. Gainesville: University of Florida Press/FMNH.

1987   Corn and Calusa; De Soto and Demography. In *Coasts, Plains and Deserts: Essays in Honor of Reynold J. Ruppé,* edited by Sylvia Gaines, pp. 173–184. Anthropological Research Papers, Arizona State University, no. 38. Tempe.

1994   *Archaeology of Precolumbian Florida.* Gainesville: University Press of Florida.

Milanich, Jerald T., ed.

1991   *The Hernando de Soto Expedition.* New York: Garland Publishing.

Milanich, Jerald T., and Charles Hudson

1993   *Hernando de Soto and the Florida Indians.* Gainesville: University Press of Florida/FMNH.

Milanich, Jerald T., and Kenneth W. Johnson
   1989   *Santa Fe: A Name out of Time.* Miscellaneous Project Report 41. DA.
Milanich, Jerald T., and Rebecca Saunders
   1986   *The Spanish Castillo and the Franciscan Doctrina of Santa Catalina, at Santa María, Amelia Island, Florida (8Na41).* Miscellaneous Project Report 20. DA.
Milanich, Jerald T., and William C. Sturtevant
   1972   *Francisco Pareja's 1613 Confessionario: A Documentary Source for Timucuan Ethnography.* Tallahassee: Florida Department of State.
Milbrath, Susan
   1989   Old World Meets New: Views across the Atlantic. In *First Encounters, Spanish Explorations in the Caribbean and the United States, 1492–1570,* edited by Jerald T. Milanich and Susan Milbrath, pp. 183–210. Gainesville: University of Florida Press/FMNH.
Miller, James J.
   1991   The Fairest, Frutefullest and Pleasantest of all the World: An Environmental History of the Northeast Part of Florida. Ph.D. diss., University of Pennsylvania, Philadelphia.
Mitchem, Jeffrey M.
   1989a   Artifacts of Exploration: Archaeological Evidence from Florida. In *First Encounters, Spanish Explorations in the Caribbean and the United States, 1492–1570,* edited by Jerald T. Milanich and Susan Milbrath, pp. 99–109. Gainesville: University of Florida Press/FMNH.
   1989b   Redefining Safety Harbor: Late Prehistoric/Protohistoric Archaeology in West Peninsular Florida. Ph.D. diss. University of Florida, Gainesville.
Mitchem, Jeffrey M., and Dale L. Hutchinson
   1989   The Ruth Smith, Weeki Wachee, and Tatham Mounds: Archaeological Evidence of Early Spanish Contact. *Florida Anthropologist* 42:317–339.
Mitchem, Jeffrey M., and Jonathan M. Leader
   1988   Early Sixteenth Century Beads from the Tatham Mound, Citrus County, Florida: Data and Interpretations. *Florida Anthropologist* 41: 42–60.
Mitchem, Jeffrey M., and Bonnie G. McEwan
   1988   New Data on Early Bells from Florida. *Southeastern Archaeology* 7:39–49.
Mitchem, Jeffrey M., Marvin T. Smith, Albert C. Goodyear, and Robert R. Allen
   1985   Early Spanish Contact on the Florida Gulf Coast: The Weeki Wachee and Ruth Smith Mounds. In *Indians, Colonists, and Slaves: Essays in Memory of Charles H. Fairbanks,* edited by Kenneth W. Johnson, Jonathan M. Leader, and Robert C. Wilson, pp. 179–219. Florida Journal of Anthropology Special Publication, no. 4. Gainesville.

Mitchem, Jeffrey M., and Brent R. Weisman

1984   Excavations at the Ruth Smith Mound (8Ci200). *Florida Anthropologist* 37:100–112.

1987   Changing Settlement Patterns and Pottery Types in the Withlacoochee Cove. *Florida Anthropologist* 40:154–166.

Moore, Clarence B.

1894a   Certain Sand Mounds of the St. John's River, Florida. *Journal of the Academy of Natural Sciences of Philadelphia* 10:5–128.

1894b   Certain Sand Mounds of the St. John's River, Florida, Part II. *Journal of the Academy of Natural Sciences of Philadelphia* 10:129–246.

1896a   Certain River Mounds of Duval County, Florida. *Journal of the Academy of Natural Sciences of Philadelphia* 10:448–502.

1896b   Two Sand Mounds on Murphy Island, Florida. *Journal of the Academy of Natural Sciences of Philadelphia* 10:503–517.

Morison, Samuel Eliot

1974   *The European Discovery of America: The Southern Voyages.* New York: Oxford University Press.

Morrell, L. Ross, and B. Calvin Jones

1970   San Juan de Aspalaga: A Preliminary Architectural Study. *Florida Bureau of Historic Sites and Properties Bulletin* 1:25–43.

Mowers, Bert, and Wilma B. Williams

1972   The Peace Camp Site, Broward County, Florida. *Florida Anthropologist* 25:1–20.

Neill, Wilfred T.

1968   An Indian and Spanish Site on Tampa Bay, Florida. *Florida Anthropologist* 106–116.

1978   *Archeology and a Science of Man.* New York: Columbia University Press.

Oré, Luís Gerónimo de

1936   *The Martyrs of Florida (1513–1616).* Translated by Maynard Geiger. Franciscan Studies, no. 18. New York: Joseph F. Wagner.

Parks, Arva Moore

1985   *Where the River Found the Bay: Historical Study of the Granada Site, Miami, Florida.* Vol. 2 of *Archaeology and History of the Granada Site.* AHRM.

Pearson, Charles

1977   Evidence of Early Spanish Contact on the Georgia Coast. *Historical Archaeology* 11:74–83.

Pearson, Fred L.

1968   Spanish-Indian Relations in Florida: A Study of Two *Visitas* 1657–1678. Ph.D diss., University of Alabama, Tuscaloosa.

Piatek, Bruce John

1992   Archaeology and History at Tomoka State Park. *Florida Anthropologist* 45:314–325.

Priestley, Herbert I., ed.
  1928   *The Luna Papers: Documents Relating to the Expedition of Don Tristán de Luna y Arellano for the Conquest of La Florida in 1559–1561.* 2 vols. Florida State Historical Society Publication no. 8. Deland.

Purdy, Barbara A.
  1987   Hontoon Island, Florida (8Vo202) Artifacts. *Florida Anthropologist* 40:27–39.

Quinn, David B., ed.
  1979   *Major Spanish Searches in Eastern North America. Franco-Spanish Clash in Florida. The Beginnings of Spanish Florida.* Vol. 2 of *New American World: A Documentary History of North America to 1612.* New York: Arno Press.

Ramenofsky, Ann F.
  1987   *Vectors of Death: The Archaeology of European Contact.* Albuquerque: University of New Mexico Press.

Ranjel, Rodrigo
  1922   A Narrative of de Soto's Expedition. In *Narratives of the Career of Hernando de Soto in the Conquest of Florida,* vol. 2, edited by Edward G. Bourne, pp. 41–158. New York: Allerton.

Reitz, Elizabeth J.
  1990   Zooarchaeological Evidence for Subsistence at *La Florida* Missions. In *Columbian Consequences.* Vol. 2, *Archaeological and Historical Perspectives on the Spanish Borderlands East,* edited by David Hurst Thomas, pp. 543–554. Washington, D.C.: Smithsonian Institution Press.
  1993   Evidence for Animal Use at the Missions of Spanish Florida. In *Spanish Missions of La Florida,* edited by Bonnie G. McEwan, pp. 376–398. Gainesville: University Press of Florida.

Ribau[l]t, Jean
  1964   *The Whole & True Discoverye of Terra Florida.* Gainesville: University of Florida Press. [Facsimile of the London edition of 1563.]

Rogers, Nikki L.
  1992   The French Connection: A Subsistence Analysis of the Oyster Bay Site, Canaveral National Seashore, Florida. Undergraduate honors thesis, Department of Anthropology, Florida State University, Tallahassee.

Rouse, Irving
  1951   *A Survey of Indian River Archeology, Florida.* Yale University Publications in Anthropology, no. 44. New Haven: Yale University Press.

Ruhl, Donna S.
  1990   Spanish Mission Paleoethnobotany and Culture Change: A Survey of the Archaeobotanical Data and Some Speculations on the Aboriginal and Spanish Agrarian Interactions in *La Florida.* In *Columbian Consequences.* Vol. 2, *Archaeological and Historical Perspec-*

tives on the Spanish Borderlands East, edited by David Hurst Thomas, pp. 555–580. Washington, D.C.: Smithsonian Institution Press.

1993   Old Customs and Traditions in New Terrain: Sixteenth- and Seventeenth-Century Archaeobotanical Data from *La Florida.* In *Foraging and Farming in the Eastern Woodlands,* edited by C. Margaret Scarry, pp. 255–283. Gainesville: University Press of Florida.

Saunders, Rebecca

1987   *Excavations at 8Na41: Two Mission Period Sites on Amelia Island, Florida.* Miscellaneous Project Report 35. DA.

1990   Ideal and Innovation: Spanish Mission Architecture in the Southeast. In *Columbian Consequences.* Vol. 2, *Archaeological and Historical Perspectives on the Spanish Borderlands East,* edited by David Hurst Thomas, pp. 527–542. Washington D.C.: Smithsonian Institution Press.

1993   Architecture of Missions Santa María and Santa Catalina de Amelia. In *Spanish Missions of La Florida,* edited by Bonnie G. McEwan, pp. 35–61. Gainesville: University Press of Florida.

Scarry, C. Margaret

1993   Plant Production and Procurement in Apalachee Province. In *Spanish Missions of La Florida,* edited by Bonnie G. McEwan, pp. 357–375. Gainesville: University Press of Florida.

Scarry, John F.

1984   Fort Walton Development: Mississippian Chiefdoms in the Lower Southeast. Ph.D. diss., Case Western Reserve University, Cleveland.

1990a   Beyond Apalachee Province: Assessing the Evidence for Early European-Indian Contact in Northwest Florida. In *Columbian Consequences.* Vol. 2, *Archaeological and Historical Perspectives on the Spanish Borderlands East,* edited by David Hurst Thomas, pp. 93–106. Washington D.C.: Smithsonian Institution Press.

1990b   The Rise, Transformation, and Fall of Apalachee: A Case Study of Political Change in a Chiefly Society. In *Lamar Archaeology: Mississippian Chiefdoms in the Deep South,* edited by Mark Williams and Gary Shapiro, pp. 175–186. Tuscaloosa: University of Alabama Press.

1994   The Apalachee Chiefdom: A Mississippian Society on the Fringe of the Mississippian World. In *The Forgotten Centuries: Indians and Europeans in the American South, 1521–1704,* edited by Charles Hudson and Carmen Chaves Tesser, pp. 156–178. Athens: University of Georgia Press.

Seaberg, Lillian M.

1955   The Zetrouer Site: Indian and Spanish in Central Florida. Master's thesis, University of Florida, Gainesville.

Sears, William H.

1967   Archaeological Survey in the Cape Coral Area at the Mouth of the Caloosahatchee River. *Florida Anthropologist* 20:93–102.

1982   *Fort Center: An Archaeological Site in the Lake Okeechobee Basin.* Gainesville: University Press of Florida.

Shapiro, Gary

1987   Archaeology at San Luís: Broad-Scale Testing, 1984–1985. *Florida Archaeology* 3:1–271. BAR.

Skelton, R. A.

1977   The Le Moyne-De Bry Map. In *The Work of Jacques Le Moyne de Morgues, a Huguenot Artist in France, Florida and England,* vol. 1, by Paul Hulton, pp. 45–54. London: British Museum Publications Ltd.

Sleight, Frederick W.

1949   Notes Concerning an Historic Site of Central Florida. *Florida Anthropologist* 2:26–33.

Smith, Buckingham, trans.

1866   *Narratives of the Career of Hernando de Soto in the Conquest of Florida as Told by a Knight of Elvas and in a Relation by Luys Hernández de Biedma, Factor of the Expedition.* New York: The Bradford Club.

Smith, Hale G.

1948a   Two Historical Archaeological Periods in Florida. *American Antiquity* 13:313–319.

1948b   Results of An Archaeological Investigation of a Spanish Mission Site in Jefferson County, Florida. *Florida Anthropologist* 1:1–10.

1956   *The European and the Indian.* Florida Anthropological Society Publication no. 4. Tallahassee.

Smith, Marion F., Jr., and John F. Scarry

1988   Apalachee Settlement Distribution: The View from the Florida Master Site File. *Florida Anthropologist* 41:51–364.

Smith, Marvin T., and Mary Elizabeth Good

1982   *Early Sixteenth Century Glass Beads in the Spanish Colonial Trade.* Greenwood, Miss.: Cottonlandia Museum.

Solís de Merás, Gonzalo

1964   *Pedro Menéndez de Avilés: Adelantado, Governor and Captain-General of Florida.* Translated by Jeannette Thurber Connor. Gainesville: University of Florida Press.

South, Stanley, Russell K. Skowronek, and Richard E. Johnson

1988   *Spanish Artifacts from Santa Elena.* Anthropological Studies, no. 7. Columbia, S.C.: South Carolina Institute of Archaeology and Anthropology.

Spellman, Charles W.

1948   The Agriculture of the Early North Florida Indians. *Florida Anthropologist* 1:37–48.

Stirling, Matthew W.

1935   Smithsonian Archeological Projects Conducted under the Federal Emergency Relief Administration, 1933–1934. *Annual Report of the Smithsonian Institution* 1934:371–400. Washington, D.C.

Sturtevant, William C.

1976   First Visual Images of Native America. In *First Images of America,* vol.
1, edited by Fredi Chiapelli, pp. 417–454. Berkeley: University of
California Press.

1977   The Ethnological Evaluation of the La Moyne–De Bry Illustrations.
In *The Work of Jacques Le Moyne de Morgues, a Huguenot Artist in France,
Florida and England,* vol. 1, by Paul Hulton, pp. 69–74. London:
British Museum Publications Ltd.

1978   The Last of the South Florida Aborigines. In *Tacachale: Essays on the
Indians of Florida and Southeast Georgia during the Historic Period,* edited
by Jerald T. Milanich and Samuel Proctor, pp. 141–162. Gainesville:
University Presses of Florida.

1992   The Sources for European Imagery of Native Americans. In *New
World of Wonders: European Images of the Americas, 1492–1700,* edited
by Rachel Doggett, pp. 25–33. Washington, D.C.: Folger Shake-
speare Library.

1993   The First America Discoverers of Europe. *European Review of Native
American Studies* 7(2):23–29.

Sturtevant, William C., ed.

1985   A *Seminole Sourcebook.* New York: Garland Publishing.

Swanton, John R.

1922   *Early History of the Creek Indians and Their Neighbors.* Bulletin 73.
BAE.

1929   The Tawasa Language. *American Anthropologist* 31:435–453.

1946   *The Indians of the Southeastern United States.* Bulletin 137. BAE.

Swanton, John R., ed.

1985   *Final Report of the United States De Soto Expedition Commission.* Washington, D.C.: Smithsonian Institution Press.

Symes, M. I., and M. E. Stephens

1965   A-272: The Fox Pond Site. *Florida Anthropologist* 18:65–72.

Tesar, Louis D.

1980   *The Leon County Bicentennial Survey Report: An Archaeological Survey of
Selected Portions of Leon County, Florida.* Miscellaneous Project Report
Series 49. BHSP.

1981   Fort Walton and Leon-Jefferson Cultural Development in the Tallahassee Red Hills Area of Florida: A Brief Summary. *Southeastern
Archaeological Conference Bulletin* 24:27–29.

Tesar, Louis D., and B. Calvin Jones

1989   In Search of the 1539–1540 de Soto Expedition Wintering Site in
Apalachee. *Florida Anthropologist* 42:340–360.

Thomas, David Hurst

1987   *The Archaeology of Mission Santa Catalina de Guale, 1. Search and Discovery.* Anthropological Papers of the American Museum of Natural
History, vol. 63, pt. 2. New York.

1993   Archaeology of Mission Santa Catalina de Guale: Our First Fifteen
        Years. In *Spanish Missions of La Florida*, edited by Bonnie G. McEwan,
        pp. 1–34. Gainesville: University Press of Florida.
True, David O., ed.
1945   *Memoir of D. d'Escalante Fontaneda Respecting Florida, Written in Spain,
        about the Year 1575*. Coral Gables, Fla.: Glade House.
Vargas Ugarte, Rubén
1935   The First Jesuit Mission in Florida. *Historical Records and Studies*
        25:59–148. The United States Catholic Historical Society.
Varner, John G., and Jeanette J. Varner, eds. and trans.
1951   *The Florida of the Inca*. Austin: University of Texas Press.
Vernon, Richard, and Ann S. Cordell
1993   A Distributional and Technological Study of Apalachee Colono-
        ware from San Luis de Talimali. In *Spanish Missions of Florida*, edited
        by Bonnie G. McEwan, pp. 418–441. Gainesville: University Press
        of Florida.
Wallace, Ronald L.
1975   An Archaeological, Ethnohistorical, and Biochemical Investigation
        of the Guale Indians of the Georgia Coastal Strand. Ph.D. diss., Uni-
        versity of Florida, Gainesville.
Weber, David J.
1992   *The Spanish Frontier in North America*. New Haven, Conn.: Yale Uni-
        versity Press.
Weddle, Robert S.
1985   *Spanish Sea: The Gulf of Mexico in North American Discovery, 1500–1685*.
        College Station: Texas A&M University Press.
Weisman, Brent R.
1992   *Excavations of the Franciscan Frontier: Archaeology of the Fig Springs Mis-
        sion*. Gainesville: University Press of Florida/FMNH.
1993   Archaeology of Fig Springs Mission, Ichetucknee Springs State
        Park. In *Spanish Missions of La Florida*, edited by Bonnie G. McEwan,
        pp. 165–192. Gainesville: University Press of Florida.
Wenhold, Lucy L.
1936   A Seventeenth-Century Letter of Gabriel Díaz Vara Calderón,
        Bishop of Cuba. *Smithsonian Miscellaneous Collections* 95(16). Wash-
        ington, D.C.
Wheeler, Ryan J.
1992   The Riviera Complex: An East Okeechobee Archaeological Area
        Settlement. *Florida Anthropologist* 45:5–17.
Widmer, Randolph E.
1988   *The Evolution of the Calusa: A Nonagricultural Chiefdom on the Southwest
        Florida Coast*. Tuscaloosa and London: University of Alabama Press.
Willey, Gordon R.
1954   Burial Patterns in the Burns and Fuller Mounds, Cape Canaveral,
        Florida. *Florida Anthropologist* 7:79–90.

Williams, Wilma B.

1983   Bridge to the Past: Excavations at the Margate-Blount Site. *Florida Anthropologist* 36:142–153.

Worth, John E.

1992   The Timucuan Missions of Spanish Florida and the Rebellion of 1656. Ph.D. diss., University of Florida, Gainesville.

1994   Late Spanish Military Expeditions in the Interior Southeast, 1597–1628. In *The Forgotten Centuries: Indians and Europeans in the American South, 1521–1704,* edited by Charles Hudson and Carmen Chaves Tesser, pp. 104–122. Athens: University of Georgia Press.

1995   Fontenada Revisited: Five Descriptions of Sixteenth-Century Florida. *Florida Historical Quarterly* 73: 339–352.

In press *The Struggle for the Georgia Coast: An Eighteenth Century Spanish Retrospect on Guale and Mocama.* Anthropological Papers of the American Museum of Natural History. New York.

Zubillaga, Felix

1941   *La Florida: La Misión Jesuitica (1566–1572) y la Colonización Española.* Rome: Institutum Historicum S.J.

Zubillaga, Felix, ed.

1946   *Monumenta Antiquae Floride.* Monumenta Historica Societatis Iesu, 69, Monumenta Missionum Societatis Iesu, 3. Rome.

INDEX

Page numbers italics refer to figures and tables.